tice

Global

incorpo   cal

landsca

world a   ly

on issue   -to-

date ac   r

significa

change,

are brou   e

connect   ssues'

sections   y to

comma

Chris   on,

where h   s

publish   *tical*

Philoso   . He

is currently working on global egalitarianism as an approach to global justice
and on the question of rights over natural resources.

Global
Distributive Justice

Chris Armstrong

CAMBRIDGE
UNIVERSITY PRESS

CAMBRIDGE UNIVERSITY PRESS
Cambridge, New York, Melbourne, Madrid, Cape Town,
Singapore, São Paulo, Delhi, Tokyo, Mexico City

Cambridge University Press
The Edinburgh Building, Cambridge CB2 8RU, UK

Published in the United States of America by Cambridge University Press, New York

www.cambridge.org
Information on this title: www.cambridge.org/9781107401402

First published 2012

Printed in the United Kingdom at the University Press, Cambridge

A catalogue record for this publication is available from the British Library

ISBN 978-1-107-00892-2 Hardback
ISBN 978-1-107-40140-2 Paperback

Contents

Text boxes

Introduction

Protests in favour of 'global justice' are becoming a familiar part of the political landscape. Placards demanding a more just, fair or equal world present a colourful accompaniment to every major meeting of world leaders. Social movement scholars are busily researching – and arguing about – whether a 'global justice movement' can be said to be emerging. There are also many organisations which campaign to try and raise awareness of global issues – such as Make Poverty History, Oxfam and the World Development Movement. And, sure enough, the idea of global justice is slowly creeping into the mainstream of political debate. When the leaders of the G8 wealthiest countries met at Gleneagles, Scotland, in 2005, they committed themselves to securing debt cancellation for the poorest countries, an additional US$50 billion in overseas aid and a (somewhat) more just system of international trade. Partly under pressure from organisations such as Make Poverty History, political leaders appeared to recognise that issues of global justice were going to be an important part of the political agenda for the twenty-first century.

But what *is* global justice, and what does it mean? Judging from the organisations and individuals who campaign about it, it incorporates issues such as global poverty, trade justice (and also fair trade), aid to the developing world, debt cancellation, and perhaps human rights too, as well as issues such as how to spread the costs of responding to climate change. But what, if anything, have these issues got in common? Broadly speaking, we can describe them as issues of *distributive justice* – that is, they concern how the benefits and burdens of living together are to be shared out between us. Advocates of global justice are arguing – typically, at least – for more equal access to international trade networks for poorer countries or the provision of more aid, or are arguing that people in wealthier countries ought to reduce their carbon emissions because they are, currently, disproportionately large. As issues of distributive justice these are *normative* concerns – they relate to what people *ought* to get (what they are morally entitled to), as well as what they ought to do, or give (what their moral duties are).

The idea of global justice has also been a growth area – perhaps even *the* growth area – within political theory or philosophy in recent years. Very many, and perhaps most, universities now teach courses on the topic. Political theorists and philosophers have supplied *theories* of global justice – attempts to explain to us, or persuade us, what our entitlements and duties are, and where they come from. These theories provide the building blocks for courses on global justice. This book presents an overview of these theories, and shows how they might apply to some of the issues described above.

The book has two main aims. The first is to help students to navigate their way through debates on global justice and to orient them in the by-now extensive literature. Students on courses on global justice (and sometimes 'global distributive justice', 'international justice' or 'global ethics') can find that literature rather complex and difficult. It is undoubtedly a sophisticated and fast-moving set of debates, which does make certain demands on the reader. For that reason, an introduction or companion to academic debates on global justice is an important addition to the resources available to students. The book is not intended as a substitute for reading and engaging with theories of global justice directly, which is something for which there is really no substitute. But it is intended to provide a map of the territory and an accessible overview of the issues with which students will be faced – which should make the process of studying global justice less bewildering and more rewarding.

The second main aim of the book is to preserve the link between the important and engaging political issues mentioned at the outset and the theories which students will actually be spending much of their time studying. While the first part of this book provides an overview of the more important theories or *accounts* of global justice, the second and slightly longer part moves on to the *issues* to which they might apply. These, after all, are what students are often most interested *in*, and what the theories discussed in part I are actually intended to provide guidance *on*. So the attention in Part II shifts to a series of significant political issues: human rights, the ownership of natural resources, trade justice, climate justice, and justice and migration. These issues all have resonance with political debates in the real world, and to bring that point home each of the chapters in part II includes a case study addressing contemporary issues or events. And, just as importantly, in each of the chapters of part II we try to assess just what the theories discussed in part I can tell us about the issue in question. Readers should get a sense both of what normative standards different theorists have suggested we ought to apply to global politics or the global economy, and what some of the practical implications of applying those various standards would be.

The scope and approach of the book

In any book of this kind decisions have to be made about what to put in and what to leave out. The book does not attempt to cover the entire field of global or international ethics. There is a series of important normative issues in international relations – such as just war, the ethics of humanitarian intervention, the morality of nuclear weapons or the appropriate response to terrorism – which will be left to one side. Our focus will be firmly on *distributive* questions: how ought the global economy to be organised? Do people every-where have an entitlement of justice that their basic needs should be met? What level of carbon dioxide emissions should each person be allowed to cause? Who owns the world's natural resources, and how should rights over them be shared? This restriction is neces-sary to keep the book manageable, but should also reflect the content of many courses on global justice, which overwhelmingly focus on such distributive issues.

Generally speaking, this book should be accessible to students and general readers interested in issues of global justice, and it does not assume prior knowledge of political theory or philosophy. But its most likely audience will be students taking optional courses on glo-bal justice, in their second or third year of undergraduate study or on master's-level courses. Although there are now some very good anthologies of key essays on global justice, bringing together contri-butions from leading theorists, these courses are not yet well served by introductory guides or companions to the literature. This book addresses that gap. Two other features of the book should make it especially valuable to most readers. The first is the extensive treat-ment not only of *theories* of (or approaches to) global justice, but also of *issues* on which those theories might give us guidance. The case studies, in particular, attempt to make the connection with contemporary politics and current affairs a strong one. The second feature is the emphasis on charting the fast-growing literature. Each of the chapters of part II ends with a section on 'Further issues', which discusses emerging debates or controversies within the field which appear likely to command increasing attention in the coming years.

In terms of the order in which readers ought to tackle the chapters, the three chapters of part I provide the theoretical underpinning for the issues discussed in part II, and so ideally should be read first. But each of the five chapters of part II could potentially be read in isolation. They could also be read in any order, which should be helpful, given that many university courses on global justice divide up and arrange the topics in different ways.

The structure of the book

Part I of the book aims to set out the most important theories of global justice:

- Chapter 1 introduces the *idea* of global distributive justice. We investigate just what a theory of global distributive justice is, and why we might think that one is necessary. Theorists disagree about exactly why we need global justice, with some suggesting that in a globalised world we need principles of justice to regulate the institutions that affect all our lives, and others arguing that it is because we are all human, with a right to equal dignity and respect, that global justice is necessary. We also briefly examine a distinction which will recur throughout this book, between *egalitarian* and *minimalist* approaches to global justice.
- Chapter 2 then examines egalitarian approaches to global justice – approaches which, in some way or another, argue that we should try to arrive at a more equal world. We take two prominent global egalitarian thinkers as examples and work through some of their more important arguments.
- Chapter 3 moves on to examine minimalist approaches to global justice. These approaches are less ambitious than their egalitarian rivals, and aim instead at securing the

foundations for a decent life for everyone. We examine
three such accounts and address their implications for global
justice.

Armed with these theoretical foundations, we move on in Part II to
discuss a set of important issues.

- Chapter 4 discusses human rights. It is particularly
  concerned with a contentious issue: whether we can be
  said to have rights, as a matter of justice, to such things as
  food and shelter and housing. We shall assess the argument
  for these 'socio-economic' rights and also discuss the
  implications of a human right to health.
- Chapter 5 discusses issues of resource distribution. Many
  countries have access to plentiful natural resources buried
  under their territories, such as oil, coal or diamonds. For
  some theorists this raises issues of justice. We examine
  recent arguments about the 'resource privilege' or 'resource
  rights', which are said to implicate wealthy Western states
  and citizens in continuing global poverty. We also address
  broader questions about who ought to own the world's
  natural resources.
- Chapter 6 discusses various approaches to international
  trade. We are often told that international trade should be
  made more just, or that we should buy 'fair trade' goods.
  But what does this mean? The chapter examines various
  arguments for reforming the World Trade Organization's role
  in achieving trade justice, for 'fair trade', and for 'linking'
  international trade with labour standards.
- Chapter 7 addresses the challenge of climate change,
  and in particular discusses how we should distribute the
  costs of responding to it. Assuming that the ability of the
  atmosphere to absorb carbon dioxide is limited, how should
  we distribute the right to emit? What guidance can theories
  of global justice give us?
- The final chapter, chapter 8, examines the challenge
  of international migration. Broad arguments in favour
  both of free movement across borders, and of restricting
  immigration, will be considered. But we shall also discuss

the relationship between migration and distributive justice: would opening borders to more immigrants be a good response to problems of global injustice or a bad one? If richer countries gave more aid to poorer ones, would this entitle the former to keep their borders closed?

part I

Approaches

chapter 1

Global distributive justice: what and why?

This chapter introduces the idea of global distributive justice, and looks at some arguments in favour of it. Although some people might think that the gulfs in income or living standards across the various countries of the world are regrettable, this does not commit us to thinking that they are *unjust*. Similarly, while we might think that more privileged people – such as citizens of developed countries – have some kind of responsibility to respond to the fact that other people lack access to clean water, adequate nutrition or basic education, this does not necessarily imply that they have obligations of *justice*. Theories of global distributive justice do, though, pick out some such facts – say, that many people lack access to basic education, or that some have a great deal more than others simply because of the country they happen to have been born into – and declare them to be unjust. They also tell us that, at least sometimes, we have obligations of justice to respond to such facts.

This chapter sets the scene, in section 1.1, with some brief facts about global poverty. How we respond to these kinds of fact, from a normative point of view, determines whether we shall be convinced by theories of global distributive justice. Section 1.2 then examines the idea of global distributive justice. Just what is a theory of global distributive justice? When is something a principle of justice as opposed to something else, like a principle of charity or humanitarianism? Although there are a number of different approaches to defining principles of distributive justice, theorists tend to converge on the idea that *duties* of justice are especially firm or stringent, and that they are also enforceable. So, for many theorists of global justice, saying that someone has an entitlement (to clean drinking water, say, or to a fair wage) as a matter of justice, means that we should also be prepared to say that someone else is acting unjustly if that entitlement is not delivered on. Section 1.2 also distinguishes between two important types of duty: positive and negative duties of justice.

Assuming that principles of global distributive justice are quite stringent and also enforceable, the justification of such principles is important. Why do we believe that there are principles of global distributive justice? Is it because we live in an interconnected or globalised world, for example? Section 1.3 examines two kinds of answer to the question, *why* global distributive justice? The first kind of answer, which we can call a *relational* answer, does indeed suggest that there is some fact or set of facts about the world that makes distributive justice relevant at the global level. More particularly, relational accounts emphasise the way in which individuals across the world are united by certain kinds of relationship – that they share certain kinds of institutions or are all part of a global economy, for example. *Non-relational* accounts do not consider such factors to be important – or, at least, while they might be important in some ways they do not tell us why we need principles of global distributive justice in the first place. Non-relational accounts emphasise facts such as our humanity or dignity or individuality – facts which do not depend on the existence of common institutions or relationships. While in practice the conclusions of relational and non-relational accounts may overlap – they may both tell us that global distributive justice is necessary – the differences in justification are nevertheless interesting, and each kind of justification has been subjected to its own set of criticisms.

The chapter, up to this point, will have given us a general account of what global distributive justice *is* and also have provided an overview of competing arguments about *why* we should think it important. But we will not know much yet about the content of principles of global distributive justice. Just what are they trying to achieve? And just how much will they ask of us? Section 1.4 introduces a distinction between minimalist and egalitarian accounts of global distributive justice which will be significant throughout this book. Broadly speaking, a minimalist account suggests that we should set our sights relatively low, and try to achieve for everyone in the world access to the conditions of a decent or minimally decent life. As such, minimalists are troubled by the facts about poverty set out in section 1.1, because they suggest, for example, that some people are falling below, and often well below, some line demarcating a life of dignity and autonomy from one of drudgery and deprivation. But minimalist accounts are *not* directly concerned by global inequalities – by the fact that some people have very much more than others. Egalitarian accounts certainly are, and tend to suggest some dimension along which we ought to equalise distribution, or at least minimise important inequalities. Egalitarians may well agree with minimalists that we ought to act to reduce deprivation or to meet basic needs. But doing so is not *enough*: we also need to tackle the inequalities themselves. Within the circle of those who are concerned about global distributive justice in the first place, the debate between egalitarian and minimalist accounts of global distributive justice is a hugely important one, and it will be examined further throughout the remaining chapters of this book.

1.1. Some facts about global poverty

Statistics on global poverty are collected by such organisations as the United Nations (UN) and the World Bank. The World Bank has two chief indicators of poverty. It defines being in poverty as having less than US$2 per day to live on, and extreme poverty in terms of having less than $1.25 per day. This is very little, but we might think that $2 would go a long way in a poor country where basic goods were presumably quite cheap. That would be mistaken, however. The World Bank uses a measure called 'purchasing power parity', so that when it says that someone in India (for example) lives on less than $2 per day, it means that they can afford in India roughly what $2 would buy them *in the United States* – in other words, very little indeed.

These statistics are not the whole story, of course, and organisations such as the World Bank are sometimes criticised for focusing too much on monetary income as the measure of poverty. We might also think of people as poor because they lack access to education or basic health care, for example (Pogge and Reddy 2010). The UN's Millennium Development Goals (which will be discussed in chapter 3) move us some distance away from a focus solely on monetary income, including as they do indicators of education, literacy, health care and so on. So there is ongoing disagreement as to how best to conceive of, and measure, poverty.

In terms of the World Bank's figures, how many people are in poverty and how has this changed over time? The Bank suggests that the number of people living on $2 a day or less increased slightly, from 2.5 to 2.6 billion people, over the period 1981 to 2005. But as a proportion of the (rapidly rising) world population, this represents a decline from 70 per cent to 48 per cent of all people living now. The numbers living in extreme poverty ($1.25 per day or less) actually fell in the same period from 1.9 billion to 1.4 billion (a decline from 52 per cent of the world population to 26 per cent). So the big picture suggests that the absolute numbers of people in poverty remain fairly static, although extreme poverty is declining. But this big picture does conceal important regional variations. It appears that most of the decline in extreme poverty has occurred in China and to a lesser extent in India, while it has declined much less in other areas, such as sub-Saharan Africa. So the rapid economic growth of some developing economies may be concealing a reality of very little economic progress for the 'bottom billion' of humanity, who are falling further and further behind the rest of the world (Collier 2007). Box 1.1 gives some key figures about global poverty.

Box 1.1. **Some key figures on global poverty**

- 2,600,000,000 people live on less than $2 per day.
- 1,400,000,000 people live on less than $1.25 per day.
- Around 27 per cent of children in developing countries are estimated to be underweight or to have stunted growth (UN 2007a).
- 72 million children of primary school age were not in school in 2005, 57 per cent of them girls (UN 2007b).
- 1.8 million children die each year from diarrhoea, and almost half the inhabitants of developing countries are, at any given point in time, suffering from health problems related to poor water and sanitation (UN 2006).

1.2. The idea of global distributive justice

Justice is an elusive term which is turned to many different uses. In international relations, for example, people talk – and argue – about just and unjust wars, just responses to terrorism and the justice of various interrogation tactics. Those issues are interesting but fall outside the concerns of this book. Our topic is *distributive* justice. Here, a very general definition would say that distributive justice concerns the way in which the benefits and burdens of our lives are shared between us. A *principle* of distributive justice is then a principle which tells us how some particular benefit or burden – or set of benefits and burdens – *ought* to be shared out. So a principle which says that people ought to receive free basic education, or that jobs ought to go to the best qualified person, would count as a principle of distributive justice.

People sometimes limit the scope of distributive justice to broadly 'economic' issues. Lamont and Favor, for example, tell us that 'Principles of distributive justice are normative principles designed to guide the allocation of the benefits and burdens of economic activity' (1996: 1). That is a little contentious, because it might exclude some 'goods' which are important to us but which are not usually considered part of economic life (such as education or health care). But still, a great many of the issues discussed in this book have some recognisably 'economic' dimension – including issues of trade justice, the ownership of resources, our duty to give material assistance to the global poor and so on.

The point about benefits and burdens is certainly important, though, because it points our attention to the two faces of distributive justice. On the one hand, theories of distributive justice will usually give us an account of what our *entitlements* or *rights* are (these correspond to the benefits, of course). For instance, a theory of distributive justice might pick out some key interests or needs that people share – say, the need for food, water and housing – and suggest that we have an entitlement of justice to those things. This is to say that, in the normal course of things, we ought to be provided with them. If we are not, an injustice has occurred. This does not tell us yet who ought actually to provide us with food, water or housing. For that, we need an account of our *duties* (which correspond to the burdens mentioned earlier). Living together, we might say, imposes certain duties or obligations on us – to refrain from mistreating those around us in various ways, or actually to provide others with certain goods if they prove unable to secure them for themselves.

Theories of distributive justice will differ on the content of the entitlements and duties that they suggest we have. Some will suggest that we have only some basic entitlements, and therefore that we only have some rather basic duties of justice. Others will defend a fuller set of entitlements and accordingly demand much more of us in the way of duties. We shall return to this issue in section 1.4, where we distinguish between minimalist and egalitarian accounts of justice. But there is another controversy that we need to recognise from the outset. As well as disagreeing about the *content* of principles of distributive justice, theorists also disagree about their *scope*. We said at the outset that theories of distributive justice tell us how to distribute the benefits and burdens that we share between us. But who is the 'we' and 'us' that we are talking about? Here, we again face the fact of substantial disagreement. While some theories of distributive justice set their sights 'only' on regulating the distribution of benefits and burdens of a single society, others set their sights far wider – on the entire world, in fact. Still others will suggest *some* principles of distributive justice for individual societies, and *others* for the entire world. For the purposes of this book we can define an account of *global distributive justice* as any theory which suggests that there are some entitlements of justice which have global scope and which also suggests that there are some duties of justice which have global scope. An account of global distributive justice need not tell us that *all* valid principles of justice are global in scope. But it will tell us that at least *some* valid principles have global scope. It will seek to regulate the distribution of at least some benefits or burdens at a global level.

So an account of global justice will tell us that individuals will have some entitlements – say, to clean drinking water or basic education – as a matter of justice. It will also tell us that people the world over have duties of global distributive justice. There are certain things we are obliged to *do*, or *not* do, and these duties are sufficiently weighty that it makes sense to say that we are behaving unjustly if we do not measure up to them. In the rest of this section we shall focus on duties, as this gives us a relatively clear picture of the distinction between accounts of global distributive justice and accounts which focus on humanitarianism or charity. First, in section 1.2.1, we shall investigate the difference between humanitarian duties and duties of justice. Then in section 1.2.2 we shall move on to the distinction between positive and negative duties.

1.2.1. Duties of justice and duties of humanitarianism

When reflecting on the facts about poverty cited in section 1.1, we might have a variety of responses. We might think that there is nothing normatively troubling about such facts. We could agree that some people's lives offer them a fairly poor set of opportunities, but simply say, 'so it goes'. Alternatively, we might agree that some people have poor opportunities, but believe that those poor opportunities are the results of bad decisions that people in their country have made over the years. Admittedly this argument gets a little difficult when we focus on children newly born in such countries, who presumably are not responsible for what political leaders have done in the past, but who still end up suffering worse opportunities. But still, some people will be unmoved by such facts. They might, for example, think that we have duties to assist those close to us, but no duties at all to people who live so far away (an idea to which we shall return at the end of this section).

Alternatively, we might think that there is something significantly wrong which is highlighted by these facts. We might think that it is wrong that some people lack access to clean water, adequate nutrition or basic education. We might also be troubled by the fact that people in developed countries tend to spend considerably more money on their pets than they do on helping to tackle poverty overseas. We might actually think that tackling global poverty would be formidably difficult – or even that giving overseas aid is counterproductive. But still, we might find it hard to reconcile ourselves to a world in which some people have so very little. And we might wonder whether we therefore have some kind of duty to do something to address a situation where some people have so much less than ourselves.

If so, there are two important questions. The first is just *who* has the duty in question, and the second is what *type* of duty it is. To take the first point first, if we want to suggest that there is an obligation to tackle global poverty, for example, then we need to specify just who that duty attaches to. We could provide both individual or collective answers to that question. An individual answer would say that it is separate people – individuals – who have a duty to address global poverty, perhaps by giving money to organisations helping people in developing countries or by refusing to buy goods from authoritarian regimes which keep their citizens in poverty, or else by lobbying governments to improve their policy on the alleviation of global poverty. Alternatively, we might prefer collective answers, which would suggest that collectives of people, or even organisations, have the duties in question. For instance, we might believe, assuming for the purposes of argument that only nation states have the resources and the capacity to address global poverty, that it is indeed the job of nation states to address it. Or we might specify that multinational corporations, for example, have a duty to contribute towards achieving the goals of global justice. Of course, theories of global justice might well provide a mixed answer, which suggests that both individuals and collectives such as nation states have the relevant duties. By way of example, section 1.3.1.1 will address the work of Thomas Pogge, a theorist of global justice who wants to suggest both that states should not (and have a duty not to) abuse their power globally by setting unfair terms of global co-operation, and that individuals have a duty to lobby their own states to act more justly within the global arena.

In terms of types of obligation, broadly speaking there are two alternatives. We might think we have an obligation of charity, founded on *humanitarian* principles, to respond to poverty. Or we might think we have a duty of *distributive justice*. The distinction between humanitarianism and distributive justice is very common in the literature on global distributive justice. But what is the difference between them? There are a variety of positions on the difference between the two kinds of duty, and we shall begin by examining a false start, which suggests that duties of humanitarianism are somehow 'superficial', whereas duties of justice tackle the 'root' of global problems.

This first way of explaining the distinction – which turns out not to be wholly useful – suggests that duties of justice are somehow more *fundamental* in their objectives, whereas duties of humanitarianism are *superficial*. On this distinction the idea is that thinking about poverty and inequality through the lens of global justice rather than humanitarianism directs our attention rather better to what is really at stake. Humanitarian principles tell us that we ought, generally speaking, to respond to global poverty because of the basic humanity of the people affected by it. But Kok-Chor Tan (2004: 21) suggests that humanitarian approaches tell us that we should redistribute resources to tackle poverty abroad but fail to adequately address 'the root of the problem'. Humanitarian approaches are rather superficial because they argue for a redistribution of wealth without asking fundamental questions about who is entitled to that wealth in the first place, why there is global poverty and what features of the global system might be contributing to it. As such they are condemned endlessly to redistributing money without ever quite breaking the links that perpetuate injustice in the first place. At worst, they are a kind of window dressing which makes us feel better about the world and our place in it, while allowing the privileged among us to benefit from the institutions of a fundamentally unjust world. Theories of global justice, for Tan, direct our attention directly towards these more fundamental issues. Similarly, Thomas Pogge has argued that characterising our duties to the world's poor as duties of humanitarian 'assistance' diverts our attention from the various ways in which we actually contribute to their poverty (Pogge 2004). Whereas the idea of 'assistance' seems to indicate that we are morally blameless but still, generously, giving help to the poor, accounts of justice ask more difficult questions about the origins of that poverty and our complicity in it (an argument we shall examine further in section 1.3.1.1).

This distinction is not all that helpful, however. To be sure, Tan and Pogge may be right about the misleading nature of the language of 'assistance'. And it is certainly the case that Tan's and Pogge's favoured accounts of global justice *do* ask some profound questions about how poverty is created and sustained, and how the global 'system' contributes to it. Still, it is not a conceptual truth that all accounts of global justice *must* ask such questions. Indeed, a given (fairly undemanding) humanitarian account could be identical in its implications to a given (fairly undemanding) account of global justice. They might both agree, for example, that countries should give 0.7 per cent of their national income in overseas aid (which many countries have agreed to do in order to meet the UN's 'Millennium Development Goals' discussed in chapter 3). They would disagree on the status of those duties – whether they were best characterised as duties of justice or not – but they could still both fail to ask the kind of difficult questions that Pogge and Tan want us to ask. Accounts of global justice *can* ask such fundamental questions – and both these theorists believe that they should – but this does not mean that an account which does not is not an account of global justice. So the 'superficial'/'fundamental' distinction does not really help us.

So what *does* the difference between duties of justice and duties of humanitarianism really consist of? Many theorists agree that duties of distributive justice – which we shall call duties of justice from here onwards – are more *stringent* than humanitarian ones, and that they are *enforceable*.

A stringent duty is one which is firm and difficult to avoid. So to say that a duty is stringent is not the same thing as saying that it is demanding or expensive to perform. But this is a potentially confusing difference, so an example might help. Let's assume that I have a duty of justice to contribute £5 per week to the cause of eradicating global poverty. That's fine for me, since although I have spent most of my week's wages I still have £20 left. However, I also told my friend that I would lend her £20 to buy a new pair of shoes. So here I seem to have two competing duties – a duty of justice to give £5, and some kind of moral duty to lend my friend £20 as I promised I would. The moral duty is more demanding or costly in this case, since it would use up all my money, whereas the duty of justice would only cost me £5 to discharge. But we could still say that the duty of justice was more stringent. If we said this, what we would be suggesting is that it would be worse to fail to perform it than the moral duty. The stringency of a duty corresponds to the importance of fulfilling it. If theorists say that we have stringent duties of global distributive justice, they are claiming that those duties are important and weighty, and that they ought not to be ignored simply because there are other things on which we would rather spend our money. And it might be thought that duties of justice are on this basis more stringent than duties of humanitarianism. When theorists argue whether our duties towards the world's poor are humanitarian duties or duties of justice, they are often arguing about how firm those duties are.

But perhaps the most compelling way of explaining the difference is to say that unlike humanitarian duties, duties of justice are morally *enforceable*; we mean by an enforceable duty a duty that it would potentially be justified for someone to compel you to perform, if you were not prepared to perform it otherwise. In the domestic context giving to charity is not generally seen as enforceable. That is, no one seems to believe that a miserly person who refuses to put a penny in the collection box of a fund-raiser should be compelled to do so. But most of us believe that someone refusing to pay their taxes – part of the goal of which will be to secure some domestic justice objective – should be compelled to do so. We believe that in principle some sanctions could be applied – so long as they are proportionate and effective, let us say. Most of us think that there is an enforceable duty of justice to pay taxes, then, assuming at least that we think that our government is more or less legitimate and that its objectives are themselves more or less just. For many theorists of global distributive justice, we should think about principles of global justice in a similar way. If we are using the language of justice to pick out interests or entitlements which are very significant, and which in turn imply stringent duties on other individuals, then we should be prepared to put our money where our mouth is and say that such duties are enforceable. We might be prepared to say that we are required to meet our duties of justice even though the cost to us may sometimes be a high one (Miller 2007: 248).

So by and large there is agreement that duties of justice, as opposed to duties of humanitarianism, are enforceable and stringent. There is not universal agreement on this, to be sure. Thus Samuel Freeman (2006: 34) argues that a principle does not count as a principle of global distributive justice unless it distributes *all* available resources. A principle which picks out some key resources – such as clean water or basic education – is not really, by this definition, a principle of justice. But this seems much too strict a definition. A principle that states that everyone's basic needs should be met as a matter of justice, across the world, would still be a principle of global distributive justice according to the standard we have described. So would one which was far more ambitious, and governed the distribution of all of the world's resources. So when, in this book, we discuss the idea of global distributive justice, we are assuming that people have both entitle-ments and duties as a matter of justice, and that by and large those entitlements and duties apply wherever in the world they happen to be. We are not saying that all our duties are global duties, because some accounts suggest that we have some general duties towards everyone, but separate and perhaps stronger duties towards our fellow citizens. But a feature of any account of global justice is that it will pick out at least some entitlements which apply globally, and specify at least some duties, applying across national borders, to respond to those entitlements.

1.2.2. Positive and negative duties of justice

One other distinction which is important to many theorists of global justice is that between positive and negative duties. This cuts across the distinction between justice and humanitarianism (so that a posi-tive duty, for instance, could be either humanitarian or a duty of just-ice). So what is the distinction between positive and negative duties? The answer, as John Rawls put it, is that a positive duty 'is a duty to do something good for another', whereas a negative duty 'require[s] us not to do something that is bad' (Rawls 1971: 114).

So a positive duty, as it is normally understood, often involves an obligation to deliver some material good for someone else – to pro-vide food for the starving or to give money to others in the form of international development aid, for example. Many people, as we have seen, will be sceptical about the existence of this kind of duty, at least its existence as a stringent and enforceable duty of justice. But we are also usually taken to have certain negative duties, and often these are assumed to be duties of justice too. A negative duty, as Rawls put it, is a duty not to do something to someone. For example, we are often taken to have a duty not to infringe the autonomy of other communi-ties, to harm their basic interests – for instance by polluting them – or to exploit or oppress them. In section 1.3.1.1 of this chapter, for instance, we shall discuss Thomas Pogge's argument that we have a negative duty of justice not to impose an unjust institutional order on other people. For some theorists, such as Pogge, accepting even these basic negative duties can take us quite a long way towards building a satisfactory account of global justice. Delivering on negative duties may have significant implications for the inhabitants of developed countries who do in fact benefit from imposing an unjust institutional order on others.

Negative duties are sometimes taken to be more stringent than positive duties. That is certainly Pogge's view. His argument depends on the assumption that even if we do not believe ourselves to have positive duties towards people on the other side of the world, it should still be very clear to us that there are certain things we should *not* do to them. That is a widespread view, but, as Pogge observes, it might have some interesting implications for people who otherwise think of themselves as sceptics about global justice. Recall that at the beginning of this section I suggested that, according to some people, we simply do not owe anything to people outside our community, or perhaps even our immediate circle. A 'realist' about international relations might take this view. I suggested that we would come back to that idea because things are not quite as simple as they seem. There are, of course, many strands of realism, which make slightly different kinds of claim. One claim would be that we have no moral duties at all outside our own community, and that our community's survival and flourishing is all that matters from a moral point of view. A slightly different claim would be that communities ought to defend their own self-interest because *in so doing* we shall be able to create a secure world in which people's basic interests might be protected. Both claims would at first sight seem to agree that we do not owe anything to 'outsiders'. But the point about negative duties is important here. For we might respond to the realist (or to the general sceptic about the idea that we might have duties of justice towards anyone outside our community) by asking: are you really saying that we do not have even *negative* duties of justice? Is there nothing at all, from the point of view of justice, that we ought not to do to people in other communities? Can it be right to kill or impoverish foreigners simply because they are foreigners? Most people, on reflection, would agree that there are some negative duties which specify what we may not do to other people wherever they happen to live. The chief disagreement will be about their precise content.

1.3. Why global distributive justice?

It seems as though theories of global distributive justice may impose some quite stringent and enforceable duties on us, wherever we happen to live, as well as granting us certain important entitlements. If we are going to be persuaded by these theories, we need an account of why global justice is necessary. Just why are we talking, increasingly, about issues of global justice? What makes them relevant and important? Very broadly speaking, theories of global justice will seek to persuade us by pointing either to facts about the world or to facts about our nature as human beings. Theories which point to facts about the world – to the effect that we share certain institutions or are bound together in some other significant way – can be called relational approaches. Theories which point to facts about human beings and are motivated by what we share simply by virtue of being human can be called non-relational approaches (Sangiovanni 2007). We shall examine each in turn.

1.3.1. Relational approaches

Relational approaches suggest that distributive justice becomes relevant between people when they exist in a certain kind of relationship with each other. That relationship could take a variety of forms. As we shall see in chapter 3, some people actually *oppose* global distributive justice for broadly relational reasons – they may believe that there is something very special about the relationship of sharing citizenship with someone, or being governed by the same state as them. They believe, also, that the specialness of that relationship makes justice relevant within that relationship but not outside it. So that kind of relationist might then want to *limit* distributive justice to the level of the state, and to reject the idea of global distributive justice altogether. But the kind of relationist in which we are interested right now is the kind who believes that there is some relationship that all, or more or less all, people share which makes justice relevant between them.

One very broad view might be that justice applies between people who share a single world. That really suggests that global distributive justice has always been applicable between all people, and continues to be. Most relationists, though, want to get a little more specific than that. But when we make the relationship slightly more specific, the practical implications change.

Another view, then, might be that distributive justice becomes relevant between people who can potentially affect each other's lives. When we factor in other people's actions when making our own decisions, we are already in the kind of relationship with them that triggers concerns of distributive justice (O'Neill 1986). If we were to focus purely on economics, we might then say that distributive justice applies to the global economy, which is a large-scale system where every individual's actions potentially have a small but nevertheless real impact on everybody else. As the global financial crisis of 2009 shows, there is substantial interdependence, so that an initially small-scale crisis quickly becomes a generalised one. However, there might be people who are not part of the global economy. There are probably not many of them nowadays, but there are some indigenous communities which are self-sufficient and which play no role in the global cash-driven economy (if it helps, consider them as inhabiting a small island, relatively untouched by contact with the rest of the world). We might then say that duties of distributive justice are owed neither to nor by those people. (We might still think that we had duties of humanitarianism towards them, or that they had such duties towards us – but they would not be part of our scheme of distributive justice. Neither would they have any entitlements of global justice.) For many, even this exclusion is a little far-fetched. For, moving away from the economy, consider the global climate. Here, it is clear, they will say, that we share a single global ecosystem, and as a result our actions potentially have an impact on many people outside our community, and perhaps on everyone else. As such, even if our islanders are not part of the global economy, they may be affected by our ecological decisions. If enough of us buy gas-guzzling cars, or if enough of us take our energy from fossil-fuel-burning power stations, there could be an ecological impact on our islanders. At the extreme, rises in sea level might destroy their way of life entirely. If so, the implication would be that, at least in terms of ecological issues, they should be considered as part of our scheme of distributive justice too.

That last view suggests that global justice is relevant because we each, potentially or actually, *impact* on each other's lives. But some relational accounts want to be more specific still. Indeed, it is probably fair to say that most relational accounts emphasise *institutional* relationships, and principally those institutions of the global economy or the organisations which regulate it. Institutionalist accounts of justice argue that the existence of common (social, political or economic) institutions make an enormous difference from a normative point of view. Note here that 'institutions' might well be used in a broad sense, incorporating general rules and patterns of interaction, as well as more formal organisations. As such the global economy itself could qualify as an institution, depending on how tightly we are defining institutions. In any case, principles of justice apply to (social, political or economic) institutions, and, as such, the scope of institutions determines the scope of justice. If there were no significant global institutions, global justice would not be necessary. The thinking often goes something like this: assuming that global institutions do not simply command us to act in one way or another without regard to our views, people across the world are presumably being asked to accept the 'global institutional order' as legitimate. If we are going to accept its legitimacy, it will have to offer us some kind of justice, minimal or otherwise. For institutionalists, then, principles of justice are primarily principles we use to appraise *existing* institutions, which we believe ought to meet certain standards of justice – to treat us equally, say, or perhaps to make sure that our basic needs are met wherever possible.

So for relationists empirical facts about the contemporary world are clearly hugely significant – some such facts have determined, in fact, that distributive justice has become applicable and given us a reason to pursue it. Globalisation may, as such, have fundamentally transformed the normative terrain, creating duties of global distributive justice where none existed before. Theories based on the idea that societies are more or less independent and self-sufficient – as many of the classics of political theory assumed – must now be seen as out of date.

1.3.1.1. Pogge on the global institutional order

Thomas Pogge's ideas on the global institutional order are set out in his book *World Poverty and Human Rights* (Pogge 2002). The starting point of Pogge's argument is the relational claim that there is now a 'shared institutional order' at the global level. This order is made up partly of formal institutions such as the World Bank, the International Monetary Fund (IMF), the World Trade Organization (WTO), the UN and so on. But it also comprises less formal institutions, such as the terms of international trade and conventions governing the way in which we deal with the sale of natural resources (see chapter 5).

If the first important consideration, for Pogge, is that there is a *shared* global institutional order, the second is that this order is in a sense *imposed* on people. More particularly, this 'shared institutional order ... is shaped by the better-off and imposed on the worst-off' (2002: 199). The better-off enjoy much greater power over defining the terms of global economic interaction, making agreements that largely suit their own economic interests because of their superior bargaining power within organisations such as the WTO. They also pay large subsidies to their own agricultural industries, for example, at the same time as placing import tariffs on goods produced by poorer countries (2002: 18). This effectively locks poorer countries into a position of ongoing disadvantage which they find it very hard to break out of. But, morally speaking, we should not just go around imposing institutions on people without paying any attention to the consequences. From the point of view of distributive justice, in particular, we have a duty to make sure that the evolving institutional order meets at least certain minimal conditions. Pogge expresses these conditions in terms of human rights. He wants to say that we are acting unjustly when we impose an order on people that prevents their basic human rights from being fulfilled.

A third relevant consideration, for Pogge, is that the poverty produced by this shared, imposed order is *avoidable*. It is avoidable in the sense that there are feasible alternative scenarios for which we could opt, in which 'such severe and extensive poverty would not exist' (2002: 199). Although surveying the facts about global poverty mentioned at the beginning of this chapter can be a forbidding process, we should not be tricked into thinking that there is nothing people can do about such statistics. According to Pogge, there is such wealth in our world that shifting only 1 per cent of total global income from the wealthiest to the poorest would eradicate severe poverty as the World Bank currently defines it (2002: 2). Short of actually redistributing resources, there may be a whole host of things we could do to reduce our role in sustaining poverty. We could, for instance, stop paying subsidies to our farmers, or refrain from making the most of our superior bargaining power within the WTO and allow fairer terms of trade to develop globally (see chapter 6). Other ways of acting, which would have less catastrophic effects on the global poor, are open to us. If we refuse to opt for such alternatives, we are knowingly violating their human rights.

Clearly, in the terms of the distinction we discussed in section 1.2.2, Pogge's is an argument about our *negative* duties. Although he does seem to believe that we also have positive duties to assist the poor of the world, it is not wholly clear whether he believes that they are duties of justice (Gilabert 2005). But he is committed to demonstrating to us that even if we only accept that we have negative duties towards everyone, this should already be enough to make us very uneasy about our complicity in the reproduction of global poverty. Given that Pogge focuses on negative duties, exactly *what* negative duty is it that he believes we are infringing in our relationship with the global poor? His most precise formulation of the relevant duty is that 'one ought not to co-operate in the imposition of a coercive institutional order that avoidably leaves human rights unfulfilled without making reasonable efforts to aid its victims and to promote institutional reform' (Pogge 2002: 170). According to Pogge, as we have seen, the global institutional order *does* avoidably leave human rights unfulfilled. Many people have poor access to nutritious food, clean water and so on, and these deficits are avoidable. If developed countries were to act differently when they negotiated international trade rules at the WTO, for example, they could reduce or minimise these human rights deficits. They have not yet shown the political will to do so, but they ought to. Citizens, too, ought to lobby their governments to fulfil their duties.

To return to our starting point, Pogge's account is *relational* in the sense that his arguments take their impetus from the fact that there is a global institutional order. Its existence, and the fact that it is both shared and imposed, means that we have a duty to make sure that its effects do not prevent the fulfilment of human rights. As Pogge puts it, 'the *global* moral force of human rights is activated only through the emergence of a *global* institutional order' (2002: 171). Because this order exists, we need to make sure that the terms by which we interact with the other people of the world are at least minimally fair, defined in terms of their impact on human rights. These relational facts, then, account for the urgency of what he sees as our (negative) duties of global justice.

1.3.2. Non-relational approaches

In contrast to relational approaches, non-relational approaches typically suggest that humans have entitlements simply *as* humans, and not because we happen to share certain institutions, for example. They suggest that our humanity, or dignity, ought to be respected, and that doing so has distributive implications. Contemporary human rights discourse tends to make just this kind of claim: all humans have certain entitlements as humans. And for *some* theorists of human rights, these rights exist whether or not there is a global institutional order. In contrast to Pogge, for instance, non-relationist accounts do not require *any* further facts about human interaction for the standards of justice to become relevant. Although it might be wrong in this globalised world for some not to have their human rights met, it would still be wrong if the world were less globalised. It is the fact of our humanity which creates entitlements and duties of justice. (Note, though, that the reference to humanity does not mean that non-relationist arguments for global justice are the same as humanitarian ones. Whereas they both justify duties by pointing to our basic humanity, proponents of global distributive justice are using that platform to argue for stringent and enforceable duties of justice).

Some critics find this latter argument a little unworldly, at least when it extends to positive duties. Imagine a world divided into two separate communities, they might ask us, where the two communities do not even know of each other's existence. Imagine also that the lives lived by the two communities are very different. In the first community the ingredients of a life of luxury and leisure are readily available: the inhabitants just have to pick nutritious fruit from the trees, or collect pure water from abundant streams. In the second community life is much tougher: there is a shortage of nutritious food, the climate is unpredictable, and locating and transporting clean water is very hard work. Should we *really* say that inequalities between these communities are unjust? That citizens of the better-off community might have positive duties to reduce those inequalities, even though they are presumably incapable of acting on them? Non-relationists – at least those who are concerned about inequalities in the first place – typically do not find this an absurd conclusion. Although our initial intuition – that the inequalities are unjust – may not have any concrete implications (in the sense that we are unable at present to do anything about the situation), that intuition is still basically correct. For non-relationists, then, a reference to humanity, or a need for the protection of human dignity, is enough to trigger concerns of distributive justice. And the fact that those concerns might sometimes be hard to act on should not trick us into accepting as just situations which are, in fact, not just at all.

In their more evangelical moments, non-relationists sometimes argue that, if only they would realise it, supporters of most contemporary political theories are really committed to such genuinely global views. Theories such as liberalism and socialism have tended to argue that all citizens – regardless of sex, ethnicity or class – should be treated equally because they have a common human nature, or rationality, or capacity for autonomy, for instance. Those arguments are absolutely standard within political theory, and have a great deal of normative appeal. Such theories, though, have also tended to 'forget' or ignore the fact that *all* of us are humans with identical capacities for autonomy or rationality, and not just our fellow citizens. But the logic of these claims is clearly *universal*. As Simon Caney (2005a: 107) puts it, 'the standard justifications of principles of distributive justice' therefore also entail that there are *global* principles of distributive justice. For if we think that citizens deserve equal opportunities because, say, people should not suffer because of the race, class or gender into which they are born, then we should recognise the obvious fact that all humans are people, and therefore neither should they suffer inferior opportunities because of such unchosen characteristics (indeed, defenders of global equality of opportunity would suggest that nationality itself might be one such unchosen characteristic which should not affect our life chances; see chapter 2 for a discussion of that idea).

Non-relationist accounts tend to emphasise *continuity*, in two senses. First, they tend to see no really important difference between domestic and global realms. If we have good reasons to accept principles of justice within the individual nation state, then we probably have the same reasons for accepting them at the global level. The two realms – national and global – are not fundamentally different. We are, after all, dealing with the same human beings in each case. This is not to say that the two realms are not *empirically* different – it might be the case, for instance, that co-citizens within France have much more in common with each other than they have in common with people from Argentina. It might also be that the institutions which regulate their common life, within France, are much stronger, and have a much more direct impact on their lives, than any truly global institutions. But non-relationists will not see those empirical facts as *normatively* important. They might make the achievement of global justice much harder, but they do not tell us that we should not *try* (they do not, that is, provide us with any normatively convincing reason why we should restrict the scope of justice). Second, and relatedly, non-relationists do not place great store by the transformations which have characterised the contemporary world – transformations which are often grouped together under the term 'globalisation'. The fact that we live in a world with instantaneous communication, where the media are capable of confronting us with the facts of other people's misery on a daily basis, may mean that we are now more likely to reflect on our duties of justice. Moreover, given the facts of economic and political integration, we may be more able to *act* on them than we were before. But the facts of globalisation have not really transformed the moral landscape. Our entitlements of justice as human beings have not, fundamentally, been affected or altered by changes within the contemporary global system. They may, to repeat, have made global distributive justice a more lively possibility. But they have not created the *need* for global justice in the first place.

1.3.2.1. Caney on justice beyond borders

Simon Caney presents a non-relationist argument for global distributive justice in his book *Justice beyond Borders* (Caney 2005a). Caney notes the 'striking' fact that, until recently, in most political theorising, 'it was assumed that principles of distributive justice should operate at the state level' (2005a: 102). But the arguments for this restriction of the scope of justice have not always been obvious. Most often, Caney notes, theories of justice suggest that people have certain normatively crucial characteristics or attributes – such as rationality, the potential for autonomy, equal dignity and so on – but to then confine justice to the domestic level makes no sense. For very few people think that, for instance, only inhabitants of one state possess these characteristics. We simply – at least potentially – possess them *as humans*. Of course, as we shall see in chapter 3, there are other relational arguments for why we might restrict the scope of justice, or equality, to the domestic level. We might think there is something special about the ties between citizens, or the specific institutions that we share. There is a variety of such views, but in a later paper Caney has suggested that they, too, are vulnerable to the slide into global justice, because the relations which are supposed to be special do not, in fact, neatly coincide with state borders (Caney 2008).

Caney therefore makes a series of what we might call 'extension' arguments – which suggest that the standard arguments for distributive justice at the domestic level also apply at the global level. As such there are no important *discontinuities* between the two realms, and no justification for restricting distributive justice to the level of individual states. What makes Caney's a non-relational perspective is that, in the end, he does not believe that empirical facts about the world are important in determining our entitlements as human beings. He suggests that it is 'hard to see why', for instance, 'economic interaction has any moral relevance from the point of view of distributive justice' (Caney 2005a: 111). He is therefore prepared to accept the kind of conclusion that relationists appear to consider absurd. Turning back to our 'divided world' case in which two communities have no interaction at all, but in which one fares better than the other for reasons of brute luck, Caney is adamant that this situation is unfair. There is simply no good moral ground on which the better-off community can claim to be entitled to be better off; as such the situation is unjust (2005a: 111). We should also resist an unfortunate real-world implication of relationist accounts of global justice, which would be that if someone *were* genuinely born into an impoverished society with no connections with other societies, we would have no duties of justice towards them (2005a: 112).

Caney's proposals for principles of global distributive justice are complex. They include the idea that we should give priority to the worst off, that we should meet everyone's basic or subsistence needs, and that we should try to achieve global equality of opportunity (on which see chapter 2). But, added together, they are challenging (and certainly more challenging than Pogge's), and represent a demanding account of what justice requires of us at the global level. They also, unlike Pogge's account, incorporate both negative and positive duties of justice. They require us, that is, not only to refrain from acting in certain ways, but also in many cases to seek proactively to improve the position of the disadvantaged of the world.

1.4. Egalitarian and minimalist approaches

We have already seen in the last section that the content of theories of global justice varies. Some theorists, such as Pogge, set their sights on the fulfilment of basic rights and the eradication of severe poverty. Others, such as Caney, set their sights higher and are prepared to say that even if we eradicated poverty and protected human rights, we should still have reasons of justice to object to many of the inequalities that would remain. For Pogge it is not clear that the inequalities would be normatively troubling, because his account would seem to be satisfied in a world where we did not impose on others a global institutional order which failed to protect their human rights. So clearly different standards are at work even among theorists who otherwise agree that global distributive justice is necessary and important. This means that, when we hear someone arguing for greater global justice or for a more just world, we still need to know more. We need to know more, specifically, about the distributive *standards* they would apply to the world as a whole. In this section we shall distinguish between *egalitarian* and *minimalist* approaches to this question – a distinction that will resonate throughout many of the remaining chapters of this book.

An egalitarian approach to distributive justice is one which places a high value on equality. It might specify that some important resource should be distributed equally between all people, or that people should at least have an equal chance to obtain it for themselves if they work hard enough. It might specify that since people's lives matter equally, then global institutions should seek to equalise their welfare or well-being. But it might not, perhaps, be that strong. Some egalitarian accounts suggest that inequalities are sometimes acceptable, but try to specify and to place limits on the kinds of inequalities that are justified. They might say, for example, that inequalities are acceptable just so long as they are necessary to create incentives within the economy. What such accounts tell us is that equality is generally to be desired, and that we should pursue it within certain limits. Not everyone would recognise such accounts as strictly egalitarian in nature. But if they do seek substantially to decrease the inequalities that characterise a society or the world as a whole, the description of them as egalitarian seems to make sense.

Egalitarian accounts will generally aim to substantially narrow global inequalities and, where they remain, to challenge us to provide good reasons for them. They will therefore tend to perceive global inequalities as unjust. Although we cannot necessarily achieve perfect equality – perhaps because perfect equality would be incompatible with other values, such as freedom or autonomy or even national self-determination – we should still be suspicious of such inequalities. When we survey the facts about global poverty outlined at the beginning of this chapter, it is significant that many people clearly do not have enough to lead a decent life, at least according to standards we would recognise in the developed world. For that reason egalitarians, like minimalists, can support the kind of basic human rights which we shall discuss in chapter 4. But, unlike minimalists, they will not limit their attention to such basic standards. For egalitarians the *inequalities* which characterise the contemporary world are also objectionable. It matters not just that some have too little, but also that some have too little while others have more than enough.

Simply identifying these inequalities might not be enough to be able to describe them as unjust, of course. While we might just be suspicious of them from the start, a relationist global egalitarian, for instance, might want to ask a further set of questions about them. Do they provide evidence that global institutions are operating unfairly? That global institutions are paying insufficient regard to the interests of the worst off? But global egalitarians are united in their belief that we have *some* compelling reasons of justice to object to at least some global inequalities.

Minimalist accounts are quite different. Generally speaking they set their sights lower, although achieving their goals might still be formidably difficult in the contemporary world. A minimalist account will suggest that global injustice occurs where some people do not have enough to get by or to lead lives of decency and dignity (or perhaps they will suggest that this is only problematic where it is not the fault of the individual concerned). They will attempt to draw a line between what is necessary for a decent or minimally accept-able life, and what is surplus to that requirement. Crucially, once the goal of securing a decent minimum for all is secured, inequalities in the distribution of various goods over and above that will not be condemned as unjust. Thus a minimalist account might tell us that it is unjust that children born in Mozambique often lack access to adequate education or even nutrition. Here the reason why minimal-ists object is because in many cases, in such countries, the minimum standard is not available for many people. But there are many coun-tries which *do* secure a decent minimum for all their citizens. We should not be concerned about inequalities between such countries: we should not, for instance, be concerned about the fact that gross national income per head is substantially higher in Denmark than in Portugal (see chapter 2). We should not care because – assuming that the decent minimum standard is not set very high – we can be rea-sonably confident that everyone in Portugal has enough. This con-cern with everyone having enough, or a decent minimum, defines the broad standard we should apply to issues of global distributive justice. If we do still care about global inequalities we care about them not in themselves – for they are not objectionable in them-selves – but because they stand in the way of achieving other things we think are valuable. Perhaps excessive global inequalities prevent political equality between nations, or allow some nations to exploit other nations too easily. Minimalists can express such indirect or instrumental concern with inequalities without fear of contradicting themselves. But they will not be objecting, here, to the injustice of the inequalities in and of themselves.

Interestingly, those who are minimalists about global distributive justice – including Rawls (1999), Miller (2007) and Nagel (2005), whose work will be discussed in chapter 3 – will not tend to reject the ideal of equality altogether. Indeed, the minimalist approaches we shall discuss in chapter 3 tend to *embrace* the importance of equality *within* individual societies. Between citizens equality may be hugely important, and fellow citizens may, for instance, be committed to an ideal of equal citizenship that is just incompatible with large inequalities between the various members of that society. But these concerns for equality simply do not *extend* to the global level. Minimalist theories often supply relationist explanations for their simultaneous support for equality at the domestic level but rejection of it at the global level. They will emphasise, that is, the special relationships between citizens which make equality appropriate and which do not apply beyond the individual nation state.

What, if anything, is the connection between the two distinctions we have been discussing, between minimalism and egalitarianism on the one hand, and relationism and non-relationism on the other? The chief division that runs through the literature, at least as this book understands it, is between global egalitarians and global minimalists. Global egalitarians could be either relationists or non-relationists. They could defend extending equality globally, that is, either by pointing to facts about the world like globalisation, or the existence of global institutions (a relational defence of global egalitarianism), or by pointing to our basic humanity (a non-relational defence). Global minimalists could also either be relationists or non-relationists, but, as it turns out, all the global minimalist theorists discussed in chapter 3 of this book are relationists. Their arguments all suggest that equality is relevant at the level of individual states, and generally speaking this is for reasons of the special relations that exist between co-citizens or co-nationals. But they also suggest that our standards at the global level should be much more modest – because the important relationship which triggers distributive egalitarianism does not apply there.

So to some extent the two distinctions cut across each other, and our position on one issue does not determine our position on the other. The distinction between egalitarianism and minimalism tells us something about the *content* of what people owe to each other and are in turn entitled to. The distinction between relationism and non-relationism tells us something about *why* that might be so – about the different reasons theorists give for extending justice globally. As such it is really a question about *justification*. One of the most important questions in contemporary debates about global justice is thus whether global egalitarians can provide good (relational or non-relational) grounds for justifying the extension of equality to the global level, or whether, by contrast, global minimalists can provide good (relational) reasons for refusing to extend equality in this way.

Conclusions

This chapter began with some facts about global poverty, and suggested that we might respond to them in a number of different ways, normatively speaking. We examined the distinction between humanitarian duties and duties of justice as a way of putting flesh on the bones of the idea of global distributive justice. We also examined the distinction between positive and negative duties of justice, with the former requiring us actively to help others and the latter requiring us not to mistreat them in certain ways. We then moved on to different views about *why* we should adopt principles of global distributive justice. While relationist accounts emphasise the interconnections between people, non-relationist accounts focus on our humanity. Although the implications might be very similar – relationists and non-relationists might both agree on the need for global justice – there are still interesting differences in the justifications they each offer.

Finally, we turned to the distinction between egalitarian and minimalist accounts of global justice. As I shall try to show in the next two chapters, the most interesting division in debates on global justice these days is between proponents of egalitarian and minimalist approaches. Chapter 2 will move on to examine some of the arguments for, and implications of, egalitarian approaches. Global egalitarians might be either relationists or non-relationists, but they agree on the idea that at least some egalitarian distributive principles are applicable at the global level. The implications of that are, in many cases, really quite radical. Minimalist accounts are addressed in chapter 3. They are sceptical about the extension of such egalitarian approaches to the global level. Most often they are relationists, and believe that there is some normatively significant difference between the national and global realms. Although they tend to be egalitarians at the level of individual nation states, they support more minimal, non-egalitarian principles at the global level. In chapter 3 we shall examine both the minimalist accounts themselves and some of the more important reasons given for rejecting global egalitarian accounts. The debate between global egalitarian and global minimalist accounts will play out through the various chapters of part II of this book, where it will often be obvious that egalitarians and minimalists view concrete problems of global injustice quite differently, and recommend quite different solutions.

chapter 2

Egalitarian approaches

This chapter examines egalitarian approaches to global distributive justice. Whereas the minimalist accounts we shall examine in chapter 3 set their sights relatively low in aiming to secure a decent minimum for all (although this could still be a very challenging objective in practice), egalitarian accounts are less easily satisfied. Even if everyone's basic needs were met, they would still offer reasons to be uneasy about the inequalities which might remain. In fact, we could object to global inequalities for a wide range of reasons, and different egalitarian theories will pick out different reasons on which to focus. But one important point to bear in mind from the outset is that egalitarian approaches to global justice will tell us that some inequalities are unfair or unjust *in their own right*. Other theories – such as the minimalist theories we shall examine in chapter 3 – could suggest that we have *instrumental* reasons for objecting to some global inequalities. Perhaps inequalities, if they become too wide, could stand in the way of *other* things that we value, such as the ability of nations to be self-determining, or to co-operate on fair terms. But pointing to such instrumental reasons would not make such theories egalitarian in themselves. Egalitarian theories are distinctive because they suggest that inequalities would matter *even if they did not* prevent us from achieving self-determination or fair co-operation for example. As such egalitarian positions on global justice will be more demanding, and less easily satisfied, than minimalist ones.

Section 2.1 of this chapter provides some brief empirical information about key global inequalities and their trends over time. It also examines what we *mean* by global inequalities – with most global egalitarians expressing concern about inequalities between individuals rather than inequalities between nation states. Section 2.2 moves on to discuss one of the first and most important arguments for a broadly egalitarian position on global justice, that of Charles Beitz. We examine his argument that the distribution of natural resources is 'arbitrary' and should be remedied by a 'resource redistribution principle', and we also examine the case he makes for a global 'difference principle'. Section 2.3 moves on to address the work of Simon Caney, another significant global egalitarian theorist. Again we sketch the contours of his account and pay particular attention to his argument for another global egalitarian principle: the principle of 'global equality of opportunity'. Section 2.4 then shifts our attention to a somewhat different issue. The various chapters of this book are principally engaged in examining the rivalry between global egalitarianism and global minimalism as opposing approaches to global distributive justice, and assessing their implications across a range of political issues. However, the literature on global justice also abounds with references to 'cosmopolitanism' and 'cosmopolitan justice'. It is often assumed that the major division is between 'cosmopolitans' and 'statists', and this could leave the reader somewhat puzzled. Section 2.4 examines the relationship between statism and cosmopolitanism, on the one hand, and global egalitarianism and minimalism on the other. Ultimately it suggests that the distinction between statism and cosmopolitanism is potentially misleading in a number of ways, whereas the language of global egalitarianism and minimalism is more useful for our purposes. But readers who are already comfortable with the language of global egalitarianism and minimalism, and who remain un-puzzled by the language of statism and cosmopolitanism, may prefer to skip this final section.

2.1. The nature and extent of global inequality

Egalitarians frequently tell us that the degree of inequality at the global level is immense. Charles Beitz, for instance, tells us that 'We live in a world whose massive inequalities dwarf those found within the domestic societies familiar to us' (2001: 95). Darrel Moellendorf observes that 'Our world is marked by deep and pervasive inequalities' (2009a: 2). Simon Caney tells us that 'The world that we inhabit is characterized by staggering inequalities' (2006: 121). Here Beitz, Moellendorf and Pogge apparently agree that global inequalities are profound, and morally serious. But we should not assume from this that they agree about the nature of that inequality or, indeed, that they necessarily mean exactly the same thing when they talk of global inequality.

There are, in fact, at least two issues on which there could still be disagreement. The first is the 'stuff' or 'currency' of equality and inequality. The second is the 'subjects' of equality and inequality. In terms of the first point, whenever we diagnose an inequality we presumably have a sense of what it is that divides people – what they have unequal shares of, or what it is that they have unequal chances to achieve. But philosophers disagree about which goods are important. Some have suggested that what matters is our *welfare*, well-being or happiness – so that equality is satisfied when all individuals have equal welfare, measured in some way or another. Others suggest that it is the *resources* we have, or have access to, that is important. Note that resource-egalitarians might interpret 'resources' quite broadly, so that all kinds of things that individuals might want in order to lead happier lives would count as resources. Still others suggest that what matters is what we can *do* – what we have the capability to achieve in our lives. In the philosophical literature we tend to find a debate (the so-called 'equality of what' debate) between proponents of equality of (or equal opportunity to achieve) welfare, resources or capabilities (for an introduction to that debate see e.g. Wolff 2007). This does have one important implication when we come to survey the facts about global inequality that are detailed in box 2.1. For resource-egalitarians, unequal shares of resources such as income or of carbon dioxide emissions are important inequalities in their own right. For welfare- or capability-egalitarians they may not matter in themselves, but are likely to be important insofar as they allow some better opportunities than others to achieve welfare or to exercise important capabilities. Furthermore, some theorists have suggested that what really concern us as egalitarians are hierarchies of power and status or the existence of oppression (see Anderson 1999; Armstrong 2006), and this approach is also beginning to make its presence felt in the global justice literature (see e.g. Altman and Wellman 2009).

Box 2.1. **Key global inequalities**

1. Gross national income per capita ($US equivalent)

China 2,360
Denmark 54,910
India 950
Portugal 18,950
Sierra Leone 260
United States 46,040

2. CO_2 emissions per capita (metric tonnes)

China 3.9
Denmark 9.8
India 1.2
Portugal 5.6
Sierra Leone 0.2
United States 20.6

3. Life expectancy at birth (years)

China 72
Denmark 78
India 64
Portugal 78.5

Sierra Leone 42.5
United States 78

4. Adult literacy rate (per cent)

China 91

Denmark 99

India 66

Portugal 94

Sierra Leone 35

United States 99

Adapted from World Bank 2009 (income, CO_2 emissions and life expectancy) and UN 2009 (literacy).

A second thing about which egalitarians might disagree is just *whom* global inequalities exist between. Although global egalitarians will insist that there are at least some egalitarian principles with global scope, that leaves open the question of to whom those principles ought to apply. Global egalitarianism, strictly understood, could include many different kinds of *subject*. We might be interested in global inequalities between units such as families, tribes or ethnic groups. Or we might be referring to differences between *countries* – we might be concerned by the fact that some countries have, in total, much greater wealth than others, for example. A principle that says that all countries should have equal opportunities, or equal shares of natural resources, say, would be a kind of global egalitarian principle. However, most global egalitarians are really interested in differences between *individuals* across the world. These are certainly the inequalities to which Beitz, Moellendorf and Caney are pointing. They agree that it is individuals, and what happens to them, that really matter, and if we care at all about inequalities between countries, we shall only be concerned because of the impact of inter-country inequalities on the individuals who live in them.

When we discuss global inequalities in this chapter, therefore, we shall principally be referring to such differences between the positions of individuals. That said, we have very little good-quality data on inequalities between individuals on the global scale (Ghose 2004). We often, therefore, end up using proxies such as differences in the average gross national income per capita of different countries (see Milanovic 2005 for a discussion of the different ways of measuring global inequalities). One obvious problem with such figures is that they reveal nothing about inequalities *within* countries. The poorest in a country with a high average income could, after all, be worse off than the poorest in a country with a lower average income, and brute averages do not tell us whether that is the case or not. Bearing this limitation in mind, picking out the different situations that individuals face in different countries is one, admittedly limited, way of highlighting the differences (between individuals' positions) that we really care about. The figures in Box 2.1 give figures for income, carbon dioxide emissions, life expectancy and adult literacy.

Although in a sense these kinds of figures are familiar – they do get cited in the media from time to time, after all – they can still be shocking. They suggest that some people have very inferior access to certain key goods, such as income (on which we have direct evidence), basic education (judging from the evidence on literacy) and health care (judging from the evidence on life expectancy). They also suggest that, at least in terms of carbon dioxide emissions, some people are making a very great contribution to the increasing concentration of greenhouse gases in the atmosphere, whereas others seem to be making a very small impact. So we can observe large inequalities in at least these dimensions. And the differences, in some cases, are very great. Carbon dioxide emissions are a striking example (with the average US citizen responsible for the same emissions as a hundred citizens of Sierra Leone). Income is another (with each Dane earning as much, on average, as two hundred Sierra Leoneans). Moreover, although the consensus seems to be that the number of people living in poverty has not changed radically over recent decades (see chapter 1), at least on some measures (and it matters a good deal which measures we use) key inequalities have grown markedly over recent decades (Ghose 2004; Wade 2004). The World Bank's Development Report for 2000/01, for example, suggested that income inequalities had increased sharply over the previous forty years (World Bank 2001). As in the case of poverty (discussed at the beginning of chapter 1), it is important to recognise that there are strong regional patterns. Whereas China has experienced rapid economic growth, other regions have fallen behind. Whereas the average North American had an income eight times that of the average African in 1900, by 2000 it was 18.5 times as great (Sutcliffe 2007: 57).

If we want to understand this rise in global inequality then we need to recognise that, whereas large (and relatively consistent) numbers of people remain in serious poverty, the income and wealth of inhabitants of developed countries has *risen* rapidly. Pogge estimates that, in terms of income and consumption expenditure, the average citizen of one of these affluent countries is better off than 300 individuals in serious poverty (2007a: 132). There is a serious fear, then, that the gulf between the 'haves' and the 'have-nots' shows every chance of growing further. As such, global inequality appears to be an enduring issue. Whether it is a *problem*, from the point of view of justice, is another question. Minimalists believe that it is not, but the egalitarian theorists discussed in this chapter seek to persuade us that it *is*.

2.2. Beitz on global distributive justice

Charles Beitz's 1979 book *Political Theory and International Relations* made a very significant contribution to the emerging literature on global justice. In it Beitz took what was the most important theory of justice at the domestic level, and argued that it, or something very much like it, should be applied at the global level too. In this section we shall see why he believed that to be the case.

First and foremost, when Beitz wrote his book he wanted to tackle the widespread belief that, since the domestic and international realms were so very different, the kinds of principles of justice that should characterise domestic societies simply do not apply beyond their borders. Many people appeared to believe that international relations was a basically amoral realm, or one where nation states were required to respect each other's independence, but in which more demanding moral values – such as justice and equality – were out of place. Beitz argued that the emergence of a single global economy challenged that picture, so that 'the international realm is coming more and more to resemble domestic society in many of the features thought relevant to the justification of (domestic) political principles' (Beitz 1979: 8). As such, statements to the effect that 'the existing global distribution of income and wealth is highly unjust' become possible and meaningful (1979: 9).

Beitz's direct aim was to offer a 'critique and reinterpretation' of John Rawls's theory of justice, contained in his hugely influential book *A Theory of Justice* (Rawls 1971). In that book, Rawls worked out a set of principles of justice, but argued that they ought not to apply beyond the borders of individual nation states (Rawls eventually suggested that, internationally, we should go for a much less demanding account of justice, which we shall discuss in chapter 3). Beitz wanted to argue for the extension of at least two Rawlsian arguments to the international level. The first suggests that the distribution of natural resources is, to use a Rawlsian term, 'morally arbitrary' and should somehow be corrected, and the second is that, given international economic co-operation, we should embrace a global version of what Rawls called the 'difference principle'. In the end, the argument for the global difference principle is the more important part of Beitz's argument, but the claim about natural resources does itself raise interesting questions, some of which we shall address in more detail in chapter 5. For now, we shall briefly examine Beitz's argument for redistributing natural resources in section 2.2.1. The argument for a 'global difference principle' is then examined more fully in section 2.2.2. Finally, in section 2.2.3 we shall examine some criticisms that have been levelled at Beitz's arguments.

2.2.1. The (re)distribution of natural resources

What principles, if any, should govern the distribution of natural resources, such as oil, coal, diamonds or gold? For many people that is simply an odd question, so accustomed are we to the apparently uncontroversial idea that such resources belong to the nations in which they are to be found (Wenar 2008a). But is the distribution of natural resources fair? Is it right to say that nations in some sense deserve to keep 'their' resources simply because they happen to be buried under the ground of their various territories? Peter Jones has argued that

> Nature has spread its resources unevenly across the globe, but, morally, that uneven distribution is a matter of mere chance and should be of

> no significance … It would seem indefensible, therefore, that access to
> those resources, or to the benefits that flow from them, should be limited
> to those who happen to be standing on them or near them … Yet that
> is effectively how we distribute natural resources across mankind at the
> moment. (Jones 2000: 171)

Beitz's argument runs along similar lines. Like Jones, he appeals to Rawls's argument that some distributions are 'morally arbitrary'. This is a contentious and potentially misleading idea, which can be interpreted in a variety of different ways (for evidence see Armstrong 2010). But the gist of it is that a distribution is arbitrary when there seems to be no good reason of justice for accepting it as it stands. Most often, theorists argue that a distribution is arbitrary because it is a matter of *brute luck* (or, as Jones puts it, mere chance), as opposed to being based on the choices individuals have made, and for which they therefore ought to be held responsible. To give an example, we might think that women should not enjoy more limited opportunities than men. After all, no one chooses to be born a woman. That, too, is mere brute luck. So a distribution which responds to such unchosen facts is arbitrary; we have no reason of justice to accept it, and we might have good reasons to try and alter it. If, on the other hand, you and I bet our wages on a game of poker and you end up with all the cash, that is not an arbitrary distribution because we can both plausibly be held responsible for what has happened.

Although it is not important for our purposes, Rawls argued in *A Theory of Justice* that the distribution of talents – the fact that some people are born with very marketable skills and others are not – is arbitrary. It is a matter of brute luck, rather than something people have chosen, and so there seems to be no obvious reason why we should just accept a distribution where those with more talent also turn out to earn more money (Rawls 1971: 72). Beitz does not attempt to defend this argument about talent. His claim is that if we think that *some* distributions are morally arbitrary – because they respond to factors of brute luck which really ought not to influence distributions – then surely the distribution of natural resources is one such case. There seems to be nothing that individual nations have done to earn those resources. On the other hand, how many resources your nation has will clearly influence its chances of developing economically. Industrialisation will tend to be easier (although not necessarily ecologically sustainable) with plentiful supplies of coal, iron and running water. Large oil reserves will be a great asset too. Resource-poor countries, on the other hand, could be on the back foot from the beginning. If some countries control the bulk of certain key resources, this will disadvantage others. As Beitz put it, 'The appropriation of valuable resources by some will leave others comparatively, and perhaps fatally, disadvantaged' (Beitz 1979: 139). Notice, here, that our concern about the arbitrary distribution of natural resources does not depend on 'relational' facts about the integration of the world economy. Even if nations were more or less autonomous and separate, the distribution of natural resources – and its impact on chances for development – would still appear unfair.

If we accept Beitz's argument, what are the political implications? Beitz suggests that, ideally, everyone should have an entitlement to an equal share of the natural resources of the world (or perhaps, an entitlement to an equal share of their *value*). But in practice, at the very least, we should embrace 'a resource redistribution principle that would give each society a fair chance to develop just political institutions and an economy capable of satisfying its members' basic needs' (1979: 141). So in some way or another, natural resources should be redistributed so that every nation had enough to allow it to function minimally well, and meet its members' basic human rights. A distribution of natural resources which did not allow them to do that would be an unjust one.

2.2.2. A global difference principle

The argument for a global difference principle is the most important part of Beitz's argument, because it responds directly to the nature of the contemporary world as he sees it. As we noted just previously, Beitz believes that the argument for a resource redistribution principle would apply even if we assumed that the world was divided into more or less isolated national communities. But that is not what he thinks the world is like. In fact, 'states participate in complex international economic, political and cultural relationships that suggest the existence of a global scheme of social cooperation'. And the implication of this is that 'international economic interdependence lends support to a principle of global distributive justice similar to that which applies within domestic society' (Beitz 1979: 144).

This idea of social co-operation requires closer scrutiny. Domestically, Rawls saw society in terms of the more or less active pursuit of mutual advantage. Terms such as 'the common good' are intelligible within single societies, because citizens are working together to achieve shared goals. Do we really have that kind of co-operation at the global level? Beitz admits that we probably do not. International economic 'co-operation' might be much less oriented towards a common good, and in fact some people in poorer countries might not even benefit from it at all. But we should not be too fixated on this difference. The idea of international co-operation still makes sense, because there is 'social activity' which produces benefits and burdens for those party to it. The global economy creates wealth (at least for some), which is no doubt why economic globalisation has continued apace over recent decades. It also produces its own costs and risks. These are benefits and burdens which would not exist otherwise, and it makes sense to appraise them from the point of view of principles of distributive justice (1979: 131).

If that argument is right, what principle should we apply to international economic co-operation? The 'difference principle' was one of the key elements of John Rawls's account of justice within individual societies (Rawls 1971). At the domestic level, a difference principle suggests that we should be prepared to accept inequalities (only) if they are to the greatest benefit of the least advantaged people in our society. So, for instance, we might prefer to opt for equal wages for all citizens – say, $500 per week – if we were thinking exclusively about the desirability of equality. But that might not actually be in the interests of the worst off. A society in which everyone earned the same might see its productivity decline, as highly skilled citizens no longer had any incentive to seek out demanding, highly skilled jobs or to work hard at them. An alternative might be to accept a degree of inequality in wages, in the hope that highly skilled citizens would indeed work harder, with the result that more wealth would be created. And if the greater wealth that is created ends up lifting the wages of the worst-off higher than $500 per week – even if the high earners are commanding perhaps $800 per week themselves – it would be wrong not to embrace this option.

The difference principle, as a result, looks rather like an argument for inequality. It tells us that a situation where one group earns $600 and another $800 should be preferred to a situation where everyone earns $500. But what the principle really does is to set down the conditions under which we should accept inequalities. Are the inequalities genuinely necessary to benefit the worst off? Will they really deliver improvements for the worst off, or is this simply some general hope? If we cannot answer affirmatively, the principle tells us to stand fast behind equality. We might also think of the difference principle as a kind of pact we all make with the worst off. We hope that the worst off will find the nature of social and political institutions acceptable – that they will buy into the system as it appears to them. After all, if 'the system' looks to them to be fundamentally unjust – if it does not meet their basic needs, say, or give them opportunities for advancement in life – then that will provide a recipe for unrest and social turmoil. It certainly would not provide for stability and a healthy society. In a sense the difference principle offers a guarantee to the worst off that their needs will be considered, and that social and political institutions will place a very high priority on their advancement. When the worst off ask the question, what does this system do for us? the answer will be readily available. The system works to their greatest benefit. Even though it contains inequalities, no other achievable system would benefit them more.

Although we have just addressed an example based on setting wages for different workers, the difference principle is really a principle of institutional design. Rather than governing micro-level decisions such as determining wage levels, it is meant to guide our thinking about the nature of just institutions as a whole. If we were designing institutions from scratch, we might well work out various ways of balancing equality with the desire to advance the position of the worst off in society. The difference principle encourages us to reject any inequalities that are not truly necessary for the advancement of their position. Of course, we do not often get a chance to create or rethink institutions in this way, although each elected government will have its own influence on the distribution of income and wealth between citizens. For some global egalitarians, though, the current global order *does* provide possibilities for the application of the difference principle. In our rapidly changing world, in which we *are* in a sense designing and redesigning global institutions on a continual basis, the difference principle provides an essential moral compass. If we were engaged in designing or reforming global institutions, a global difference principle would have us select those arrangements that would benefit the least advantaged the most (Beitz 1979; Moellendorf 2002).

Here we might return to the idea of a difference principle as a pact we make with the worst off. Globally, there are people who are radically deprived of opportunities, who see no real prospect of substantially improving their incomes, for instance, and who are sometimes prepared to endanger their own lives travelling, often illegally, to other nations where they might be able to pursue better opportunities. What can we say to such people when they ask of us, what does the system do for us? Can we genuinely reply that it works to their greatest advantage? Is there no attainable system that would provide them with better opportunities? Some might think that there is not. For example, a stout defender of the free market might argue that the only achievable route to advancement for the worst off of the world is that of free trade and open markets. But even if we did believe this, there would still be direct political and economic implications: we might then think that the countries of the developed world, for example, should work to open their borders to goods and services from the developing world, and stop dumping their own goods on markets in the developing world.

More likely, for global egalitarian theorists such as Beitz, we would seek to advance the position of the globally worst off by some more ambitious programme of institutional reform. This would almost certainly require us to reduce current inequalities both between and within countries (Beitz 1979: 153). As opposed to a global order which responds to the interests of powerful states and economic actors, a global difference principle would tell us to try and build structures and policies seeking rapid advancement for the poorest of the world. Although Beitz's main goal is to establish the normative argument for the global difference principle, he does investigate some policies that might further it in practice. One application might be to the rules of international trade (see chapter 6). Perhaps these could be redesigned so that they promoted redistribution towards poorer countries. More specifically, perhaps we could investigate possibilities for adopting preferential tariffs that allowed developing countries to establish lucrative industries at the same time as removing barriers to the import of their goods on the part of developed countries. We could also try and make the International Monetary Fund a more effective tool of development (Beitz 1979: 174). Other advocates of a global difference principle have argued that it produces a strong argument for cancelling the debts of poor countries (Moellendorf 2002: 94), or that it provides guidance on how to deal with the costs of addressing the problem of global warming (see chapter 7).

2.2.3. Responses to Beitz

Beitz's intervention was very influential, but it did not pass without criticism. We shall address here two specific objections that were made to his argument. The first suggested that he was wrong about the normative significance of 'international social co-operation'. The second attacks the idea of a global difference principle.

The first criticism levelled at Beitz, then, centred on the justification he offered for his account of global distributive justice, which appeared to be broadly relationist. Here Beitz was criticised from both relational and non-relational directions. From the *relational* point of view, it was questioned whether the global economy really embodied ideals of co-operation, or reciprocity, as opposed to being some relatively amoral free-for-all. If ideals of co-operation or reciprocity were not already embedded in the global economy, then it might provide an unsuitable subject for principles of justice. Some consider this a dubious argument, however. It seems to suggest that the issue of fairness only arises when we have already, in some sense, entered into certain relations with other people, and perhaps even when we have already undertaken to act with an eye to their interests. It seems to suggest, by extension, that if we do not undertake to further someone's interests alongside our own, then we would be justified in treating them unfairly. But this seems wrong. If we decided to interact with a part of our own domestic population in terms which had nothing to do with reciprocity or co-operation, and which were basically exploitative and self-serving instead, would that mean that we had no obligations of justice towards them? That seems to be a perverse conclusion, as Beitz suggested (see also Abizadeh 2007). But if we reject that conclusion, we might want to say instead that principles of justice apply wherever there is sustained interaction, and not just where we can observe deliberate co-operation aimed at some common good.

The position has also been criticised from a *non-relational* point of view. Here, the relevant question is, is it really the case that principles of global justice only become valid once international institutions or sustained co-operation come into existence? For some non-relationists this also seems to get the moral reasoning the wrong way around. Principles of justice might tell us to create institutions, or to reform them, but this is not the same thing as arguing that they only exist, or are only valid, where such institutions exist already (see Caney 2005b). Perhaps as a result of this kind of criticism, Beitz seems to have come to embrace a more explicitly non-relationist position (Beitz 1999a). In the 'Afterword' to the second edition of *Political Theory and International Relations*, Beitz returns directly to a key question which divides relationists and non-relationists: 'what role is played in the argument for global principles of justice by facts about the extent and character of the world political economy?' (Beitz 1999a: 204). Here Beitz wants to say that 'it now seems wrong' to suggest that economic globalisation makes standards of global justice appropriate. But it still might be the case that international social or economic co-operation provides a subject to which to *apply* such principles where none existed before. The emergence of such co-operation, we might say, gives global distributive principles something to get their teeth into, even if those principles were in some sense 'valid' even before it emerged.

Our second objection centres specifically on the idea of a global difference principle. Although the idea of foregrounding the advancement of the world's poor is an attractive one, the notion of a global difference principle has been subjected to a number of overlapping criticisms. While its defenders have often suggested that it is supposed to apply precisely to institutional orders or schemes, and that a relevant global institutional order exists to apply it to (see e.g. Tan 2004: 109), it has been objected that this is not quite what Rawls had in mind. Rawls believed that principles of justice should apply to the *basic structure of society*, where society is conceived as a scheme of social co-operation, as Beitz says. That basic structure is made up of the web of overlapping economic, political and social institutions that make up the 'system' at the domestic level (Rawls 1971: 7–9). That basic structure has huge effects on the life chances of those subject to it and it also, for example, regulates property relations. Although Beitz does suggest that there is an 'international basic structure', some critics have suggested that this is very different in form from, and much weaker and less direct in its impact on our life chances than, the domestic basic structure. Given the huge differences between domestic basic structures and the international (so-called) equivalent, it is not clear that a suitable target exists for the principle or a suitable agent to apply it (see also chapter 3, section 3.4). As Samuel Freeman puts it, 'There is no global political authority to apply the difference principle; nor is there a global legal system or global system of property to apply it *to*. So a global difference principle is doubly infirm, without both agency and object' (Freeman 2007: 444). If there is no agent or structure which distributes property or property rights in the first place, it cannot sensibly be asked how property, for instance, might be distributed more fairly.

Two responses might be offered. First, it might be said that whether or not we can tick the boxes of any given definition of a basic structure, it still matters whether the global institutions that *do* exist could reasonably be accepted by those subject to them, and reflection on this question might still encourage us to seek to limit the inequalities that arise from them or demand that any inequalities operate in everyone's interests (see e.g. Tan 2006: 335). These institutions might have distributive effects even if they do not directly allocate either property or property rights. Second, perhaps the criticism again concentrates inappropriately on the question of what institutions already exist, to the neglect of what institutions *should* exist. Beitz could argue that we have good moral reasons to try and *construct* effective institutions to help achieve a more equal world. This does not mean that the ideal is invalid just because we cannot put it into practice right now (Beitz 1979: 156). The debate about the kinds of institution to which principles of justice and equality should apply continues, however, and we shall return to it in the next chapter.

2.3. Caney on global distributive justice

· ·

In the years since Beitz's intervention, defences of global distributive justice, and particularly of broadly egalitarian accounts, have proliferated. One of the most careful and consistent arguments in favour of an egalitarian approach to global justice has been put forward by Simon Caney. In this section we again set out the broad contours of his position, and show why he thinks that we should be committed to an egalitarian account of global justice. In section 2.3.1 we shall address one distributive principle which he has defended at length – the principle of global equality of opportunity. We investigate what this challenging ideal might mean, and why Caney believes that we should recognise its normative appeal. Finally, in section 2.3.2, we look at some criticisms of Caney's position.

We already know from chapter 1 that Caney defends a non-relationist approach to global justice. There are certain entitlements that we have as humans, and we do not need to be able to point towards facts about globalisation or the emergence of global institutions to see that this is the case. We also saw that Caney thinks that conventional arguments for domestic distributive justice can be extended to the global level. If people have entitlements of distributive justice at the domestic level because they are all autonomous individuals or people with the capacity for rationality, for instance, then we should realise that those facts do not mysteriously cease to be true when we look across national boundaries. Caney thinks that relational arguments are also vulnerable to such a slide towards global justice. If we believe (and Caney does not) that justice is relevant because of some relational fact – say, that there are powerful coercive institutions at the domestic level, or because citizens co-operate together – then we should also realise that these empirical facts do not reliably demarcate citizens from non-citizens (Caney 2008). In fact Caney suspects that no good arguments can be made for restricting justice to the domestic level. The arguments presented so far, at least, are not compelling.

What about the *content* of Caney's approach to global justice, though? In his book *Justice beyond Borders*, Caney (2005a: 122–3) actually presents a somewhat complex picture of distributive justice at the global level, comprising at least four principles. One states that everyone has a human right to subsistence – to the meeting of their basic needs. A second suggests that we should prioritise improving the position of the worst off. A third suggests that we should embrace equal pay for equal work. A fourth and final principle defends something called global equality of opportunity, which we shall examine shortly.

One question which might occur to the reader at this point is, in what sense is this complex set of principles egalitarian? After all, the argument that our basic needs should be met is a minimalist principle and, indeed, it is similar in form to some of the minimalist arguments we shall examine in chapter 3. The second principle resembles the global difference principle, although strictly speaking it does not call for equality in itself. The third and fourth principles are recognisably egalitarian, but they are only part of the normative picture Caney is painting for us. In line with the distinction we drew in chapter 1, it nevertheless makes sense to describe Caney's as an egalitarian approach to global justice. This is, first, because it aims to achieve a substantially more equal world in which inequalities are limited. Second, it suggests that some inequalities (in opportunities, or in pay, for instance) are bad in themselves. This argument would not be accepted by minimalist accounts, and does mark Caney's position out as distinctively egalitarian.

2.3.1. Global equality of opportunity

The ideal of equality of opportunity can be unpacked in a variety of ways. A relatively weak version of the ideal would suggest that when a job is offered it should go to the best qualified candidate. The reason why it is a weak conception of equality of opportunity is that it does not address the possibility that some people, perhaps because of their parents' wealth, might have a much better chance to obtain qualifications in the first place. It could even be satisfied in a world where members of a particular ethnic group are barred from attending university, but where all the best-paid or high-status jobs demand a university education. So a stronger version would go much further, perhaps suggesting that people born with equal potential or equal natural ability should have an equal chance of obtaining the best jobs (if they make the same effort). That is the gist of John Rawls's conception of 'fair equality of opportunity'. This principle demands that individuals with 'the same level of talent and ability and the same willingness to use these gifts should have the same prospects of success ... In all parts of society there are to be roughly the same ... prospects of achievement' (Rawls 2001: 44).

What is important about this argument, according to some commentators, is that it effectively selects some characteristics that people have – say, gender, class or ethnicity – and says that they should *not* affect our opportunities. It also selects some characteristics – either talent or hard work or both (on which many egalitarians disagree) – and says that these are the only factors which *should* affect our opportunities. If we accept this argument, which many of us intuitively do, then many global egalitarians believe that the logic of this stronger position – which they support – pushes us in the direction of *global equality of opportunity*.

Why might that be? The argument goes like this. Most of us believe that individuals' lives should not offer them worse opportunities because of their ethnicity or gender, as we have just said. Many of us are also prepared to add class to that list. Perhaps, like Rawls, we have a general belief that our lives should go well, or badly, according to our talents or the hard work we are prepared to put in, and not according to other factors which are after all a matter of 'brute luck'. For no one chooses to be born part of one ethnic group rather than another, or male rather than female. Note that what egalitarian theorists are doing here is describing class, gender and ethnicity as 'morally arbitrary' characteristics. Recall from our discussion of the distribution of natural resources that a morally arbitrary characteristic is one that is not held to give someone a good claim to better resources (or opportunities) than anyone else. But should we not add another aspect of our 'identity' to this list of arbitrary features: *nationality*? If we are committed to the idea that individuals' lives should not start at a disadvantage because of the unchosen facts of their ethnicity, gender and so on, then why not add nationality to that list? Who, after all, chooses to be born in Mozambique rather than Monaco, with the radically different advantages that the latter entails? Of course, according to some recent commentators, that is just what does predictably happen. Being born into a poor country deals just as bad (and arbitrary) a blow to one's prospects as being born a serf rather than a lord used to in feudal times (Shachar and Hirschl 2007). If we object to the inequalities of feudalism, we should object to *global* inequalities of opportunity too. If this is right, then, as Caney puts it, 'The logic underpinning equality of opportunity entails that it should be globalized' (2005a: 123).

The argument, then, suggests that nationality is a 'morally arbitrary' feature of people, like race or gender. As Caney puts it, 'It is difficult to see why such arbitrary facts about people should determine their prospects in life' (2005a: 123). It is worth noting that the very same argument underpins Caney's separate argument for 'equal pay for equal work'. As he puts it, 'What is relevant when determining someone's pay is the quality of their work or the demand for the product but their nationality is surely simply not germane' (Caney 2005a: 123). It is once again hard to see, Caney is suggesting, why a fact such as the country in which one is born should determine the market value of the hours one is prepared to work.

Caney's precise formulation of the argument for global equality of opportunity is this: 'persons of different nations should enjoy equal opportunities: no one should face worse opportunities because of their nationality' (Caney 2005a: 122). But what might that mean in practice? One question which any ideal of equality of opportunity has to answer relates to its range. Just what is it that we ought to have an equal opportunity to achieve? It might be thought that if Caney is serious that nationality is a morally arbitrary characteristic, then it should not affect *any* of our opportunities to achieve anything important to us in life (or at least anything with which a theory of justice would normally concern itself). But the principle is usually connected to the question of access to what Rawls called 'favoured social positions' (Caney 2001: 114). It concerns the chances of obtaining favourable jobs or positions, with all the rewards that come hand in hand with them. Global equality of opportunity suggests that, when it comes to distributing jobs or the rewards attached to them, our nationality should not make a difference.

Caney suggests that the demands of global equality of opportunity would be 'relatively light' (2001: 116), and in that sense we might consider it (and Caney himself seems to consider it) to inhabit a position somewhere between minimalist and egalitarian approaches to global justice. After all, it is compatible with inequalities in outcomes (so long as people have equal opportunities in the first place), and also appears to confine itself to access to (and rewards from) occupations. Even so, though, it is worth noting how radically transformative of the existing global scene implementing even such a limited principle might be. Moellendorf is almost certainly right to point out that, in order to achieve the principle,

> A great deal would have to be spent on infrastructure among the world's poor. Educational opportunities would have to be equalized across the globe and between the sexes, health care access and facilities would have to be approximately equal, and all persons would have to be free of persecution on the basis of race, ethnicity, gender, religion and political affiliation … in light of current global inequalities, its requirements would be very demanding. (Moellendorf 2002: 79)

It is worth noting, then, that achieving equal opportunities for all individuals would run counter to conventional views on the place of women in many societies, as well as on the proper place of religion (since in some societies a number of privileged positions will currently be readily available not to all, but instead to members of some particular religion or caste).

2.3.2. Responses to Caney

Like Beitz's, Caney's global egalitarian argument is an apparently demanding one, and it has not passed without criticism. We shall focus here on two main objections. The first concerns the idea of moral arbitrariness that we have by now seen discussed at a number of points in this chapter, and which appears to be quite important to global egalitarian arguments. The second concerns the specific demands of the principle of global equality of opportunity. We shall address each in turn.

First, then, it has been suggested that the argument that nationality is morally arbitrary is misleading. We might mean a number of things by this. On the one hand, we might question whether the possession of a particular nationality is always unchosen (since egalitarians usually want to identify arbitrary characteristics with unchosen ones). This is usually true, but it is a generalisation. Many people, for example, deliberately change their nationality during their lifetime. Is it wrong for their life chances to suffer as a result? The answer is not clear (Armstrong 2010). A more complicated question concerns *identification* with one's nation. Is it wrong for my life chances to suffer because of my nationality if I readily accept it and identify with it, and see its decisions as somehow arising from values that I share with my fellow nationals? For some critics this is also far from clear. Indeed some have suggested as a result that nationality is not a morally arbitrary characteristic at all (see Miller 2007). A related criticism suggests that eradicating the influence of nationality will leave no space at all for national self-determination – for the kind of local variation whereby nations can make routine decisions about just how to educate their citizens, how to prioritise spending on health care, how to structure welfare benefits and so on. While Caney suggests that his approach is compatible with some degree of national self-determination, this is not altogether certain. For won't the decisions made by nations with a degree of self-determination immediately thwart the goal of equal opportunities (Moore 2007)? This raises the question whether global egalitarians are prepared to sacrifice a degree of equality in favour of achieving some degree of national self-determination, a question on which they appear to disagree. We shall pursue these questions further in chapter 3, section 3.3. These debates look likely to continue, but suffice it to say that the exact meaning of the argument about moral arbitrariness and the role that idea should play in defences of global egalitarianism remain open to question. That said, it is a rhetorically powerful idea with which many global egalitarians appear very reluctant to part company.

Second, despite the apparent power of its founding intuition (that our lives should not go worse simply because of the country in which we happen to be born), the practical implications of the notion of global equality of opportunity have also been called into question. David Miller (2007) has questioned whether it can make sense, given the diversity (across, rather than within, communities) of goods or positions that we value. After all, what would an equal opportunity to become a banker mean to members of a community which only valued spiritual advancement (for allied critiques see Boxill 1987; Moore 2007; see also Miller 2005a)? The question that therefore immediately presents itself is just *which* positions individuals should have equal opportunities to achieve. Are we talking about positions which all individuals, no matter where they live, should have the same opportunity to fill? One defender of global equality of opportunity, Darrel Moellendorf, has suggested just that, arguing that all individuals should have equal opportunities to achieve specific valued social positions. As he puts it, 'one way to imagine fulfilment of the goal is that a child born in rural Mozambique would be statistically as likely to become an investment banker as the child of a Swiss banker' (Moellendorf 2002: 79). Whatever job we might specify – banker, lawyer, footballer or film star – for justice to be achieved we should be able to say that individuals the world over are equally well placed to fill it. Caney, though, is more circumspect, perhaps anticipating one criticism which might be levelled at that idea. After all, who is to say that in all societies becoming an investment banker *is* the most valued position? Some societies might value quite different positions, such as healer, farmer or religious leader. In specifying a particular set of valued positions, aren't we running the risk of cultural imperialism – of imposing our own sense of what is valuable in life on others (Miller 2007; Walzer 1983)? Caney accordingly defines global equality of opportunity somewhat more loosely, in terms of the ability to attain a similar number of different positions, with comparable standards of living attached to them. As he puts it, people 'ought to have equal opportunities to gain positions of equal worth', rather than necessarily competing equally for the very same positions (Caney 2001: 120).

It is not wholly clear that this avoids the difficult questions Miller is pointing towards, however. Is it possible to say what we mean by 'positions of equal worth' or comparable standards of living? We might, of course, simply measure the incomes attached to jobs, with most currencies, after all, being readily convertible. We could apply a standard of US dollars and measure incomes at the going exchange rate. But it is likely that Caney means something more general than monetary income when he talks of equal worth. It is likely that he is referring to a broader set of goods than this, perhaps comprising key human capabilities – opportunities to enjoy a healthy life, to obtain education, to interact with others and so on. If this is right, then the question about cultural imperialism reappears. While some are confident in describing genuinely human capabilities that anyone would have reason to value (Nussbaum 1992), others are less clear that we can draw up such a list in a culturally neutral way. Of course, another response which we could make – a response which Caney makes himself – is to suggest that this kind of measurement problem is not a problem that should deter us at the level of ideal theory (Caney 2007; see also Caney 2001). We are interested in the question of whether global equality of opportunity is defensible at the level of principle (and Caney thinks that it is). But that is a separate question from that of how we would achieve or measure equal opportunities at the global level. Still, if global egalitarians are interested in seeing their ideas translated into practice, progress will need to be made on supplying a general means of measuring equal opportunities.

2.4. Cosmopolitanism and global justice

This chapter has concentrated thus far on what distinguishes global egalitarianism as an approach to global distributive justice, and has also surveyed the ideas of two prominent global egalitarian thinkers. The suggestion has been that the most interesting opposition, in approaches to global justice, is between thinkers who would defend egalitarian approaches (discussed in this chapter) as opposed to minimalist approaches (discussed in the next).

In the literature, however, we sometimes find a different set of oppositions. One of the most common of these is between *statists* and *cosmopolitans* (see e.g. Beitz 1999b). Here, statists are those who would restrict distributive justice to the state level, and cosmopolitans are those who would extend it to the global level. The meaning of statism looks quite straightforward, but the term 'cosmopolitanism' may be less familiar and, indeed, potentially confusing. But many global egalitarian thinkers – including Beitz and Caney – have identified themselves as 'cosmopolitan' thinkers. It is therefore important to be clear about just what they mean by this, and just how the opposition between statism and cosmopolitanism relates to the opposition between global egalitarianism and global minimalism. Although I am suggesting that the distinction between egalitarianism and minimalism is more important for the purposes of this book, the reader would still be well advised to proceed through the literature armed with an understanding of the idea of cosmopolitanism. In this final section we shall examine this complex idea – or set of ideas.

'Cosmopolitanism' is a word which is used to describe many different things. Sometimes, in international relations, it appears to signify an approach to international politics which seeks to build a form of *global citizenship* or even a *world state*. In its literal meaning, from the Greek, 'cosmopolitanism' means being a citizen of one universal community (from *cosmos* – the world or universe – and *polites* – a citizen). The term also has meanings beyond the academy, though; sometimes we use the word 'cosmopolitan' to describe the attitude or identity of someone who is not particularly rooted in one specific place ('Julia is very cosmopolitan. She's just as at home in Athens or Moscow as she is in Pittsburgh'). Here, 'cosmopolitanism' refers to an outward-looking attitude. It is also sometimes connected to the idea that the various cultures of the world are becoming more and more intermingled, and therefore less distinct (see Scheffler 2001: 111–30).

These ideas about global citizenship or the world state, or about attitudes and culture, fall outside the scope of this book. We're interested in cosmopolitanism, if at all, as a claim about the *scope of principles of justice*. According to Thomas Pogge, there are three key elements to cosmopolitanism from a *moral* point of view. The first is *individualism*: cosmopolitans believe that 'the ultimate units of concern are human beings, or persons – rather than, say, family lines, tribes, ethnic, cultural or religious communities, nations or states' (Pogge 2002: 169). Organisations that act as intermediaries between individuals can have only indirect importance. This accords with the idea we noted in section 2.1, which suggested that the inequalities that matter are not those between countries, which are not directly important, but those between individual people. The second element is *universality*: cosmopolitans believe that equal concern must be shown to all individuals equally. There is no set of humans to whom we do not owe equal concern, perhaps because of their ethnicity, or gender, or nationality. The third and final feature is *generality*: cosmopolitans believe that this concern must be shown by all to everyone; this suggests binding obligations on all of us (Pogge 2002: 169).

Although cosmopolitanism as a moral position is relatively clear and straightforward, two confusions often threaten to slip in. The first confuses cosmopolitanism as a *moral* position with cosmopolitanism as a view about *institutions* – that is, the view that there should be a world state, or a form of global citizenship. In fact, the kind of (moral) cosmopolitans in whom we are interested could believe that their principles were best achieved in all kinds of ways. While some might argue for global citizenship or a world state, others might disagree about the best way of seeing their moral position furthered in practice. As Charles Beitz puts it,

> Cosmopolitanism about ethics does not necessarily imply cosmopolitanism about institutions. It is consistent with moral cosmopolitanism to hold that something like the state system is better than anything like a world government – perhaps because human interests are best served in a world partitioned into separate societies whose members recognize special responsibilities for one another's well-being. (Beitz 1999b: 287)

So the first point to make is that we need to be clear that there is no necessary connection between moral and institutional cosmopolitanism. A second source of confusion, which is more troubling, is that there does not seem to be a very clear connection between moral cosmopolitanism and support for principles of global distributive justice. Pogge might disagree. He might believe that anyone accepting his three principles – which combine to suggest, roughly, that we all matter equally, and that this places demands on all of us – will be pushed in the direction of embracing principles of global distributive justice. But it is not clear that this is true – and this is where the term 'cosmopolitanism' can turn out to be particularly misleading in debates on global justice. The cosmopolitan principles Pogge sets out are quite thin – most people would accept them, at least on reflection. Indeed, it is worth asking just who would reject them. Realists might; they might argue that the state only has a moral duty to protect its own citizens, and has no real obligations to anyone else, except perhaps for obligations to keep to the terms of any treaties it has signed and so on. Some might reject the claim of universality on other grounds. For instance, racists might reject it; they might argue that equal concern need not extend further than the racial group to which an individual belongs. But that idea is not often defended openly. The real problem for Pogge, though, is that we might accept his three principles but still refuse, in good faith, to adopt principles of global distributive justice. For instance, we might believe that individuals are due equal concern and respect and that this places moral demands on the actions of all of us. But we might also believe that belonging to a self-determining national community is an absolutely crucial good for individuals, and that adopting principles of global distributive justice – at least reasonably demanding ones – would be incompatible with securing that good for everyone.

So we might, therefore, reject global distributive justice in favour of a world of largely self-determining nation states, with no (or at least no positive) duties of global distributive justice. That would be a version of cosmopolitanism about morality that rejected global distributive justice (see e.g. R. Miller 1998). Of course, someone else might adopt Pogge's three principles but argue that the (equal) interest of individuals in securing the material conditions of a good life is paramount, and go on to adopt some robustly global egalitarian principles. In this case cosmopolitanism about morality does lead directly to support for global distributive justice. But who is to say that the latter is any more 'cosmopolitan' than the former? They both start from the same morally cosmopolitan premises, but go on to reach quite different conclusions in terms of distributive justice. This rather suggests, as I have said, that there is no necessary link between acceptance of Pogge's principles and support for principles of global distributive justice. Cosmopolitans about morality might *tend* to embrace global distributive justice, but the connection is not a conceptually tight one.

David Miller (2002) has levelled a similar challenge at cosmopolitanism. He argues that it is ambiguous, offering both a very weak version and a very strong version. The very weak version only requires us to accept that all individuals count equally and that we should show equal concern and respect for them, but need not require us, for example, to adopt any robust redistributive principles at the global level, as the above example shows. The very strong version, by contrast, argues that any valid distributive principle should be global in form, which Miller believes has the implication that individual nation states could not be genuinely self-determining. In response, some cosmopolitans have tried to carve out space for a moderate or intermediate version of cosmopolitanism, which might be compatible with some local variation (Caney 2002; Pogge 2002). But the original problem remains, which is that weak cosmopolitanism – which seems, despite being weak, to keep faith with Pogge's three principles – does not appear necessarily to have any specific distributive implications.

This is why, in this book, we are concentrating on the opposition between those who embrace robust principles of global distributive justice (global egalitarians), and those who reject them and embrace a much less demanding version, if any (minimalists). The debate about cosmopolitanism, although it characterises much of the literature on global justice, at times threatens to obscure this distinction. One reason why it is less useful is that both global egalitarians and global minimalists *can* describe themselves as cosmopolitans, although not all of them do. It is also confusing because cosmopolitanism has so many other 'lives', both inside and outside the academy. Although it is too early to say, it may be that the debate is leaving the distinction between statism and cosmopolitanism behind to some degree. As we suggested in the last chapter, a more profitable and pertinent distinction is the one between egalitarian and minimalist approaches to global distributive justice.

Conclusions

This chapter has examined what it might mean to defend an egalitarian approach to global distributive justice. We began by examining some prominent global inequalities – in income, life expectancy, carbon dioxide emissions and literacy levels. Global egalitarians will object to at least some of these inequalities and suggest that they are wrong in themselves and not merely because such inequalities stand in the way of achieving other goals that we care about. But they may disagree about just which inequalities matter most, and may have different ideas about what we should have equal shares of at the global level, if anything. We moved on to examine two prominent global egalitarian accounts, put forward by Charles Beitz and Simon Caney respectively. Whereas Beitz defends both a resource redistribution principle and a global difference principle, Caney defends a principle of global equality of opportunity. In both cases, we have also examined some of the more prominent criticisms levelled at these global egalitarian principles, as well as some ways in which Beitz or Caney might respond to them. We concluded by examining the idea of cosmopolitanism, since both Beitz and Caney have identified their own positions as cosmopolitan ones. The opposition between statists and cosmopolitans does not coincide neatly with the distinction between global egalitarianism and minimalism. Both egalitarians and minimalists could plausibly claim to be cosmopolitans in some way, although substantial differences might remain between them. By the same token, minimalists are not necessarily statists – although their ambitions for global justice may be more basic than those of global egalitarians, this does not necessarily mean that they want to restrict distributive justice to the level of individual states. Some minimalists may want to, but others will endorse a programme of global distributive justice, although if they do so it will be aimed at securing the basic needs or basic human rights of all people. We shall move on to examine such minimalist positions in the next chapter.

Minimalist approaches

This chapter introduces a number of minimalist approaches to global distributive justice, and investigates their reasons for scepticism about global egalitarianism, their chief rival. The three minimalist theories examined in this chapter all embrace the value of equality within individual societies, but reject the extension of egalitarianism to the global level. Minimalists would send us back to the figures about global inequality which were cited at the beginning of chapter 2, and ask a question of us. While we might be convinced that our normative objection is to the *inequality* involved, minimalists will ask us whether it is not, after all, the *poverty*, or some people's lack of access to a decent life, which troubles us, once we have properly reflected on our objections. We might well be troubled by the inferior life chances available to many people in Sierra Leone — which are far worse, according to key indicators, than those available in Denmark. But is the *difference* between life chances in Sierra Leone and Denmark really the problem, or merely the very low level of the life chances available in Sierra Leone? As a way of examining our normative intuitions about this, consider the smaller, but still real, inequalities between Portugal and Denmark. Do these bother us at all? There are substantial differences in gross national income per capita in the two countries, but do these really matter from the point of view of justice, so long as we are content that the average citizen of Portugal has ready access to the material ingredients of a decent life? To push our intuitions still further, are we bothered at all that per capita national income is higher in Denmark than in the United States? If we *are* still at all troubled by the inequalities, we are likely to be resolute global egalitarians. But minimalists will try to persuade us that these inequalities at the 'top end' of the scale are not, in the end, normatively troubling, and that what we are really bothered by – and what we are *right* to be bothered by – are the poor life chances available to inhabitants of Sierra Leone. We are bothered by them because they will often fall below what we see as a level compatible with a life of dignity and decency. But it is that minimalist measure of decency, dignity or (as the philosophical literature often puts it) sufficiency that does the work in explaining our normative unease. We might object to such great inequalities *inside* a single country – and we might be right to do so. But outside the borders of the nation state, we should endorse some form of global minimalism. Delivering on that minimalism will itself present enough of a challenge to the contemporary world.

Section 3.1 of this chapter briefly sets out some facts about giving in the form of overseas aid, and examines the UN's Millennium Development Goals, to deliver on which wealthier countries have been asked to give 0.7 per cent of their national income in the form of aid for international development. While an egalitarian might think this a puny proportion, if it helped to eradicate poverty a minimalist might be satisfied. So examining our views about such targets can be instructive. We then move on to our three minimalist accounts. Section 3.2 introduces the account presented in John Rawls's hugely significant essay *The Law of Peoples*. While Rawls did not quite reject the idea of global distributive justice entirely, he was certainly very sceptical about the more ambitious accounts of global distributive justice – including egalitarian ones – and recommended instead that wealthier societies embrace a 'duty of assistance' to help poorer societies meet the basic needs of their members. This section examines the reasons for Rawls's reluctance to accept more demanding views on global justice, and seeks to explain the reasons for his adoption of a more minimal standard.

Section 3.3 discusses David Miller's minimalist account of global justice. Miller is often labelled a 'liberal nationalist' thinker, so we try to unpick the significance of nationality to his account, which suggests that co-citizens have egalitarian duties towards one another based on the special bonds that unite them. By contrast, although Miller does not reject the idea of global distributive justice, he does believe that it should have much more limited aims. Specifically, rather like Rawls's account, the aims of an account of global justice should be to help nations deliver on the basic human rights of their members in cases where they prove unable to do so unaided. This does not mean that those human rights are best seen as entitlements of global distributive justice. For the most part they are rights held against the nation state in which we happen to live. But in certain circumstances, outside states can have duties of justice to aid in their delivery. Beyond this, Miller also rejects the extension of equality to the global level. Indeed, he probably provides the most developed and multi-faceted argument against global egalitarianism of any of the theorists discussed in this chapter.

Section 3.4 examines Thomas Nagel's defence of an even more minimalist account. Nagel rejects global distributive justice entirely, and suggests that any duties we have to try and alleviate global poverty are duties of humanitarianism, and not of justice. The explanation he gives for this focuses on the normatively special character of coercive state institutions. Since they are in a sense responsible for the inequalities they impose on each other through the coercive institutions of the state, co-citizens owe each other egalitarian distributive justice – they owe it to each other, that is, to make sure that the state presents each citizen with distributive outcomes that do not unfairly burden any of them, and which can be defended from an egalitarian point of view. But global inequalities are not 'imposed' by coercive global institutions, and so global inequalities are simply not unjust in the way in which domestic inequalities could be said to be.

The principal aim of this chapter is to understand how Rawls, Miller and Nagel each come to embrace a minimalist approach to global justice. But we are also interested in the various reasons they provide for rejecting global egalitarianism as a rival approach. Section 3.5 therefore concludes by collecting together the various challenges to global egalitarianism and arranging them a little more systematically. But the real battle between minimalist and egalitarian positions, of course, is waged over the five key issues discussed in part II of this book.

3.1. Spending on overseas aid

Box 3.1. **The Millennium Development Goals**

In 2000, world leaders adopted the UN's Millennium Development Goals. These eight goals were to be achieved by the year 2015. They aimed:

1. to eradicate extreme poverty and hunger
2. to achieve universal primary education
3. to promote gender equality and empower women
4. to reduce child mortality
5. to improve maternal health
6. to combat HIV/AIDS, malaria and other diseases
7. to ensure environmental stability
8. to develop a global partnership for development.

Source: UN 2000.

Meeting the Millennium Development Goals would clearly cost money. In coming together to sign up to the goals, the leaders of developed countries were making some kind of commitment to help to pay for their delivery. But what kind of commitment? Many richer countries, including the countries of the European Union, have pledged to deliver 0.7 per cent of their gross national income per year in overseas development aid. Taken by itself, that figure of 0.7 per cent seems very low. But it seems to be proving challenging nevertheless. Current levels of aid often fall between 0.2 per cent and 0.4 per cent of gross national income, and the recent global financial crisis seems to be placing greater pressure on government revenues – although some countries, nevertheless, have met or exceed their targets.

Let us return to those figures. The fact that so many countries cluster around the 0.2–0.4 per cent figure could be taken to suggest that there is a widespread feeling that countries are justified in pursuing their own domestic agendas first and foremost, whereas the goal of global poverty relief is a relatively low priority. But perhaps, on reading these figures, you might be surprised. There is some evidence that the general public consistently overestimates the amount governments spend on overseas aid (van Heerde and Hudson 2009), and is surprised when it recognises just how low the figures really are. If a government spends roughly one dollar out of every three hundred on poverty relief, is that not a rather paltry amount? Would even the 0.7 per cent figure be enough, or would it still represent a serious breach of our humanitarian or justice duties?

There are, of course, good questions to be asked about the effectiveness of aid, which colour many people's attitudes towards this issue. Some of these suggest that recipient countries spend aid badly or corruptly, and that we might better focus on providing advice and guidance to poorer countries, rather than a constant drip feed of money to be squandered. Others suggest that donor countries themselves are rather bad at sending money where it is most needed, and are all too happy to give to nations with whom they share economic or military interests and not to those who are genuinely most needy. Either way, the basic needs of many poor people throughout the world might not be met as a result of overseas aid policy.

But in this chapter we shall be putting to one side those empirical questions about the best way to deliver help, and focusing instead on the normative question of whether relatively low levels of aid are in principle *justified*. Each of the three minimalist accounts developed in this chapter agree that our principal responsibilities to the world's poor are to provide help to make sure that they avoid suffering and serious deprivation. They understand that duty in slightly different ways – and indeed they might not agree that the 0.7 per cent target is the right one – but they all agree that we do not owe anything much more substantial than this or some similar kind of aid. Our attention should be on helping other communities to avoid serious poverty or breaches in basic human rights, and not on grander goals of securing a more equal world.

3.2. Rawls and the Law of Peoples

As mentioned in chapter 2, John Rawls's work has been taken as an inspiration by many global egalitarian accounts. Such accounts have often attempted to take the principles he suggested for individual societies – such as the difference principle, or the principle of equality of opportunity – and 'globalize' them. While Rawls had not done this in his widely influential *A Theory of Justice* (Rawls 1971), he did provide the tools for doing so, and a generation of theorists of global justice took it as their task to show the global implications of his theory (e.g. Beitz 1979; Pogge 1989). If the hope was that Rawls himself would accept this global extension of his theory, then his global egalitarian defenders were to be sorely disappointed. In his last book, *The Law of Peoples* (Rawls 1999), he unambiguously rejected egalitarian principles of global distributive justice. Instead, he presented an account of global justice which his critics saw as far too modest and presenting far too little of a challenge to the status quo. Instead of a demanding account of global distributive justice Rawls recommended a 'duty of assistance' towards poorer societies – a concession that was described by many critics as wholly inadequate to the task of addressing global economic injustice (see e.g. Pogge 2004; Tan 2004). In this section we shall examine why Rawls recommended such an approach, what his account attempted to achieve and why he rejected global egalitarianism.

With Rawls, starting points are very important. In *A Theory of Justice* he had asked us to imagine what principles would be required to govern a just society. What principles would help us to realise our idea of ourselves – and each other – as free and equal citizens? Could these principles lead to justice and stability over the generations? Could citizens be expected to show allegiance to them? These questions, we might say, illustrate the role that the difference principle plays; it represents a principle which is both just and likely to secure agreement from all in society, including the worst off, and hence also produce stability over time. When he came to look at questions of global justice, many of his global egalitarian supporters might have expected Rawls to ask what principles of justice should govern the distribution of resources across the globe. But that is not the question that he sets his sights on. His is a much more modest one. The question he has us ask ourselves is this: imagine that we have achieved some approximation of justice within our own society. How, then, should we – 'we' understood as members of one particular more-or-less-just liberal society – relate to the rest of the world? What principles would we want to see governing our interaction with the other 'peoples' of the world (Rawls uses the term 'peoples' to describe societies; he seems to have in mind something slightly different from nation states as usually understood, but the differences are not important for our purposes)? To make the question more concrete, imagine yourself as a political leader of such a liberal society – the person who in the United States is called the Secretary of State and in the United Kingdom is called the Foreign Secretary. What principles would *you* want to see governing relations between different societies in international politics? As Rawls himself put it, the goal is to 'work out the ideals and principles of the foreign policy of a reasonably just liberal people' (Rawls 1999: 10).

Rawls assumes that we should be reasonably, but not overly, ambitious in the vision of just interaction between societies that we come up with. We should not just defer to the status quo and merely redescribe it. That would be indefensibly 'realist', because we are asking a question about how societies would *justly* interact, not just how we should *expect* them to interact. So we should be 'utopian' to a degree: we should identify what we see as the more positive developments of international politics, and see how far we might plausibly push them. But at the same time we should be 'realistically utopian': we should not ask men and women to act as angels, and we should not, for instance, just wish away individual nation states as an obstacle in the way of global justice. Like the eighteenth-century German philosopher Immanuel Kant, Rawls believed that international society could be characterised by the gradual pursuit of justice, and as holding out the possibility of an ever-increasing circle of peace between more or less just peoples – what Rawls referred to as the 'Society of Peoples'. What international society does not seem to offer is some short cut to a global egalitarian paradise where nations agree to share resources, for instance, equally between them. The job of the philosopher – and perhaps of the enlightened politician – is to start with the elements of international politics that hold out the promise of decent, peaceful and just interaction between peoples, and to try to extend them.

Here, Rawls identified certain key elements of international society – in particular the ideas of what has come to be known as 'just war theory', practices of diplomacy and treaty making, and, significantly, the founding documents of international human rights law set down by the UN in the years after the Second World War. If we worked these up systematically, we would arrive, Rawls says, at something like his eight principles of the Law of Peoples (box 3.2).

Box 3.2. **Eight principles of the Law of Peoples**

- Peoples (as organized by their government) are free and independent, and their freedom and independence is to be respected by other peoples.
- Peoples are equal and parties to their own agreements.
- Peoples have the right of self-defense but no right to war.
- Peoples are to observe a duty of non-intervention.
- Peoples are to observe treaties and undertakings.
- Peoples are to observe certain specified restrictions on the conduct of war (assumed to be in self-defense).
- Peoples are to honor human rights.
- Peoples have a duty to assist other peoples living under unfavorable conditions that prevent their having a just or decent political and social regime.

Source: Rawls 1999: 37.

From the point of view of global distributive justice – which is what we are concerned with here – it is notable that, whereas the first two principles invoke freedom and equality as values, only the last two have any direct and obvious implications for global distributive justice. Rawls is clearly not intending to recommend anything approaching the scheme he suggests for domestic societies. His vision of global justice falls far short of the goals of global egalitarians.

In keeping with the practice in international politics, one of Rawls's major interests appears to be in the toleration of peoples by peoples or, we might say, the peaceful coexistence of nation states. This belief that peoples should be allowed – within limits – to remain self-determining in their internal affairs informs his rejection of robust principles of global distributive justice. But before getting to that, we should note that, for Rawls, the attitude we ('we' meaning the enlightened foreign ministers or secretaries of state of liberal societies) should take towards other societies depends on the nature of the society we are dealing with.

Rawls divides societies into various types. We might think of *outlaw societies* as akin to what are sometimes called 'rogue states': they are either internally repressive (showing disregard for the human rights of their own citizens) or externally aggressive (showing themselves willing to wage war for reasons other than self-defence, including imperialist or ideological reasons). Liberal societies are not obliged to tolerate these societies. They have the right to defend themselves against them and the right, if it is really necessary, to intervene in them to prevent gross violations of human rights. We might think of *burdened societies* as either unlucky or poorly governed societies. Such societies are not repressive or aggressive like outlaw societies, but they are subjected to 'unfavourable conditions' of various kinds – poor social and economic policymaking, sometimes a poverty of natural resources or a harsh climate, in turn sometimes made worse by the inefficiency or corruption of their governments. Such societies are simply unable to operate as well-ordered societies. Liberal societies ought not to intervene in them – because gross human rights abuses are not occurring – but they do have a duty to help them become self-supporting. These societies, as we shall see soon, are the target of the 'duty of assistance'.

That leaves *reasonable peoples*, who are deserving of toleration and mutual respect. Rather controversially, Rawls includes two kinds of society in this category. The first is societies which are liberal and just. Rawls thinks it is uncontroversial that our relations with such societies – which after all we perceive to be just like our own – should be characterised by toleration and a healthy respect for their right to self-determination. More controversially, Rawls also includes in his category of reasonable peoples a second kind of society, which he calls 'decent hierarchical societies'. A decent hierarchical society will typically be a religious republic, albeit one in which different religions are tolerated. It will not have a democratic government, although it will have a 'consultation hierarchy', a formal and open process through which grievances can be voiced and listened to. Basic human rights will be respected, and the society will be internationally non-aggressive.

What does Rawls have in mind here, and why is it so important that we tolerate decent hierarchical societies which do not, after all, match up to the standards of justice we would apply to our own societies? Rawls does not describe actual instances of decent hierarchical societies, but instead imagines a theoretical republic, which he calls Kazanistan. But many commentators have interpreted his ideas as dealing with the thorny real-world problem of coexistence between Western societies and Islamic societies. Rawls's approach suggests that – provided they meet the basic human rights of their members and are non-aggressive – our approach to them ought not to be one of condescension, hostility or even constant persuasion to adopt liberal democratic ideals. We should aim to coexist peacefully with them, as we would with other liberal societies. If this leads over time to their coming into the fold of liberal democracy, that might be a good thing. But it should not be a goal of foreign policy. This implies what the limits of our ambitions for international society should be: we should aim at a world of independent peoples who respect the basic human rights of their own citizens and do not wage war on each other. But we should not try to convert the other peoples of the world to what we would recognise as just principles of distributive justice and democracy.

3.2.1. Rawls on global distributive justice

Rawls's position on global justice suggests a focus on securing basic human rights for all. This determines the goals we should adopt in our foreign policy. Given the importance of self-determination – described in the very first principle of the Law of Peoples and reinforced in the second, third and fourth principles – we should recognise that there are only two justifications for intervening in another society. These are self-defence and the prevention of the gross violation of human rights. In the latter case war should be our last resort once the options of political and economic sanctions have been exhausted.

Human rights, then, are important. This is *not* to say that our human rights are entitlements of global justice. In the main, our rights should be fulfilled by our own government, and whereas other societies may sometimes have a duty to help them achieve this, this is not quite the same thing as saying that we have an entitlement of distributive justice that they do so. What, then, are our basic human rights? Here Rawls largely follows documents such as the UN Universal Declaration of Human Rights. He describes the right to life, to liberty, to property, to equality before the law, to freedom of movement, to freedom from discrimination and so on. Importantly, Rawls does include a right to subsistence within his list – a right, that is, to food, water and shelter (the idea of subsistence rights is an issue to which we shall return in chapter 4). Some of his critics, though, have cast doubt on whether this list is as uncontroversial as Rawls claimed. One controversy has surrounded the omission from his list of a right to fully equal political participation – or to *democratic* political participation as we would recognise it. Another disappointment, to some critics, is the omission of any robust defence of equality for women (see e.g. Nussbaum 2002). For although on Rawls's account women should (like men) have their basic human rights respected, this is compatible with a society granting *more* than basic human rights to men alone.

Human rights are also important in setting the goals of the 'duty of assistance'. Recall that this is a duty owed by reasonable peoples to 'burdened societies', which may be failing to meet the basic human rights of their members. The recipient societies may be disadvantaged by a variety of 'unfavourable conditions' preventing a just or decent regime emerging, including a lack of 'material and technological resources', of 'human capital and know-how' or of the 'political and cultural traditions' that would enable them to become well-ordered (Rawls 1999: 106). The *goal* of the duty is the development in those burdened societies of decent social and political institutions; it does *not* aim to address inequalities in wealth between societies. As Rawls puts it, after a society becomes well-ordered 'further assistance is not required, even though the now well-ordered society may still be relatively poor' (1999: 111). The *means* by which the duty is fulfilled will in large part be through the provision of advice and technical support, although material assistance may be necessary if the burdened society in question proves to be unable to meet the basic human rights of its members.

The duty of assistance is strictly limited in two ways. First, unlike many schemes of global egalitarian justice, it does not aim to redistribute resources to create some kind of ideal pattern of distribution, such as equality. It has a strictly limited goal: assistance in the creation of functioning and stable institutions. Second, Rawls does not seem to expect its demands to endure much over time. It has a defined 'target and cut-off point', in contrast to egalitarian schemes which might need to redistribute resources indefinitely.

There is some controversy over whether the duty of assistance should be characterised as a humanitarian duty (Buchanan 2000; Tan 2004) or a duty of justice (Reidy 2004; Freeman 2007). The demanding-ness of Rawls's duty is also contested, some supporters suggesting that it could be pretty demanding (thus David Reidy argues that 'Rawls's duty of assistance is a richer and more demanding requirement of a just global economy than it at first appears' (Reidy 2007: 201), while Mathias Risse claims that Rawls has formulated 'a stringent duty (shaming the status quo) in a philosophically sound manner that has a genuine chance of persuading policy-makers' (Risse 2005: 117)). But, either way, the goals of the duty of assistance are clearly limited. They take as their ultimate aim the creation of institutions which could deliver on basic human rights, and they will not necessarily demand much in the way of transfers of resources. Rawls is not adamant that we should reject the idea of global distributive justice altogether. He considers a distributive proposal of Thomas Pogge's for instance – which would tackle extreme poverty – and implies that, assuming that it would have implications similar to his duty of assistance, he has no reason to reject it (Rawls 1999: 119). By contrast Rawls *does* definitely want to reject egalitarian principles of global justice which seek to redistribute resources on a continual basis. He is quite clear about this; he asks us, for instance, to imagine a richer society and a poorer one. In the poorer society the worst-off person, as we would expect, is much worse off than the poorest person in the richer society. But Rawls tells us that the Law of Peoples is 'indifferent' to this fact, so long as the poorer society is meeting the basic human rights of its members (1999: 120).

Why might this be? What might make Rawls so keen to reject the claims of global egalitarianism? There seem to be two major reasons. The first suggests that global egalitarianism neglects the responsibilities of peoples for their own fortunes. The second suggests that it is incompatible with showing the requisite toleration to other (decent hierarchical but not liberal) societies.

First, then, Rawls believed that the causes of wealth and poverty are primarily 'internal'. As he put it,

> I believe that the causes of the wealth of a people and the forms it takes lie in their political culture and in the religious, philosophical and moral traditions that support the basic structure of their political and social institutions, as well as in the industriousness and cooperative talents of its members. (Rawls 1999: 108)

This is in contrast to Beitz (see chapter 2), who claimed that a deficit of natural resources might lead to serious disadvantage. Rawls's argument suggests that redistribution of natural resources is unnecessary. He also believed that, since peoples are essentially responsible for how they fare economically, continually redistributing resources between them to create equality would be *unfair*. He has us imagine two societies, one of which industrialises and works hard, while the other chooses a life of leisure and very little industry. 'Should the industrializing country be taxed to give funds to the second?' Rawls asks us. 'This seems unacceptable' (Rawls 1999: 117). If the second ends up being poorer – so long as it is still able to run decent institutions – that outcome should not concern us. So the goals of global egalitarians, according to Rawls, are incompatible with recognising national (or people's) responsibility for their own economic situations. They would in effect penalise industry and good decision-making, and reward laziness and poor decision-making.

Second, Rawls is far from sure that we could achieve the goals of global egalitarians without jeopardising the toleration of other societies, and in particular decent hierarchical societies. His domestic account of justice is based on ideas – including, importantly, the shared idea that we are all free and equal citizens – which are particular to liberal societies. Beyond the 'world' of liberal societies that idea is not widely accepted. This has implications as to those principles to which we can rely on gaining assent globally. It is possible, Rawls says, to draw up a scheme of justice for a liberal democracy based on what he calls its 'public political culture' – the views, beliefs and ideas present in popular debate and so on about the freedom and equality of citizens. But this is not possible at the global level. The global public political culture, such as it exists, extends simply to the familiar set of ideas about national self-determination, respect for basic human rights, just war and so forth. Beyond this there is disagreement, and to impose liberal distributive ideas beyond liberal societies would require unjustifiable coercion. So an egalitarian version of global distributive justice, in particular, would need to be *imposed* on non-liberal (decent hierarchical) societies which could not reasonably be expected to accept it. As such, according to Leif Wenar, applying it would require us to abandon a 'fundamental requirement of legitimacy' (Wenar 2006: 103).

3.2.2. Responses to Rawls

As mentioned above, Rawls's arguments in *The Law of Peoples* have gained some adherents, but have also disappointed many, perhaps most, of those who admired his original theory of domestic justice. Some have suggested that, although Rawls claims to provide us with principles which already enjoy widespread support in international relations, his approach is just outdated. It might support a world in which nation states are assumed to be more or less autonomous, but it is less well suited to our world of substantial interdependence, economic globalisation and rapid global institution-building (see e.g. Buchanan 2000). Rawls does, of course, set himself the goal of being 'realistically utopian' – of not just describing the status quo, but of suggesting how we might make important but achievable advances on it. Thus it would be an interesting question whether Rawls would have supported the UN's Millennium Development Goals, and whether he would have seen the duty of assistance as likely to make progress in that direction.

But Rawls's realistic utopianism is rather too realistic for some. Some theorists have been appalled at the suggestion that we should tolerate societies which may themselves be intolerant towards their ethnic or religious minorities, or their female inhabitants (Tan 2000). Others suggest that Rawls is rather hamstrung in his attempt to build an adequate account of global justice on the basis of ideas that are already commonly shared by people across the world. Is it illegitimate for philosophers or political theorists to try and convince us to adopt new ideas about how the world should be? If some cultures do not view their inhabitants as free and equal, should we meekly accept that fact, rather than seeking to persuade them to change their minds? On this point it is an open question whether Rawls had already overstepped the bounds of existing agreement in suggesting a duty of assistance. He actually omitted it from his original version of the essay (published in 1993), and when he did eventually include it in *The Law of Peoples* he appeared to concede that it took us on to more contested terrain (Tasioulas 2005). As such one supposed advantage of Rawls's theory – that its principles already enjoy substantial international legitimacy – turns out to be less clear (Armstrong 2009a).

The argument about national responsibility has also been hugely controversial. One line of criticism seeks to convince us that there are other significant causes of poverty beyond the simply internal. Thomas Pogge's work is one prominent example, since he tries to persuade us that even if domestic leaders *do* make bad decisions, they do so in a global context where poorer nations enjoy unfairly inferior opportunities, and where consumers and corporations based in wealthier states are prepared to sustain undemocratic and unjust leaders in power so long as we can continue to buy the natural resources of their countries (Pogge 2002; see also chapter 5 of this volume). Another line of criticism suggests that even if poorer nations are responsible for their own poverty, this does not mean that all their citizens are. For example, in a decent hierarchical society many people could be excluded from an equal role in decision-making, yet Rawls seems to consider it fair that they bear the costs of poor decisions along with more privileged citizens. Should we, therefore, restrict the idea of national responsibility to democracies, where all adult citizens can be held accountable for collective decisions? Even then, there will be minorities who vociferously disagree with the decisions made by elected leaders. Children are another difficult category. For when a nation makes very poor decisions, the consequences of those decisions will be visited not only on adult citizens, who might or might not have participated in making those decisions. They will be visited on children, too, including children who have not yet been born. Decisions to borrow money to fund ill-advised or vainglorious construction projects will leave these children, when they grow up, bearing debts which they had no role in taking on. Suffice it to say, then, that the conflict between national responsibility and the goals of global equality is complicated and contested. Citing national responsibility as a reason why we do not need a global egalitarian account leaves a number of questions unanswered.

Rawls's *Law of Peoples* does present a powerful challenge to global egalitarian accounts. But the advantages Rawls claims for his account, which purportedly make it more attractive than a global egalitarian version, are not as clear as we might initially think. Furthermore, as we shall see in part II of this book, global egalitarians remain unconvinced that his account can deliver really satisfying positions on contentious issues such as trade justice (chapter 6) and ecological justice (chapter 7).

3.3. Miller on national responsibilities

David Miller defends a minimal account of global justice which focuses on protecting basic human rights and securing fair terms of international co-operation. He does accept the idea of global distributive justice, and suggests that the need to help some states meet their citizens' basic rights can sometimes place duties of justice on the shoulders of other communities. But he argues forcefully that 'Global justice cannot mean global egalitarianism' (Miller 2007: 265). This section examines Miller's reasons for adopting instead a minimalist account, which foregrounds the special ties people have with those who share their nationality. We shall also examine the implications for global justice, and some criticisms that have been levelled at Miller's arguments.

Why, then, does Miller advance a minimalist account of global justice? First and foremost, Miller's work emphasises the normative significance of *nationality*, which is a special tie that individuals share with co-nationals but not with outsiders. Recall from chapter 2 that some global egalitarians consider our nationality to be a 'morally arbitrary' feature, which should not impact on our life chances – most likely because they do not believe that we should suffer because of something (like nationality) for which we are not responsible. Miller believes this argument to be mistaken. While we might not (always) be responsible for choosing the national community we inhabit, that does not mean that nations are not normatively important, or that we might not identify with them, for example. In fact our nationality is, for most of us, a very important fact. We identify both with our nation and with its history and commitments. Without a nationality, and the traditions and customs that come along with nationality, we might be somewhat rootless and disoriented in such a complex world as this one. In a way nations stand between us and the world and provide us with a lens that allows us to see what is important and valuable in life. Against the global egalitarians, Miller therefore suggests that

> People value the rich cultural inheritance that membership of a nation can bring them ... The idea that they should regard their nationality as a historic accident, an identity to be sloughed off in favour of humanity at large, carries little appeal. (Miller 1995: 184)

So nations are important, although global egalitarians have sometimes neglected this fact. The next part of Miller's argument may be more controversial. He suggests that, because nationality is intrinsically important to us, we might have certain special duties towards our co-nationals (Miller 2007: 34–5). Whereas we might owe 'general' duties towards all of humanity, 'special' duties are those which we owe to only some people, in this case because of our close and significant relationship with them. We shall also only owe special duties where the duties are 'integral to the relationship', so that the relationship could not really exist unless they were observed (Miller 2007: 35). Thus I might argue that while, as a human, I have a duty to treat all children with a degree of kindness and consideration, I have a special duty to extend certain kinds of treatment to my own children and them alone. Perhaps I have a special duty to help educate them morally, nurture their individuality or respond to their day-to-day problems. Not doing so would mean that I was really not acting *as* a parent.

To make a parallel with nations, Miller's position suggests that whereas we sometimes owe it to distant others to help to meet their basic human rights, there are also certain things we only owe to people with whom we share a nationality. Just what things might they be? Broadly speaking, Miller believes that social justice – including the pursuit of equality – is something that only co-nationals owe to each other. This is not to say that we have no duties of justice towards outsiders, or that these ought not sometimes to be prioritised above what we owe to fellow nationals (Miller 2007: 44). But it is to say that the set of duties we have towards fellow nationals is much fuller than the relatively thin set of duties we have towards outsiders. Miller also seems to suggest that the positive duties we have towards our fellow nationals are more stringent than those towards outsiders. While we shall sometimes have positive duties to aid outsiders in cases where they need assistance, and where the institutions of their own nation state have failed them, Miller's suspicion is that we would be justified in meeting our duties of social justice towards fellow-nationals first (2007: 50).

Thus the fact that we belong to a nation, and that this nation is very important to us, has implications for justice. On the one hand, nationality and the cohesion or fellow-feeling that it produces make political projects such as social justice and democracy possible. Complicated projects, such as pursuing social justice – establishing and maintaining a welfare state, redistributing income through taxation and so on – are far easier if we are sure that everyone will comply with what is being asked of them. This requires generalised trust, and a faith that others will also pay their dues and act according to the common good. That kind of faith is reliably provided by a shared nationality, and is unlikely to exist without it (Miller 1995: 91). On the other hand, if nationality makes social justice possible, then we should not expect it to extend to a level – such as Europe, or the whole world – where there is no shared nationality (Miller 2000). Note that this is not just a matter of practicality: Miller's argument is not that it would be a good thing to have social justice at the global level, but in the absence of national ties we are unlikely to be able to persuade people to go along with it. In fact Miller wants to say that globalising social justice is not necessary or desirable in the first place, because social justice is a reflection of what co-nationals owe to each other and do *not* owe to others. In a related point, Miller also mentions the normative importance of shared *citizenship*. While in general we do not have direct reasons for objecting to inequalities at the global level (although see the discussion in section 3.3.1.), it does make sense to say that some inequalities are incompatible with an ideal of equal citizenship (Miller 2007: 55). As co-citizens we are committed to limiting the inequalities between us, so that our social relations are not characterised by hierarchies or by the domination of some over others. To some extent those two arguments overlap, to produce the conclusion that the pursuit of equality and social justice is a project for nation states, and not one for the world at large.

3.3.1. Miller on global distributive justice

Miller's approach to global justice has two components, as we have suggested. First, he provides an account of people's basic human rights, and assesses just when the need to meet these rights can impose duties of justice on distant others. Second, he suggests we have an obligation to make the terms of international co-operation broadly fair. I will call these the *rights-based* and *co-operation-based* arguments. Whereas the rights-based argument is clearly minimalist in orientation, the co-operation-based argument has some implications for the kinds of inequality that we should be prepared to tolerate. I shall briefly outline each argument.

First, then, Miller's account of global justice is oriented around meeting *basic human rights*. The list of human rights is rather like Rawls's; it includes a right to subsistence, but again excludes democratic rights. It focuses on certain 'core human activities' which reflect 'the conditions that must be met for a person to have a decent life' in the society in which he or she lives (Miller 2007: 184). In fact, we should resist the temptation to build too much into our conception of human rights, since the language of human rights is 'supposed to set minimum standards of treatment for human beings that are uncontestable' (2007: 193).

Whose responsibility is it to secure these basic human rights? The primary responsibility falls on national communities, which is why human rights are not really entitlements of global justice as such. But, again like Rawls, Miller is not necessarily opposed to the idea of global distributive justice. His position is rather complex, so that while the *primary* responsibility for meeting basic human rights falls on the state to which an individual belongs, that responsibility might, in the right conditions, devolve to other states. There is no general duty of justice to make sure that everyone's rights are respected (2007: 248). But, when a state fails to meet the basic human rights of its members through no fault of its own, this might produce duties of justice which fall on *other* states. To be more specific, duties falling on those communities which are particularly close by, or generally well *able* to respond to undeserved poverty, may properly be considered duties of justice (2007: 254–5).

This is a clearly minimalist account of global justice. The focus on basic human rights and on decency tells us that Miller's aims are relatively limited. We also know that Miller is determined to 'break the hold that global egalitarianism has had on our thinking about global justice' (2007: 53). Miller has two chief arguments against global egalitarianism. The first suggests that it is in tension with his goal of a world of self-determining nations, which can make their own choices and which will in turn bear responsibility for those choices. The second suggests that we have no clear method for measuring global equality.

Miller suggests at a number of points that there is bound to be tension between the aims of global egalitarians and the ideal of a world where nations are able to exercise choice, and bear *responsibility* for their choices. On the one hand, equalising goods continually between nations would seem to stand in the way of those countries' ability to make decisions about what to do with their resources. On the other hand, once decisions have been made, it seems fair that nations should reap the costs or benefits of those choices. Of course, I suggested in the last section on Rawls that the idea that all citizens might be responsible for the decisions of their nation is a controversial idea. But Miller devotes considerably more time to judging when a nation's citizens are responsible for its decisions. His account suggests that we can make this judgement most easily with regard to democracies. But even in non-democratic societies it might be the case that decisions arise from shared aims and outlooks (2007: 117) or from collective institutions. So an individual might be responsible for collective decisions even if she voted against them, for example (2007: 121).

What of the argument that we do not have a method of *measuring* global equality? In the literature this has come to be known as the 'metric' objection. As it is usually expressed, the idea is that whereas we know which goods or opportunities we care about at the domestic level – so that when we talk of equality domestically we know what we mean, and can readily say that person x and person y are unequal – we do not have such agreement at the global level. Perhaps people in different cultures simply value different goods or roles. This is the gist of Miller's critique of the ideal of global equality of opportunity, which we discussed in chapter 2. Miller suggests that either we have to go down the route of carefully specifying exactly which goods matter (with the unfortunate result that some communities simply will not value some of these goods), or we provide a very general or broad list of goods. But if we take the latter route, we will not necessarily know how to compare or prioritise different inequalities within each category (2007: 64). In sum, whereas we can readily say that certain people are *poor* or are unable to meet their basic needs, it is much less clear how we can judge whether people are *equal* or unequal across all communities, and across all the different goods that matter to people. There are, Miller believes, formidable technical obstacles in the way of determining what global equality means (see also Walzer 1983).

So Miller is fairly resolute in his opposition to global egalitarianism as an approach to global justice. This is not to say that we never have reasons to resist global inequalities, however. This is where Miller's second, *co-operation-based* argument comes in. He believes that we have an obligation to make sure that the terms on which we interact with other communities are more or less fair, and that the international order gives other societies 'adequate opportunities to develop' (Miller 2007: 253). This might suggest that when we come to negotiate the terms of international trade under the auspices of the World Trade Organization, for instance, we should try to make sure that each nation's interests and perspectives are given some weight, and not simply ignored or marginalised (see chapter 6). Sometimes, though, the fairness of the international order *is* jeopardised by excessive inequalities. In fact, Miller criticises Rawls for not recognising that global economic inequalities will sometimes translate into political inequalities, which make fair terms of co-operation difficult to achieve (Miller 2006: 203; 2007: 267). How could we make fair international agreements on trade, for instance, if a few very rich nations were able to dictate terms to the rest of the world? If they did so, they would be translating economic inequality (with which we are not directly concerned) into political inequality (about which we are concerned, because it means that co-operation is unlikely to be fair). So there are sometimes good indirect or *instrumental* reasons for objecting to particular global inequalities. But these do not mean that global egalitarianism as an approach to global justice has direct appeal. If we could deal with the political inequality in its own right, it would presumably be preferable to do that. If that failed to work, then preserving the background fairness of our international institutions might demand action to limit economic inequalities. But this is not to say that global economic inequality matters in itself.

3.3.2. Responses to Miller

The most common criticism levelled at Miller's argument comes from those who do not find it plausible that common bonds of nationality are required for distributive justice. Thus some critics question whether we really *have* fuller distributive duties towards our fellow nationals. It might be that sharing a nationality with someone might make it more *likely* that you will sacrifice your self-interest to help them. But does that really mean that we have no substantial obligations of justice to people with whom we do not share a nationality? Some global egalitarians, such as Simon Caney, do not believe that good grounds have yet been given for special distributive duties towards co-nationals (Caney 2005a: 269). Others are happy to accept special duties towards co-nationals, at least for the sake of argument, but challenge the way in which Miller weighs global and domestic priorities against each other. Van der Veen (2008), for example, suggests that nations should meet a duty of justice to secure basic human rights worldwide *before* embarking at home on more grandiose projects which are less urgent in character. Miller may be right that we have special duties towards our co-nationals, this criticism suggests, but he places too much weight on them.

Other critics have probed the idea of national responsibility that is so important in Miller's argument. Some find it implausible that a population can collectively be held responsible for the decisions 'they' or their leaders make. Here we might either say that nations are not appropriate subjects to bear collective responsibility (Pierik 2008), or we might push Miller on the implications for particular groups of people – such as those who disagree with 'common' decisions. We might, alternatively, find it unjust that individuals born into nations which have in the *past* made bad decisions will now suffer the consequences.

It is also worth asking whether the two main objections Miller levels at global egalitarian accounts are convincing. First of all, it is open to question whether national responsibility or national self-determination are really incompatible with all forms of global egalitarianism or with just some of them. Global egalitarianism could after all mean a variety of different things, and global egalitarian principles could apply to some goods and not others. As such they might leave space for considerable national variation and local decision-making. Miller's assertion that the two things are incompatible is therefore too sweeping (Armstrong 2010). Second, we can ask how successful the metric-based objection is. Our response to this will of course depend on whether we think egalitarianism needs a single metric in the first place. If we do not, then we might not be troubled by Miller's criticism. Or we might say that, even if working out a metric is difficult, it is just obvious that there are major inequalities between individuals in different countries that should trouble us. There is nothing particularly controversial, we might say, about the argument that it is unfair that individuals in Sierra Leone and the United States are born with such different life expectancies, or grow up to enjoy such different incomes (see chapter 2). Although there are cultural differences between communities, it is not too controversial to assume that all people would prefer to have more rather than less money to spend on whatever they think is important in life or to live longer rather than shorter lives. Alternatively, we might say that finding a metric for global equality is going to be formidably difficult, but this does not mean that global egalitarianism is not the right approach to global justice at the level of principle (Caney 2007).

3.4. Nagel on coercion and the state

In chapter 1 we examined relational arguments for global justice. Some of these stressed the importance of *institutions* in determining the scope of justice. Theorists such as Pogge suggested that since there was a global institutional structure, we needed global principles of justice to regulate it. In making that argument, many theorists took their lead, once more, from John Rawls. Rawls argued that principles of justice at the domestic level should regulate a society's *basic structure* – generally speaking, its web of social, political and economic institutions, which combine to make a 'system' which has a great impact on our individual life chances (Rawls 1971). But, some theorists asked, is there not a *global* basic structure too? Are there not important global institutions which themselves have an important impact on the life chances of people born into both rich and poor countries (see e.g. Beitz 1979; Hinsch 2001)? Sceptics about global justice then denied that there was in fact a global basic structure, since global institutions are different in type from, and much less powerful than, domestic institutions (see e.g. Freeman 2007).

In the end this debate was not entirely helpful. For domestic and global institutions do look to be quite different – but this does not settle the questions whether they are both normatively important and whether their effects need to be appraised according to principles of distributive justice. Ascertaining that the WTO or the UN or the World Bank do not, in the end, closely resemble Rawls's definition of a basic structure does not settle the normative issues. The debate has since moved on in several ways. For one thing, proponents of global egalitarianism have clarified their positions on which (if any) institutions are important in determining the scope of egalitarian justice, and why. In this regard some theorists have changed their positions over time (see e.g. Beitz 1999a). For another, sceptics about global egalitarianism have refined their own accounts of just *why* the institutions of the state are special. Is it because they embody relations of *reciprocity* between citizens (Sangiovanni 2007; but see Armstrong 2009b)? Is it because state institutions are *coercive* in some way (R. Miller 1998; Blake 2001; Risse 2006)? Within this debate one of the most noteworthy positions has been taken by Thomas Nagel, who suggests that the coercive nature of state institutions determines that distributive justice should apply at the state level and only at the state level. We shall examine his argument in this section.

Thomas Nagel has proposed one of the starkest minimalist positions of recent years on global justice, in the sense that whereas he endorses distributive egalitarianism at the global level, he rejects entirely the idea of global distributive justice (Nagel 2005). His position therefore entails a very strong break or discontinuity between the domestic realm, within which co-citizens owe each other a fairly substantial degree of equality, and the global realm, where our only duties to outsiders are humanitarian in form. This position – that we do not owe outsiders *any* duties of distributive justice, and that our only obligations towards them are those of humanitarianism, aimed at alleviating poverty (but not inequality) – pushes him a little further than Rawls. Rawls, after all, was not in the end resolutely opposed to the idea of global distributive justice, so long as its aims were clearly limited and it did not extend its ambitions in too egalitarian a direction. But Nagel *does* reject any version of global distributive justice.

In terms of the distinction between relationism and non-relationism (see Chapter 1), Nagel's is clearly a relationist view. It suggests that citizens are joined together in a *relationship* which is important enough to make distributive justice relevant between them – and them alone. But what kind of relationship exists between co-citizens, and why is it so important? For Nagel, the relational 'trigger' for distributive justice to become relevant is the presence of *coercive political relations*. What is special about citizens – and what is not true of the relationship between citizens and outsiders – is the way in which they shape each other's fates through a set of political institutions which enjoy coercive power. Building on a theme from Rawls (1971), Nagel argues that it is because we as citizens sustain an institutional structure that in turn impacts on our individual life chances, that we owe each other a normative justification for those institutions.

Let us take an example. Imagine three people: Alice is a wealthy American, who works for a big publishing company. Deborah is a poor American, who cleans offices. Stephanie is a poor Singaporean who also cleans offices but earns a good deal less than Deborah. Here it is hugely significant for Nagel that Alice and Deborah share a common political system (the political and economic institutions of the US state). Whereas Alice may not be directly responsible for Deborah's poverty, Alice and Deborah are both nevertheless citizens of the same state. Because they live in a democratic state, their government is in a sense their agent (along with all other Americans). As such, Nagel believes they are collectively responsible for the inequalities it either produces or fails to address. If Deborah is poor because the state did not give people like her the good-quality education that it gave people like Alice, then it has committed an injustice. If Deborah is poor because she belongs to a disadvantaged racial group and the government has failed to tackle that disadvantage, then this looks unjust too. The state has what Rawls called a 'basic structure' of institutions, which has a real impact on the life chances of Americans. Justice tells us that it has a responsibility to make sure that the impact of that structure is reasonably egalitarian. And since the government is the agent of all its citizens, we can reasonably say that the citizens themselves are responsible for any inequalities that remain.

We cannot, according to Nagel, say those things of Alice and Stephanie. The inequalities between them were not produced by the US government. They may have been produced, or intensified, by the global economy or even, conceivably, by global institutions such as the International Monetary Fund (IMF). But Alice and Stephanie are not joined together in the strong political relationship which would be required to convert the inequalities between them into injustices. The global economy does not represent Alice and Stephanie, and neither is the IMF their common agent. The inequalities between Alice and Stephanie might be regrettable, but they are not unjust according to standards of distributive justice. Those standards are simply out of place at the global level.

So, rather like Rawls's basic-structure-based argument for the difference principle, the thinking is that at the domestic level, and *only* at that level, there is an institutional structure for which we are all responsible. We as citizens are therefore responsible for domestic inequalities, and for everyone to be able to accept them we need to provide citizens with a good reason why they are necessary. A principle like the difference principle, or some other egalitarian principle, might play that role of limiting and justifying the remaining inequalities. It would be invidious if we seemed to be imposing a status as inferior citizens on others without offering such a justification (as Nagel puts it, 'We are required to accord equal status to anyone with whom we are joined in a strong and coercively-imposed political community' (2005: 133)).

To be a little more precise, Nagel believes that there are three necessary conditions for distributive justice to become appropriate between a given set of individuals. First, as we have seen, relations of justice apply within the boundaries of a system of *coercively imposed* rules and institutions. 'The economy' is not a system of coercively imposed rules and institutions, for Nagel, but a state is. Second, relations of justice apply between citizens considered to be *joint authors* of such a coercively imposed system. This is the reason why citizens owe each other justice: in a real and meaningful sense they are jointly responsible for the inequalities that remain between them. Third, relations of justice apply when such citizens can be considered *involuntarily subject* to the resulting norms and obligations. We would not want to talk of distributive injustices within a sporting club, Nagel tells us – because if we do not like the inequalities within that club we can simply walk away and join another one. But states do have a habit of making us accord with their rules whether we like it or not. So they are a uniquely appropriate site for principles of distributive justice.

It is important to recognise that Nagel believes that all three criteria have to be satisfied for duties of distributive justice to arise between people. We could, for instance, make an argument to the effect that the World Trade Organization has coercive power over people (perhaps because it can impose penalties, or authorise states to impose penalties on each other), or even that subjection to it is involuntary (because choosing not to join it might technically be a choice for each state, but not joining would be a crazy choice). But Nagel would be unmoved by these arguments unless we could *also* say that the World Trade Organization is our common agent, or that all of us are joint agents of its rules and decisions. And Nagel just does not think that this is the case. As such, arguments for global distributive justice are mistaken.

3.4.1. Nagel on global distributive justice

The implications of Nagel's argument for global justice are very simple. Talk of global distributive justice is mistaken, because principles of justice apply to coercive, jointly-authored institutions to which we are involuntarily subjected, and no such institutions exist at the global level. This does not mean that we have no obligations towards the poor of the world. But it does mean that our obligations will be humanitarian in form (Nagel 2005: 118), and hence will not be stringent and enforceable in the same way that duties of justice would be. So while he might want to endorse the UN's Millennium Development Goals, he would not want to say that a country which failed to meet the target of giving away 0.7 per cent of its national income in the form of overseas aid would be acting unjustly. He is also clear that whereas domestically we are rightly concerned about relative differences between citizens – in other words, inequalities – globally the issue to which our humanitarian duties respond is absolute poverty (Nagel 2005: 119) – the fact that some people simply do not have enough to live.

It is an implication of Nagel's account that if coercive and jointly authored institutions *did* emerge at the global level (and we were involuntarily subjected to them), *then* we could reasonably ask them to conform to standards of global distributive justice. Nagel does not believe that this is likely to happen for some considerable time. But from the point of view of global justice, he suggests, our best hope is that powerful global institutions will emerge which at first look decidedly unjust (2005: 147). We can then ask or entreat them to become more just in their effects or outcomes, and the notion of global justice can at last begin to have an object to get its teeth into. But until that time, talk of global distributive justice is unwarranted.

3.4.2. Responses to Nagel

Critics have responded to Nagel's argument in two ways. A first response broadly accepts Nagel's claim as to when distributive justice becomes relevant, but tries to show that someone accepting that claim should actually be committed to global distributive justice, perhaps of the egalitarian variety. Perhaps there really are global institutions with coercive power, with the implication that Nagel is mistaken, and some kind of global distributive justice really is necessary. A second and more fundamental response suggests that Nagel is wrong about the conditions that trigger the concerns of distributive justice. Coercion is simply not important in the way that Nagel suggests that it is; establishing the presence or absence of coercive institutions does not tell us when duties of justice arise. We can examine each response in turn.

The first response, then, accepts the general contours of Nagel's account but suggests that he draws the wrong conclusions because there are in fact global coercive institutions. Perhaps powerful global institutions such as the World Trade Organization, the World Bank or the International Monetary Fund are able to ensure that members implement their rules and decisions. Alternatively, some have pointed to the fact that nation states themselves coercively control their borders, and that this coercion is felt by outsiders and not just citizens (Abizadeh 2007). Perhaps in response to this kind of argument, in recent years the coercion-based view has been developed by a number of theorists who have tried to clarify the specific kind of coercion that makes distributive justice or equality necessary. Perhaps there is something special about the very *direct* way in which states coerce their citizens. After all, if global institutions want to coerce individual citizens, they usually need those citizens' states to do so for them, on their behalf. As such their coercion is indirect at best. It is states that are directly and immediately coercive of citizens (Risse 2006).

But this first challenge probably misses the point in any case. Nagel can accept that there are global institutions with coercive power, without being led to the conclusion that we therefore need some kind of global distributive justice. This is because coercion is not the only necessary condition for justice to become necessary. We also need to say that this coercion is *jointly authored* (as well as individuals being involuntarily subject to it). But Nagel will simply deny that any coercion that might or might not be exercised by institutions such as the WTO and the IMF is jointly authored. After all, when was I, a citizen of the United Kingdom, ever consulted on one of their decisions? So, as it turns out, the more productive avenue for those unhappy with Nagel's conclusions to explore is probably the meaning of joint authorship (Armstrong 2009b). For here Nagel's account is a little ambiguous. Recall that Nagel wants to say that in a state all citizens are collectively responsible for addressing inequalities, because they are in an important sense joint authors of those inequalities. What is important here is that Nagel wants to extend this argument to all states, and not just democratic ones. It would be a pretty unpalatable conclusion if Nagel had to say that in a state which was not a democracy, leaders were not obliged to treat their citizens equally, precisely because they did not consult them about their decisions. So in this case Nagel wants to say that inequalities are still in a sense jointly authored, because an undemocratic government still makes its decisions *in the name of* its citizens (Nagel 2005: 121). The problem for Nagel is that we can try and apply this same logic to global institutions, too. After all, if global institutions such as the WTO do not make their decisions *in the name of* all individuals of the world, just whom *do* they represent? And if they do make some claim to represent all of us, even if not at all democratically, then it seems that by Nagel's standards they are responsible for treating us equally and limiting any inequalities to which their decisions give rise. This seems to make some kind of global distributive justice necessary.

So it seems likely, if we accept its premises, that Nagel's account can be redirected to justify some kind of global distributive justice. The second and more fundamental response to Nagel works quite differently, though, by denying the importance Nagel attaches to coercion in the first place. A non-relationist, for instance, might simply deny that the presence or absence of coercive institutions has any importance at all in determining the scope of justice. Coercive institutions are just not important to such a view. Although Nagel may be right that having global coercive institutions would make achieving global justice easier, this does not mean that without them we do not *need* global justice. Indeed, Nagel may just be plain wrong about the relationship between justice and institutions. Nagel assumes that the presence of institutions such as the state tells us all we need to know about when and where we need to pursue justice. But what if he has got this the wrong way around? What if justice at least sometimes tells us when we need to *create* institutions? If we restrict our attention to evaluating institutions that already exist, and are debarred from calling for the creation of new ones, we are in effect condemned continually to justify something like the status quo. Relationists could also reject Nagel's account as confused. A relationist global egalitarian could say that Nagel may be right that the presence of coercive institutions at whatever level gives us a reason to pursue global justice. But this does not at all prove that it is the *only* reason we have to pursue global justice. Relationists could suggest that, even if coercion makes justice necessary, so do other things, such as the fact that we all belong to a global economy or ecosystem, that our decisions have an impact on other people's lives and so on. Providing us with a story about why coercion is important is not the same thing as providing us with a story about why it is the *only* thing that is important. Given that he has not yet done the latter, the arguments of proponents of global distributive justice may be able to escape from Nagel's challenge.

3.5. Global minimalism versus global egalitarianism

The three accounts discussed in this chapter are all minimalist regarding global justice, but they are minimalist in slightly different ways:

Rawls's account recommends a duty of assistance which at least some supporters see as a duty of justice. Whereas he is generally sceptical about the claims of global distributive justice, he is also happy to say that his duty might be close in its implications to some proposals put forward by advocates of global distributive justice. Rawls is certainly determined to reject the claims of global egalitarianism, though. His goals are minimalist in the sense that they are exclusively oriented around delivering on basic human rights. Those human rights include a right to subsistence – to food, shelter, water and so on. But beyond this baseline, global inequalities simply do not matter in and of themselves.

Miller is also determined to reject the claims of global egalitarianism, although he does acknowledge some instrumental reasons for caring about global inequalities. He appears happy to consider his account as incorporating in at least some instances duties of global distributive justice which people in richer countries might have towards people in poorer countries. But on the whole his account is also minimalist in the sense that its goals are oriented around the protection of basic human rights – which again include rights to subsistence, but which we should be careful not to stretch too far. Miller is also concerned that global institutions offer 'fair terms of co-operation' to the nations of the world. In some cases this provides us with indirect or instrumental reasons for objecting to certain global inequalities, but in general he has attempted to define the terms of fair co-operation without explicitly invoking egalitarian principles.

Nagel's account is the most minimalist. Not only does he reject global egalitarianism, but he rejects the project of global distributive justice in its entirety, at least until we enter a very different phase of international politics where there are effective and powerful global institutions. As such, although we might have obligations to respond to suffering, these will represent humanitarian duties rather than duties of distributive justice. Unlike Miller, Nagel does not acknowledge even instrumental reasons for tackling global inequalities.

While the three accounts are minimalist about global justice in slightly different ways, they all share a commitment to rejecting global egalitarianism. In the interests of continuing the discussion between the approaches discussed in the last chapter and the approaches discussed in this one, we can briefly assemble the four challenges that are levelled at global egalitarianism as an approach to global justice. First, the *national responsibility objection* suggests that distributing goods between people in an egalitarian fashion prevents us from responding to the fact that nations are sometimes responsible for their own situations, and that individual citizens, in the right conditions, are also responsible. Second, the *national self-determination objection* suggests that global egalitarianism would stand in the way of the ability of nations to make decisions about their future, and to use their own resources in a way they saw fit. Third, there are various forms of the *relational objection*, but they all suggest that equality is only appropriate between people who share a particular relationship. In this chapter we have examined Miller's argument that it applies between co-nationals and Nagel's that it applies between people who are subject to a specific kind of coercive institution (the state). Finally, the *metric objection* suggests that even if greater global equality were a valuable goal, we might not know what it would look like, or indeed know how to move closer to it, given the lack of a common global measure of the goods that are important. Cultural difference stands in the way of such a common metric.

The debate between global minimalists and global egalitarians continues, so we should not assume that any of these objections necessarily represent decisive blows, or that global egalitarians are unable to respond to them. But we might think that the best measure of minimalist and egalitarian theories is in any case to test them on specific issues of global justice, to see whether they give plausible and useful guidance when we think about issues such as trade justice, migration, natural resources or climate justice. That is the task of part II of this book.

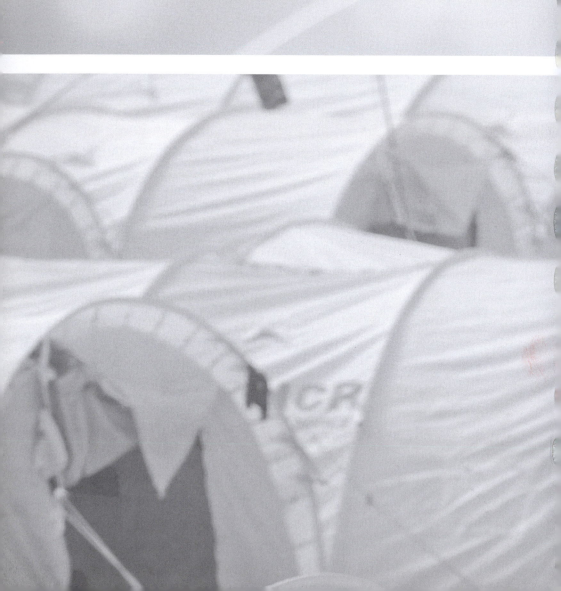

part **II**

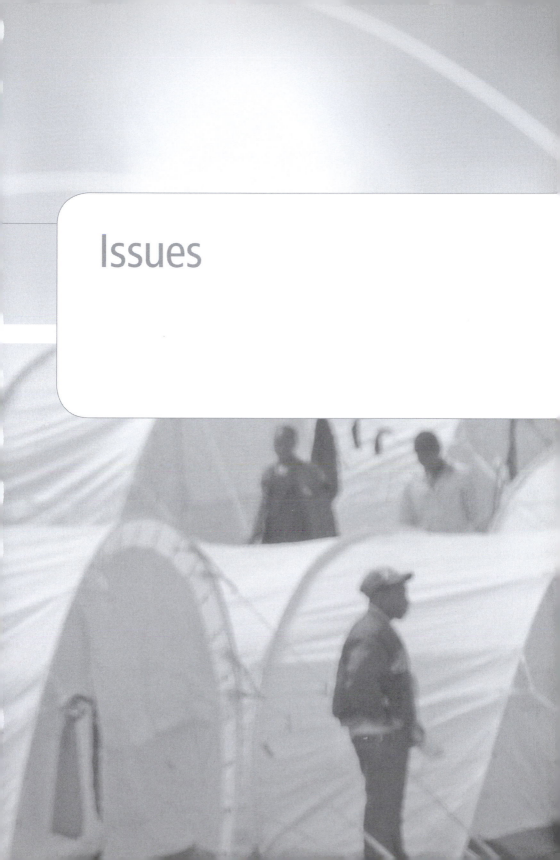

Issues

chapter 4

Global justice and human rights

It is often said that in the years after the Second World War the world witnessed a 'human rights revolution'. Documents such as the 1948 United Nations Universal Declaration of Human Rights proclaimed the universal and binding character of certain rights, and called on all nations to observe and protect them. This document was followed in due course by similar declarations from the Council of Europe, the Organization of American States and the Organization of African Unity (predecessor of the African Union), and the United Nations itself has further refined its list of human rights in a series of Covenants and Conventions. Most countries of the world have signed up to such agreements, and that apparently wide agreement is important. Whereas each of us will likely have various rights as citizens of particular countries, *human* rights are intended to pick out goods or interests which we can safely assume are important to everyone, in whatever kind of society or political system they happen to live. As James Griffin puts it, when we set out a list of human rights we focus on 'what is at the center of a valuable human life and so requires special protection' (Griffin 1986: 64). So an account of human rights concentrates on setting out a kind of 'moral minimum', of which no one should be deprived, regardless of where they live. To specify something as a human right is to accord considerable normative force to it, so that respect for someone's human rights will usually – though not necessarily always – take precedence over other moral considerations. It will also, standardly, involve a claim that someone – or perhaps everyone – has a *duty* to respect and if necessary protect that right (see e.g. Nickel 2005, Griffin 2008).

From the point of view of international politics, this human rights 'revolution' has two elements: it both *limits* the autonomy of states by imposing core standards on them, and simultaneously *affirms* their status as the major units of legitimacy and power in world politics. Let us take each in turn. First, the human rights revolution appears to have brought along with it a significant redefinition of the idea of national sovereignty (Reus-Smith 2001). By signing up to human rights treaties, the various countries of the world are (at least in theory) agreeing to fall in line with a set of minimal standards which limit how they can legitimately treat their citizens. Those standards are not then easily ignored; as Jeremy Waldron has put it, 'there is now scarcely a nation on earth which is not sensitive to or embarrassed by the charge that it is guilty of rights-violations' (Waldron 1987: 155). As a result, when national leaders visit each other – and especially when leaders of liberal democracies visit their counterparts in certain non-democratic countries such as China or Saudi Arabia – the media tend to wait eagerly for the moment when the former begin to lecture the latter, politely or otherwise, about 'the human rights issue'. Countries which do not protect human rights are prone to being labelled 'failed states', and if so, the consequences may extend well beyond simple criticism. The extreme neglect or abuse of human rights is sometimes thought to legitimise external intervention by other states (see e.g. Buchanan 2010). This is the role that John Rawls wants human rights to play, of course: the protection of human rights determines which societies we are, and are not, obliged to tolerate. To say that a society does not protect human rights is to say, quite simply, that it has no right against external intervention (Rawls 1999: 79–81).

Second, though, it is important to remember that human rights are still usually held to be standards which individual countries must meet in their treatment of their *own* citizens, rather than outsiders (Donnelly 1999: 85). In practice human rights really function as a universal but nevertheless nationally enforced set of rights, which reinforces the idea that it is states above all which are the sites of real power and authority in the contemporary world. Our understanding of *abuses* of human rights is, accordingly, almost wholly state-centric. When a policeman randomly assaults a citizen, that assault will usually be recognised as a violation of human rights. When one citizen randomly assaults another, it usually will not be – here the language of human rights is thought to be inappropriate because the local state is not directly involved in protecting or failing to protect the right under threat (Pogge 2002: 57–8). Likewise, if a child in Bangladesh is starving, we may be prepared to say that the government of Bangladesh has violated – or at least failed to protect – her human rights. Unless we knew that they were somehow involved in causing her starvation, we would not usually say that the governments of Canada or Mexico or Chad had violated, or failed to protect, her rights. This, however, is the subject of some debate. As we shall see later on in the chapter, some theorists of global justice want to see human rights supported by duties of justice across borders. Indeed, some of the liveliest controversies surround this question of just *who*, if anyone, has an obligation to deliver on the promise of human rights.

The special role played by human rights in international politics is reflected in agreement between both egalitarians and minimalists that human rights mark out especially pressing claims which deserve urgent attention. Indeed, both egalitarians and minimalists may share at least partially overlapping views on many of the rights which most matter. There is space, though, for disagreement even here. For one thing, whereas minimalists believe that human rights provide the major focus of an adequate account of global justice, egalitarian accounts will be far from satisfied with a world where human rights are protected. They would still find reason for dissatisfaction in a world where human rights were met but large inequalities remained. For another thing, as we shall see, egalitarians and minimalists may have competing ideas about whose responsibility it is to meet human rights, with minimalists placing most of the responsibility at the door of the local nation state, and egalitarians potentially spreading it more widely.

We shall begin this chapter with a case study on human rights as defended by the European Court of Human Rights (box 4.1). This case study allows us to grasp the concrete significance of human rights law, and the real constraints it now places on the actions of individual states. We then turn, in section 4.1, to examine the normative basis of human rights, and the different justifications which have been provided for them. Section 4.2 shifts our focus to the *content* of human rights and, specifically, it concentrates on so-called 'socio-economic' human rights, including, most significantly, arguments in favour of a right to 'subsistence'. Subsistence rights set out the material basis people require to maintain a 'minimally adequate standard of living' (Jones 1999: 53), and typically include entitlements to food, clothing and shelter. Many theorists of global justice, whether of a minimalist or egalitarian variety, have been prepared to defend such rights, but they have, nevertheless, proven to be the subject of some controversy. Some critics do not believe that socio-economic rights (including subsistence rights) are correct objects for human rights, and suspect that the concept of human rights has been 'inflated' too far in including them. We need to consider, therefore, the strength of the argument for subsistence rights as human rights. In section 4.3 we turn to the important question of who has a duty to *fulfil* people's human rights. In particular, if we can be said to have a human right to food, shelter and so on, this implies that others have a positive duty to help to provide us with those things. But how should we divide up positive duties to meet others' human rights? This, perhaps, is where the connection between human rights and global distributive justice comes into clearest focus, because for *some* theorists of global justice, individuals and the states to which they belong have definite duties of justice to help to meet human rights in other countries, at least in some circumstances. So here we examine debates about how to allocate those duties. Finally, in section 4.4, the 'Further issues' section, we shall examine some recent arguments about the implications of a human right to health, particularly as developed by Thomas Pogge.

Box 4.1. **Case study: the European Court of Human Rights**

The ECHR was established in 1959 by the Council of Europe, to enforce the European Convention on Human Rights. It is based in Strasbourg, France, where by 1998 it had become a permanent court with dedicated full-time judges. The Court has binding authority over the forty-seven member states of the Council of Europe, and, as such, over 800 million Europeans are able to take cases directly to the ECHR, without the permission of their own governments. Indeed, a significant number of Europeans have done so: by 2010 the Court had a backlog of over 120,000 cases.

The decisions of the Court must be respected by its member states. Although a member state could leave the Council of Europe if it chose to, on a day-to-day level its power represents a genuine check on the sovereignty of member states. While its power – and many of its decisions – have been the object of scorn from those concerned to protect national self-determination, it has succeeded in protecting the rights of many European citizens. Some key cases include the following.

Tyrer v. *UK* (1978). In this case the Court ruled against the imposition of corporal punishment on juvenile offenders, considering it to represent 'degrading treatment' in contravention of Article 3 of the European Convention on Human Rights.

Soering v. *UK* (1989). Here an EU citizen suspected of murder in the United States claimed that his right not to be subjected to 'inhuman or degrading treatment' would be jeopardised if he were extradited to the United States (and, particularly, to a state which retained the death penalty). The suspect was eventually extradited after the United Kingdom obtained a guarantee that the death penalty would not be applied. The case significantly extended the duty not to inflict degrading treat-ment: any signatory state, according to this judgment, has a duty not to expose a person to degrading treatment in *any other* state, even if the latter state has not signed up to the Convention.

Jersild v. *Denmark* (1994). A Danish journalist had been convicted of aiding and abetting an anti-immigrant group whose views he had reported in a television interview. The Court, however, determined that his right to freedom of expression had unjustly been curtailed, since although he had not challenged the views of the group in his interview, he had sufficiently 'dissociated' himself from them.

Bączkowski and Others v. *Poland* (2006). This case ruled that the Polish govern-ment's banning of a 'gay pride' parade in Warsaw violated the participants' free-dom of association and freedom of assembly.

4.1. Why human rights?

Human rights are supposedly universal, but the fact remains that they developed as a concept largely within Western societies, and moreover at a time when Western nations were dominant in world politics. The claim that they are little more than a projection of Western values or interests has never, therefore, been far away, and the challenge of providing a sound justification for them has been keenly felt. Theorists of human rights have devoted considerable effort to providing a rationale for those rights which could genuinely be accepted by the different societies of the world. As David Miller puts it, when grounding human rights 'our starting point cannot be a value that is likely to appeal only to liberals' (Miller 2007: 198). Rather, 'the justification we give should be valid across the different religious, moral and political cultures that we find in the contemporary world' (2007: 164–5).

What would it mean, though, for a justification to be 'valid' across different cultures? Much time has been spent on finding support for the idea of human rights – or something suitably close to it, such as a conception of human dignity – within traditions such as Islam, Confucianism or Hinduism (on which see e.g. Taylor 1999; Sen 1997; Donnelly 1982). But just what are we doing when we look for support for human rights in these traditions? One view would be that a minimal moral code – such as that provided by human rights – should be 'universalist' in the strictly limited sense that it builds from what is genuinely shared between different societies, and does not impose from the outside ideas which are not already present in the 'local' culture (Walzer 2007: 183–7). But that would be a very serious limitation on the enterprise of describing human rights. For we might then think that if we could identify a single culture which offers *no* support for human rights, then that counts seriously against their universality. Most theorists of human rights, though, do not want to restrict themselves simply to describing actual overlaps between different cultural traditions. Instead, they believe that our conception of human rights should be *critical* to some degree. If support for human rights really cannot be found within a given tradition, then perhaps we ought to say, so much the worse for that tradition. Similarly, a belief in human rights will, in at least some cases, support a rejection of practices which may be an authentic part of a given cultural tradition (see e.g. Caney 2005a: 90). A more realistic hope, overall, is that *some* resources can be found within different traditions to subscribe to the core idea of human rights, even if those traditions find different reasons to subscribe to them (Rawls 1999: 65, 68). We might then see the commitment to human rights as 'broadly shareable', to use a term from Pogge, rather than *broadly shared* (Pogge 2002: 54).

So even if we should not presume that we shall find total support for all elements of our conception of human rights, there has still been a concern to provide a justification for them which is likely to be broadly acceptable to people within a wide variety of traditions. When we turn to two of the most common ways of justifying human rights, we can see that each attempts to avoid the charge of 'cultural imperialism' – to avoid, that is, basing itself on claims about the good life or the good society which turn out to be obviously specific to particular cultures. Both approaches attempt to draw on facts about human beings whose truth could, in theory, be recognised regardless of which society to which we happen to belong. The first approach emphasises our moral personhood, or capacity for agency. The second emphasises certain key needs or interests which all human beings can be said to have.

4.1.1. Moral personhood and normative agency

Our first approach to justifying human rights emphasises their importance to human 'personhood'. This is the core of James Griffin's recent account, for example. On this view humans, perhaps unlike other animals, are 'persons'. Particularly, they have the capacity to make choices and to reflect on what constitutes, for them, a worthwhile life. So the 'personhood'-based justification for human rights emphasises activities such as 'deliberating, assessing, choosing, and acting to make what we see as a good life for ourselves' (Griffin 2008: 32). We need not make any assumptions here about what the content of a good life *is*. Instead, we focus on a human being's ability to formulate an idea of what represents a good life for him or for her (this distinction, presumably, allows us to sidestep the charge of cultural imperialism).

If we accept that people are moral 'persons' – insofar as they have what Griffin calls 'normative agency', the ability to reflect and to choose – then we should also see that this moral personhood needs *protection*. A person could hardly exercise this kind of agency if they were dominated by others, prevented from participating in making decisions about the society they lived in, or tortured or arbitrarily imprisoned. Their normative agency will also be undercut if they are deprived of a minimal level of both education and material resources on which to live. While theories of justice might produce an account of how we could protect or respect people's normative agency to the maximum extent, human rights focus on the 'minimum provision' necessary to protect it. If we understand human rights, then, as what Griffin calls 'protections of our normative agency' (2008: 2), we can produce a list of things without which the capacity to reflect, to choose and to direct one's life are thwarted. We would accept, Griffin suggests, human rights to life, to physical security, to a voice in political decision-making, to freedom of assembly, expression and worship, and to basic education and the material requisites of physical survival (2008: 33).

Griffin, then, believes that a focus on moral personhood provides a justification for human rights which is suitably 'universal' insofar as it emphasises qualities which are possessed by human beings simply *as* human beings. The ability to make basic decisions about your life is not a culturally specific value, but is important whatever social setting we happen to live in (2008: 48–9). As such we can ground human rights without wading into very controversial waters.

4.1.2. Basic needs and interests

A second common approach to justifying rights is to emphasise the way in which they serve important human interests (Raz 1986). On this view, although humans may differ in their culture and beliefs, there are still some things they can be presumed to have an interest in having, or being able to do, simply by virtue of their nature as human beings. Such an approach has been embraced by a number of theorists of human rights (e.g. Caney 2005a: 73). But a version of that approach has been defended at some length by David Miller, whose account we shall examine here.

Miller's argument is that when grounding human rights we should focus on basic human *needs* – specifically, on things which humans need in and of themselves, if they are going to escape serious harm. This is one variant of the interests-based approach, insofar as it emphasises those goods or opportunities which we can reasonably say are important to each human being, regardless of their culture. Basic needs are, for Miller, an appropriately universal basis on which to build an account of human rights because they do not describe what people happen to *want* or value, but rather what any human being *requires* for their continued existence (Miller 2007: 180). This is key in avoiding the charge of cultural imperialism. Basic needs can often be read off from uncontroversial biological facts about human beings, as when we describe a need for food and water – because the need for food and water does not vary to any great extent between different societies, or at least not so much that it becomes impossible to specify an adequate minimum. So although we know from chapter 3 that Miller believes that cultural diversity provides one reason why a 'metric' cannot be supplied for global egalitarian ideas, it does not prevent us from identifying *basic needs* which apply across cultures (although see Wenar 2008b for a critical discussion on this contrast).

It is important, for Miller, to distinguish basic needs from 'societal needs'. Societal needs refers to the things we need if we are to live a minimally decent life in the *particular* society to which we happen to belong (reflection on these will probably, according to Miller, lead to a fuller and more demanding list in wealthier countries than in poorer ones). Societal needs are important to the pursuit of social justice, but take us well beyond the proper basis of human rights. We should, instead, restrict our attention to the things which humans need in *whichever* society they happen to live (Miller 2007: 182). Miller's list of basic needs therefore includes 'food and water, clothing and shelter, physical security, health care, education, work and leisure, freedoms of movement, conscience and expression' (2007: 184). Provided that certain conditions are met – including, perhaps, that meeting these basic needs is feasible – then it makes sense for them to be used to ground human rights (2007: 194).

4.1.3. Controversies about the content of human rights

Griffin's and Miller's accounts converge, to a substantial extent, on a list of human rights which they both believe are important to all human beings *as* human beings. Moreover, they expect that support for their conceptions could be forthcoming from a variety of cultural traditions – although they do not necessarily believe that lack of widespread agreement would disqualify their accounts. But even if there were broad agreement on a general conception of human rights, we should not assume that controversy about the precise *content* of a list of human rights can be avoided. In fact disagreements about which rights should be on the list are enduring and sometimes intense.

One source of controversy about which rights we should include arises from underlying disagreement about the different roles we want human rights to play. For instance, human rights are sometimes thought of as standards to which governments should *aspire* – even if they cannot all measure up to them right now. As such human rights function as broad goals of domestic policy, towards which progress should be made. But on the other hand human rights are sometimes viewed as much firmer than this. Perhaps they represent very fundamental and urgent standards, and any government which does not measure up to them is simply illegitimate – and a potential target for external intervention. John Rawls held that kind of view (Rawls 1999), and his account certainly possesses a kind of neatness and economy: human rights determine the right to intervention, so we should not be prepared to say that something is a human right unless we are *also* prepared to say that intervention is legitimate if it is not observed. But, for some critics, that neatness comes at too high a price. Rawls's very limited list of core human rights has attracted some fierce criticism, not least because it omits a human right to democratic participation, or any robust defence of gender equality (see e.g. Buchanan 2000). Of course Rawls should not be expected to say that there is a human right to democracy, given that he has already stipulated that decent hierarchical societies (which are not democratic) ought to be tolerated. But Griffin, for one, believes that leaving out democratic rights is too high a price to pay for setting clear boundaries of toleration (Griffin 2010). Perhaps, we might say, the two roles of human rights must come apart to some degree, so that we could specify a subset of human rights whose violation *would* trigger intervention, but also a further subset of rights which, although important in their own way, would not normally trigger intervention.

A related source of controversy is underlying disagreement about the importance of feasibility and achievability. Many theorists are only prepared to say that something is a human right if it can be delivered by some identifiable agent with a definite duty or set of duties to uphold it – and this agent is usually the state. But some human rights do look less secure than this, and instead appear to name aspirations which governments *ought* to aim at delivering over time. For some critics, when we include such rights on our list we have strayed too far and illegitimately 'inflated' the concept of human rights. When we have a political axe to grind appeals to human rights are attractive, because such rights are internationally respected, and they often have mechanisms of enforcement attached to them (Wolff 2011). But if we try to pack too much content into human rights, we run several risks. We risk, for example, straying into areas where controversy is more intense, or where the capacity to deliver on the putative rights in question may be wholly lacking; we also risk moving away from the very basic and urgent human requirements which human rights were originally intended to defend and which give them their special character as (generally) non-negotiable moral commitments. This tension – between packing more content into our conception of human rights, and retaining the focus on very basic and urgent requirements – is an ever-present one, as we shall see in the next section.

4.2. Human rights and subsistence

Human rights are often divided into two categories. *Civil and political* rights refer to what should be fairly familiar entitlements, including the right to freedom of expression, freedom of assembly, freedom of thought and religious affiliation, and perhaps – although more controversially – the right to participate in politics on a democratic basis. Historically these were the first to be claimed and they formed the basis, for instance, of France's 1789 Declaration of the Rights of Man. *Socio-economic* rights, on the other hand, venture onto the terrain often discussed by theories of distributive justice – they focus, for example, on the availability and distribution of material goods. Depending on how expansive we want our list to be, these latter rights might include entitlements to food, shelter and clothing, to education and health care, to housing, and to certain rights in the field of employment. Their identification as human rights is a much more recent phenomenon.

It is an open question whether this division between civil/political and socio-economic human rights is conceptually helpful. We can certainly say, at the very least, that when we look at particular rights violations – such as slavery, or the restriction of the right to join a trade union – it is not always very obvious which of the two kinds of right is at stake. But, for better or worse, one thing which the distinction has allowed is debate about the relative *priority* of the two kinds of right. In fact it is frequently said that whereas civil and political rights ought to be guaranteed by all states – and indeed, *could* be guaranteed by all states without too much difficulty – socio-economic rights 'inflate' the concept of human rights, representing a kind of 'wish-list' that looks suspiciously as if it has been derived from a conception of distributive justice, rather than properly focusing on the truly minimal requisites of human life. In political practice, as Evans puts it, 'socioeconomic rights are rarely given the same status as liberal freedoms associated with civil and political rights' (2002: 197). Human rights conventions have sometimes themselves accorded the two kinds of right a different status – defining civil and political rights as rights with which governments should immediately comply, but describing socio-economic rights as rights to be 'progressively realised' over time. In this section we shall investigate arguments in favour of one very important socio-economic right: the right to subsistence. This right has gained the attention, and support, of many theorists of global justice, who have tried to establish that, since it does describe some of the requisites of a minimally decent life, it is a proper subject for human rights.

4.2.1. Basic rights and subsistence

The list of human rights contained in the 1948 Declaration is quite extensive, and includes, for example, the right to belong to a trade union, the right to equal pay for equal work and the right to choose how one's children are educated (UN 1948). Indeed, since 1948 the list of human rights has proliferated still further. For some critics, when we proclaim such rights we move further and further away from the supposed 'core' of human rights – things which are generally agreed to be absolute necessities for life –and intrude instead on the territory of general aspirations of social justice (see e.g. Cranston 1973). One response to this challenge would be to say that whereas *some* supposed socio-economic rights may really just be aspirations, a certain core of them *are* absolutely fundamental to anyone's chances of living a minimally decent life. These core socio-economic rights are just as 'basic' as rights to freedom of expression or physical security. The accounts of John Rawls (1999) and David Miller (2007) suggest this kind of strategy when they defend 'basic' human rights. Miller in particular is keen to distinguish these from projects of social justice aimed at serving 'societal' needs (see section 4.1.2).

But just how do we mark out some rights as 'basic' and others as 'secondary' or less fundamental? Henry Shue is the author of a widely influential account of how we might do so. A basic right, for Shue, is a right which must be secure in order for people to be able to enjoy other rights in turn (Shue 1980: 19). For example, we might be persuaded that people have a human right to join a trade union. But if we know that a given person (correctly) fears for her life every time she leaves her house, and is not able to communicate with the outside world without risking her personal security, then that right to join a union has no reality for her. Here we might follow Rawls in distinguishing between formally having a right and actually being able to enjoy its 'full value' (Rawls 1971: 204). In this case, we might be prepared to say that a right to join a union is all very well, but a right to physical security is necessary first in order to enjoy it. Physical security is a basic right because without it we could not enjoy other non-basic rights. Basic rights describe a true moral minimum: they pinpoint those things which every human being will need in order to live a life of any appreciable quality. Unless our basic rights are protected first, other rights will be more or less worthless.

So what are our basic rights? The most common – and very short – list describes basic rights to physical security and to liberty, to which Shue wants to add the right to subsistence. Each of these three basic rights are often endangered by 'standard threats', against which we ought to be protected. Physical security involves the ability to go about one's life without encountering continual threats to one's health, safety or physical integrity. It can be endangered by very high crime levels, or by the particular vulnerability that some people in society have to being attacked because of their sex, sexuality or religion, for example. The basic right to liberty, for Shue, includes entitlements to freedom of movement and to some kind of political participation. This can be endangered by arbitrary imprisonment or by complete exclusion from political life, for example. Finally, subsistence involves the right to 'unpolluted water, adequate food, adequate clothing, adequate shelter, and minimal preventive public health care' (Shue 1980: 23). It is endangered when people are unable to access the material means of physical survival, for example for reasons of poverty or environmental disaster. Basic rights overall, then, can be seen as 'a shield for the defenceless against at least some of the more devastating and common of life's threats' (Shue 1980: 18). It makes sense to foreground them in any account of human rights, both because of their direct importance to people and their instrumental role in securing other rights.

Shue is well aware, however, that this account of basic rights will not satisfy all critics of socio-economic rights. The inclusion of subsistence may still be objected to and, if so, the objection may make use of the distinction between positive and negative duties which we discussed in chapter 1. The objection would suggest that there is still a key difference between subsistence and the other basic rights. We can defend the human rights to security and liberty, the objection suggests, simply by observing a *negative* duty not to inflict physical violence on other people or to restrict unreasonably their various freedoms. It could be secured, we might suppose, free of charge: refraining from attacking each other does not cost anybody any money. Defending their supposed human right to subsistence, on the other hand, would invoke some supposed *positive* duty – the duty to deliver food or water or shelter to those who proved incapable of acquiring them for themselves. And as we know from chapter 1, whereas there is widespread agreement that we have basic negative rights not to harm other people's basic interests, positive duties are much more controversial.

This seems to point to an essential difference between subsistence rights and the other two basic rights, and potentially stands as a challenge to the defence of a basic right to subsistence. However, as Shue ably shows, this argument is flawed. First, the idea that subsistence rights demand that we observe positive rather than (or as well as) negative duties turns out to be incorrect. It is *not* the case that we can place rights to liberty and security on the 'negative' side of the picture and subsistence rights on the 'positive' side (Shue 1980: 37). After all, the simple observance of a negative duty not to harm others or inflict violence on them is not enough to guarantee their right to security, for instance. If your right to security was *only* protected by people recognising a duty not to attack you, it would be very insecure indeed. In fact, your right to security will only be adequately protected if the state establishes a police force, courts, prisons and so on. And these do not, of course, come free of charge. Just like subsistence rights, they require the state to tax citizens to pay for their own and other citizens' security. In fact, the protection of subsistence rights 'need not be any more expensive or involve any more complex governmental programs than the effective protection of security rights would' (Shue 1980: 39). So it seems that the safeguarding of any right will require the observance of *both* positive duties and negative ones, and in this sense rights to subsistence, security and liberty are on more or less the same normative terrain (Shue 1988: 689; see also Jones 1999: 64).

Moreover, if we are defining basic rights as those rights which need to be in place before other rights can be securely enjoyed, then it should be clear that deficits in subsistence rights lead, predictably, to deficits in the rights to security and liberty too. In that sense they are just as fundamental to a decent life as the other two. When people lack essentials such as food and water, they are often left highly vulnerable to abuse, exploitation and coercion by others (Shue 1980: 25). If so, then defending basic rights to liberty and security but excluding subsistence from the list will be self-defeating. Subsistence is just as fundamental as the others, and its neglect will jeopardise them too (Rawls 1999: 65).

The ongoing conceptual debate about the status of socio-economic rights has been mirrored in the real world. When the UN attempted to codify human rights in a single document, reflecting the progress in thought and practice that had been made in the years since the 1948 Declaration, that enterprise rapidly became enmeshed in superpower conflict. The United States, in particular, refused to accept the legitimacy of socio-economic rights such as the right to subsistence. In the end human rights were proclaimed in two separate documents, both adopted in 1966, and ratified a decade later: the International Covenant on Civil and Political Rights (which includes familiar liberties and describes rights to political participation, for instance), and the International Covenant on Economic, Social and Cultural Rights (which includes the right to subsistence, in addition to other 'social' or 'economic' rights). The US has declined to ratify the latter to this day.

Despite this, the vast majority of theorists of global justice – whether of the minimalist or egalitarian variety – are prepared to argue for subsistence rights as part of any satisfactory account of human rights. Indeed for many minimalist theorists – including Rawls and Miller, but also others such as Charles Jones (1999) and Thomas Pogge (2002) – they represent a large part of the goals of an appropriate account of global justice. For Rawls, recall, the objective of the duty of assistance is to help build stable institutions in burdened societies so that those societies could meet their members' basic human rights. Human rights, here, are not to be interpreted too expansively: they represent a 'special class of urgent rights' which protect people from the worst abuses (Rawls 1999: 79). But they do include subsistence rights, which Rawls includes under the general heading of a right to life and which he considers, following Shue, to be 'basic' (Rawls 1999: 65).

For Miller, the two goals of a satisfactory account of global justice are to secure fair terms of international co-operation and to secure people's basic human rights. Basic human rights have a special role in determining when people in one society have duties to outsiders (Miller 2007: 163–4). As we saw in section 4.1, these rights must be based on clear and identifiable human needs, and not on general aspirations towards justice. But rights to food, water and shelter certainly do fall into the category of basic human rights, and can trigger duties on the part of outsiders when the 'home' state fails to deliver them

(2007: 167). Thomas Pogge is something of an unusual case, since so many commentators suspect him of having global egalitarian sympathies (see e.g. Kelly and McPherson 2010) – an entirely reasonable suspicion given the thrust of his earlier work (see e.g. Pogge 1989, 1994). But his official position is now characterised by a focus on human rights which would include socio-economic rights such as a right to subsistence (2002: 64–9). The major objective of his work in recent years has been to emphasise the negative duty to avoid complicity in sustaining deficits in these human rights. He believes that adherence to this negative duty alone will produce great progress towards global justice (see section 4.4).

For global egalitarians, too, meeting subsistence rights can certainly be seen as a major priority in the pursuit of global justice. This is not to deny that their normative aspirations, unlike many minimalists, will extend well *beyond* securing such human rights. But they are often prepared to endorse such rights as a fundamental and urgent requirement of a just world, and to place priority on their achievement (see e.g. Caney 2009; Beitz 2009). There may still be considerable disagreement between global egalitarians and global minimalists, though, about another thorny question: the question of just *who*, if anyone, has a *duty* to protect the human right to subsistence. We shall consider some answers to that question in the next section.

4.3. Duties to fulfil human rights

Griffin describes human rights as 'doubly universal' (Griffin 2008: 51), in the sense that first we all have them simply as humans, and second that we all owe 'correlative' (or corresponding) duties as humans. But this is not quite the same thing as saying that humans owe duties *to all other humans*. That conclusion does look unavoidable in the case of negative duties – duties not to deprive people of what they have rights to, or not to kill or maim them, for instance. It is perfectly intelligible to say that negative duties are universal – indeed it would be odd to say otherwise (Shue 1988: 690). If anyone has a duty not to maim me, then surely everyone has.

But in the case of positive duties it is less clear that everyone must owe duties to everyone else. It would be perfectly coherent to say that all humans have a right to liberty, security and subsistence, but that the correlative duties fall solely on the particular states in which people live. Indeed, as we have seen, this was very much the approach of the founders of modern human rights doctrine, and is still broadly accurate as a description of the way in which human rights work in the world today. Human rights, essentially, set standards for what *my* state can and cannot do *to me*, and also for what it must provide for me.

Although there are significant controversies about the content of human rights, in which many theorists of global justice have been keen participants, from the point of view of global justice this question – of the allocation of duties to fulfil human rights – is where things get really interesting. We have already seen that global minimalists and global egalitarians could endorse much the same list of human rights, albeit perhaps for different reasons. A minimalist's account of global justice might not extend much beyond protecting basic human rights, for instance, whereas an egalitarian's certainly will – he or she will in all likelihood embrace basic human rights as a mere step – albeit an urgent one – in the direction of an adequate account of global justice. But still, there need not be extensive disagreement between them about the content of human rights.

When it comes to distributing duties to *fulfil* rights – such as the right to subsistence – the paths of egalitarians and minimalists may diverge more radically. Broadly speaking, minimalists have endorsed the status quo, albeit with some important modifications. Rawls thus believes that the governments of individual peoples have a duty to secure the basic human rights of their members. Although he also wants to argue for a duty of assistance to help them in doing that, it is not clear that he expects this to involve substantial transfers of resources (in fact he says that 'Throwing funds at [the problem] is usually undesirable' if the goal is to get a burdened society to change its culture and institutions). It may well be that the duty will be fulfilled instead by liberal peoples advising burdened societies on sound economic policy, emphasising the importance of human rights, or providing technical assistance (Rawls 1999: 108, 110). He is certainly clear that the duty is strictly limited in its goals, and seems also to expect that it will be limited in duration (unlike duties of egalitarian distributive justice, it has a 'cut-off point'). Miller, whose ideas we shall discuss in a little more detail below, also believes that the overwhelming responsibility for delivering on basic human rights falls on the nation states in which people live. While he is prepared to accept that we may in some circumstances have a duty of justice to help other countries to fulfil those rights, he is keen to specify those circumstances quite narrowly. Like Rawls, he does not appear to expect substantial redistribution of resources to be necessary. Finally, Nagel, as we also saw in the last chapter, rejects the very idea of duties of justice to help deliver on human rights overseas. At best we have humanitarian duties to alleviate absolute poverty.

Global egalitarians are likely to be unsatisfied with these approaches, and have implied that more extensive positive duties of justice will be necessary to alleviate serious deficits in human rights. However, it is important not to exaggerate the differences here. In particular, global egalitarians might still have good reasons for emphasising the importance of existing institutions such as the state as bearers of duties to fulfil human rights. We might think that individuals would be the obvious bearers of duties. But acting alone, in the absence of co-ordination and enforcement, they will be unable to achieve much. In such circumstances it can be helpful to rely on institutions. Henry Shue has spelled out at least two good reasons why this might be so. He calls the first 'efficiency': even if we believe that we have a duty to alleviate suffering, our efforts will not be effective if we all try to act individually and in an unco-ordinated fashion. Institutions, though, can achieve more than the sum of their parts. The second thing institutions provide is what Shue calls 'respite': the duty to alleviate suffering may appear overwhelming if confronted by a single individual, and could easily consume her life. But in fact 'It is not necessary or desirable for each conscientious individual constantly to confront the hollow-eyed stare of every hungry child in the world' (Shue 1988: 696–7). Institutions, by carving up duties and making them manageable, leave room for other things of value in our lives.

It is perfectly intelligible, then, to say that positive duties, unlike negative duties, can be packaged up and dispersed between different institutions or groups of people. We need not say that, in order to *be* a human right, a right to food or water has to place positive duties on *everyone.* It is enough to say that it places duties on *some* specifiable agents (Griffin 2008: 109). As Shue suggests, a 'division of labour' makes progress towards fulfilling rights more likely. Still, just *how* to distribute those duties is the difficult question. We shall turn now to David Miller's answer to that question, before considering some objections that might be made to his answer.

4.3.1. Miller's division of labour

We saw in the last chapter that David Miller believes that most of our duties of justice are held towards our fellow citizens. At the same time, he agrees that the need to protect basic human rights can place duties of justice on the shoulders of people in other countries. How are we to balance those two commitments? What are we to do in cases where we apparently have to choose – because of limited resources, for instance – between pursuing social justice 'at home' and protecting basic rights abroad?

Miller devotes some time to addressing this question, and he does not believe that the correct answer will be simple. In the case of negative duties the moral situation is straightforward: if we have the same negative duties to our co-citizens and to foreigners, to show any preference towards our co-citizens in the way in which we act on those duties would not be justified. We can conjure up a concrete example based on the negative duty not to kill people. As a key negative duty, this applies to both co-citizens and foreigners. Now, imagine that an aircraft has been taken over by terrorists, and that it becomes necessary to shoot it down to avoid a massive number of deaths. Imagine that we have the option of shooting it down just before it enters 'our' airspace, or just after. If we shoot it down before, a certain number of foreigners on the ground will probably be killed. If we leave it until later a similar number of our co-citizens will likely die. Miller believes that the negative duty to refrain from infringing basic rights 'excludes giving any greater weight to the claims of compatriots' (Miller 2007: 48). So taking the first option purely because we value the lives of our fellow citizens above those of foreigners would be impermissible.

Positive duties, though, are more complicated. In the first instance, as we would expect, Miller believes that positive duties to fulfil basic human rights lie with the local state. But this leaves open two kinds of case, where we *might* think that the positive duties in question should be placed on the shoulders of outsiders. In the first case a community, through no fault of its own, is unable to meet its citizens' basic rights – perhaps because it has been the innocent victim of an environmental disaster. In the second case a community fails to meet its citizens' basic rights, but through its *own* fault, or the fault of a sub-group within the community which holds the reigns of political power. In both cases we are concerned to distribute what we can call *remedial positive duties* – positive duties where the primary duty-holder (the local state) has already failed.

Miller is sympathetic, in the first case, to a community which has fallen victim to such a disaster. Here it is quite right to say that we can place remedial duties on the shoulders of other nation states, and these will be firm duties of justice, provided that we can find some way of assigning the duties in question to a specific state (2007: 254). It is not, though, easy to decide the state or states to which the duties should be assigned. In deciding on that, various factors seem important, including the capacity to help and any close ties a nation state might have with the one afflicted (2007: 100–4). In particular, sometimes we shall assign responsibility 'to one agent who stands out as most closely connected' (2007: 107); later on he puts this a little more firmly: 'We find the capable agent or agents most strongly connected to the people whose human rights are being infringed, and hold them responsible for bringing relief' (2007: 255).

On the second kind of case, Miller is much less sympathetic. His view appears to be that, whereas we might have duties to help in cases where local actors have failed through their own fault, our duties here are humanitarian ones, and not duties of justice (2007: 257–8, 259). Moreover, they are duties which we would be justified in acting on *after* we had met all our obligations of social justice towards fellow nationals (2007: 50; see also Miller 1995: 79). This is the case whether it is the whole society which is responsible for the failure to protect human rights, or a subgroup such as a dictatorship (2007: 257). While we ought, morally speaking, to help a country in this situation, we would not be acting *unjustly* if we refused to do so, and placed our own domestic justice goals first.

4.3.2. Responses to Miller's division of labour

Miller's vision represents an important step forward from the status quo in at least one respect – it recognises cross-border duties of justice to protect the basic human rights of people in other communities. But the circumstances in which Miller is prepared to endorse such duties are heavily circumscribed, and his moral division of labour does leave some loose ends.

One objection will suggest that there is an inconsistency between Miller's positions on the first and second cases of human rights failure. In the first case, he argues that where a society is suffering through no fault of its own, duties of justice to protect basic human rights can fall on the shoulders of other states. In the second case, though, he maintains that if a dictatorship violates basic rights, no duty of justice will fall on other states. He also suggests that *responsibility* is key here (2007: 254, 257). But look at this from the point of view of an average Zimbabwean, to draw on a case Miller mentions himself. Am I, a typical Zimbabwean, any more responsible for the fact that my country is ruled by a dictatorship than I would be responsible for its being hit by a flood? If I have a young child who lacks access to vital medicine, is Miller providing a good answer to the question: why should others have a remedial duty of justice to help in one case, but not the other? It may be true that the dictatorship is responsible for the rights violation, and that must be normatively important in some way. But the rights which are being thwarted are still just as basic, their thwarting is still not the fault of (the vast majority of) citizens, and outside states still have the capacity to help. Miller's view that in the dictatorship case any duties are merely humanitarian – and therefore rich countries would be justified in prioritising *any* pursuit of social justice above meeting such claims – will strike some as too harsh a division of moral labour.

A second objection will focus on the first case alone – the case of natural disasters and other examples of bad luck – where Miller believes that we *do* have remedial duties of justice to help the victims. To be specific, Miller believes that we have duties of justice *if we have been specifically assigned them*. The objection will suggest that his account of how to assign duties is incomplete, and perhaps unconvincing as far as it does go. The account of how to assign duties

is certainly not yet well developed. This may not be so much a criticism of Miller as an indication of just how difficult it *is* to distribute
positive duties to help in cases where the primary duty-holder (here
the local state) proves unable to defend basic rights. Miller has made
a welcome contribution here, but his position will still not be entirely
satisfying to some critics.

For one thing, he moves between the claim that a variety of factors
will influence the duty to help (2007: 100–4), and the much narrower
claim that the strength of connection between particular nations will
(provided they are capable of helping) determine the responsible agent
(2007: 255). It is not clear that this narrower claim is very plausible. In
many cases when a poor nation enters into difficulties, its most closely
connected nation will be a close neighbour. But, if so, this means that
the remedial burden will tend to fall on other poor countries, given
that poor and rich countries *tend* to be geographically concentrated
into clusters. Of course, Miller might want to rule this out by saying that those nations are not capable of helping, but he does not
define capacity in any detail and so we cannot say for sure. Either
way, the idea is not that we select the nation *most* capable of helping.
The idea seems to be that we select those who are at least minimally
capable of helping, according to some criteria, and then pick the one
with the strongest connection with the country which needs help.
But global egalitarians may feel that this emphasis on connection is
arbitrary. For at least some of them, it will make more sense to place
weight purely on capacity to help, rather than on that of 'closeness' or
strength of connection. Interestingly, even ('non-relational') theorists
who do not think that institutions are important in creating entitlements may nevertheless think that institutional capacity can play a
proper role when we think about how to divide up duties to *act* on
those attachments, so that only those best able to help are required to
do so (Caney 2009: 289; Shue 1988: 703).

A second, related thought is this. Miller tells us that duties of justice
to assist exist *when responsibility has been assigned*. He provides the
beginnings of an account of how to assign that responsibility, *morally*
speaking, although the details of a fully adequate account could no
doubt be debated at length. But he does not tell us how to distribute
that responsibility, *institutionally* speaking. Perhaps that is not a reasonable demand to place on the shoulders of a political philosopher.

For many, though, an institutional framework for dividing up remedial positive duties is highly desirable. For the precise problem with which we are dealing is that in circumstances where remedial positive duties are not clearly laid at the door of specific actors, there will be little or no progress in securing them. Indeed, some theorists of human rights argue that we can have an important duty to *establish* institutions which would secure human rights more effectively (Shue 1988: 703; Jones 1999: 69). Interestingly, Miller himself accepts this kind of duty to set up institutions to 'co-ordinate relief efforts' in meeting basic human rights (Miller 2007: 11). But his focus appears to be on the practicalities of stockpiling supplies and so on. The question here is whether institutions could be created which would convert rather general duties to help (which often go unheeded) into much more specific duties to respond in particular situations. That is not an easy question to answer. But if we want to place our faith in remedial positive duties as a vehicle for more ambitious accounts of global justice, it is a question on which progress may need to be made.

4.4. Further issues: a human right to health?

One of the key questions running through this chapter has been, how much content should we pack into our conception of human rights? Human rights are said to derive much of their normative force from the fact that they specify truly fundamental and urgent requirements for human life. If so, the focus ought not to be on securing the *best* achievable conditions for everyone's lives, but on ruling out the *very worst* kinds of deprivation, marginalisation and brutality. But, partly because the language of human rights possesses so much normative force – and partly, also, because human rights have the backing of international law and some mechanisms of monitoring and enforcement – it is tempting to pack more and more content into an account of human rights, in order that commitments in which we earnestly believe achieve the same kind of support. This temptation in turn prompts the question whether the idea that human rights name fundamental and urgent requirements of any life is being stretched beyond recognition.

This tension applies not only to the question of *which* human rights we ought to recognise, but also to the question of how ambitiously we should define any individual right. In this final section we shall examine the human right to health as an example. A human right to health appears to be a plausible contender for inclusion in a list of basic human rights. After all, if we are unable to enjoy minimally good health, then enjoying other human rights may be impossible. It also seems fairly plausible to enshrine a duty to defend people against standard threats to human health caused by waterborne diseases, preventable infections, environmental pollution and so on. But beyond that, as we shall see, the ground remains rather uncertain. Just what is a human right to health a right *to*? And just how, and by whom, ought it to be protected?

The human right to health is perhaps indirectly invoked in the 1948 Universal Declaration of Human Rights, which declares that everyone has a 'right to a standard of living adequate to the health and well-being of himself and of his family'. But the constitution of the World Health Organization declared in 1946, much more explicitly, that 'The enjoyment of the highest attainable standard of health is one of the fundamental rights of every human being' (World Health Organization 1946). That commitment to the 'highest attainable standard' of health was then repeated in Article 12 of the 1966 International Covenant on Economic, Social and Cultural Rights (UN 1966). The right to health therefore appears to have secured the status of an important human right in international law.

But the *content* of the human right to health has not always been entirely clear. Specifically, if there is a human right to the 'highest attainable standard of health', one obvious question is: the highest attainable standard *where*? There are at least two possibilities. First, a person might have a right to the highest standard of health attainable in the country *in which he lives*. But even then the word 'attainable' remains ambiguous. It might mean that Mustafa, an Egyptian, has a right to the highest standard of health currently available in Egypt right now. Or it might mean that he has a right to the best standard of health Egypt could 'progressively realize', given sufficient investment. Second, and alternatively, we might mean that Mustafa has a right to the highest standard of health attainable *anywhere in the world*. Perhaps he has a right to the standard of health 'attainable' by people in countries with the best health-care systems there are (one report suggests these are France, Japan and Australia: World Health Organization 2000).

So the human right to health could be interpreted in many different ways. Human rights are often interpreted – at least on Shue's (1980) account – as defending us against certain 'standard threats' which would otherwise undermine them (see section 4.2.1). If we followed this approach, our interpretation would likely be much less ambitious – it might focus, for instance, on a person's right to inoculation against certain prevalent diseases, on access to clean drinking water, and on certain basic health-care provisions such as the ability to see a doctor or to give birth with a medical professional present. If the human right is interpreted, by contrast, as a right to the best standard of health available *anywhere*, then this sets out a very demanding standard. Moreover, it appears to take us well beyond the usual focus on eradicating the worst instances of deprivation. This more demanding standard has not, so far, commanded much support in domestic legal decisions based on human rights law. Cases drawing on the human right to health have not succeeded in obtaining access to the 'best available' health care for litigants, even if we interpret that requirement as the best standard progressively realisable in a particular country. Instead, judges have recognised the difficult budgetary constraints faced by individual countries with conflicting spending commitments. Successful cases have largely concentrated on eliminating discrimination in the provision of whatever level of health care is currently on offer in a particular country (Wolff 2011).

A further question concerns just who has a duty to deliver on the human right to health. Case law, as mentioned above, has focused on the positive duty of states to deliver health care for their own citizens, and this is in line with the broad thrust of international law, which chiefly understands human rights to define standards which individual countries should observe in their treatment of their own citizens. An interesting alternative to this general trend appears in the work of Thomas Pogge (2005), who focuses on the *negative* duty of citizens, governments and corporations in developed countries to refrain from imposing a global health protection system which leads to foreseeable deficits in human rights amongst the world's poor.

Pogge is interested in the system for developing new medicines, and for financially rewarding companies which develop them. In a perfectly free market, there would be little incentive to develop new medicines at all. Drugs are extremely expensive to research, develop and then test. But, in a free market, once a given company *had* developed a new drug, competing companies would quite quickly be able to develop their own versions and bring them to market more cheaply. It would be very hard for the developing company to make enough profit in the interim to recoup the considerable costs sunk into development. The current intellectual property rights system responds to this incentive problem by granting patents. A patent is, in effect, a promise that a given company will be able to exploit a new drug exclusively for a fixed period (typically twenty years), and thereby turn a profit on its research. If a company is fairly sure that a market exists which will allow it to turn a profit in future, then research and development into new drugs comes to make sense. Its 'intellectual property' will be defended internationally by the rules of the World Trade Organization (see chapter 6).

For Pogge (2005) this system has very serious shortcomings when examined from a moral point of view. For a period of twenty years companies are able to name their price for drugs which could alleviate massive human suffering if they were made available more cheaply and easily. But companies have no incentive to make them cheaply available. There has been *some* progress on this issue in the high-profile case of HIV/AIDS – where developing countries have been able to supply their citizens with cheaper versions of antiretroviral drugs – but still, only about 0.1 per cent of Africans with HIV/AIDS have access to antiretroviral therapy (Cullet 2003: 143). Meanwhile, the problem that poorer governments often cannot afford key drugs remains a widespread one (Muzaka 2011). A related problem is that the current patent system means that it makes sense for companies to develop drugs which will realise good profits and not necessarily those which will realise the most significant health benefits. As a result, much attention is given to developing drugs which produce minor improvements to the quality of life of people in richer countries, and relatively little attention is given to finding treatments for diseases which have a huge impact, and claim many millions of lives, in the developing world (Pogge 2005: 190). As a result, Pogge argues, victims of these diseases 'are deprived of some of the objects of their human rights', and specifically the means for meeting their human right to health (2005: 197).

Pogge has an alternative proposal which shifts the incentives towards alleviating the most pressing instances of human suffering. His 'global public good' scheme depends on countries or other morally inclined investors paying into a global Health Impact Fund (on which see Hollis and Pogge 2008). That fund would then pay money out to drug companies in proportion to their impact on eradicating the 'global disease burden'. This reform would generate far greater investment in the diseases that kill or seriously harm most people in the world today. As such it 'would align and harmonize the interests of inventor firms with those of patients ... interests that, under the current regime, are diametrically opposed' (Pogge 2005: 189).

Pogge's argument does *not* appear to 'inflate' the idea of a human right to health, in one respect at least. He is concerned to enhance the ability of governments to protect people against major threats to health such as malaria, pneumonia, diarrhoea and tuberculosis (2005: 190), and these goals are hardly overly ambitious. But there are still interesting questions to be asked about his account.

One question relates to Pogge's depiction of who is currently preventing the right to health being achieved in practice. Is Pogge claiming that the current patent scheme *itself* violates people's human rights? If they do not reform that system along the lines Pogge is suggesting, are citizens and governments of developed countries violating those rights, or merely making it harder for governments in developing countries to protect those rights? Pogge's argument appears to be that a rights violation occurs whenever a system is imposed – or maintained – which avoidably and foreseeably prevents human rights being realized (2005: 196). If we impose or maintain such a system we *are* violating an important negative duty. To recall from chapter 1, Pogge believes that the best formulation of this negative duty is that 'one ought not to co-operate in the imposition of a coercive institutional order that avoidably leaves human rights unfulfilled without making reasonable efforts to aid its victims and to promote institutional reform' (Pogge 2002: 170). There is scope for conceptual disagreement here, though. For example, we might say that acting in a way that makes it more difficult or more expensive for someone else to fulfil their rights is not quite the same as violating those rights ourselves.

A second, related question asks whether Pogge is packing too much content into the idea of negative duties. Even if we accept that we are violating a negative duty by imposing an unjust system for rewarding pharmaceutical innovation, would respecting that duty be enough to secure the human right to health for everyone? Let us put this a little more concretely. Pogge suggests that we could act on our negative duty here by establishing a Health Impact Fund, so that pharmaceutical companies could profit from alleviating the global burden of disease. For this to be effective, that fund needs money in it. But do we have a *duty* to pay money into it? Pogge is silent on this question. He may believe that we have a humanitarian duty to pay funds into it. But he appears to be committed to saying that we do not have a positive duty of justice to pay into it. But if this is so we could discharge our negative duty by setting up the fund and then refuse – without acting unjustly – to pay any money into it. If we did that, the world would continue much as it is. It is for this kind of reason, presumably, that some theorists of justice believe that we *do* have a positive duty of justice to contribute in some way to the eradication of ill-health or poverty (see e.g. Caney 2009). As even some minimalists (such as Miller) recognise, a focus on both positive and negative duties of justice appears necessary to tackle serious deficits in human rights.

chapter 5

Global justice and natural resources

Natural resources are distributed very unevenly throughout the world. The territories of some nation states contain abundant mineral resources which can command high prices on world markets – think of Saudi Arabia and its oilfields, or South Africa and its diamonds. Likewise, the fact that Britain was the first country to undergo an industrial revolution is considered to be at least partly due to its ready supplies of coal, iron and fast-running water. But some countries possess resources in much more meagre quantities, and may not even have secure access to the essentials of life. Millions of people currently have insecure access to clean drinking water, for instance, and while the most severe problems are faced by the inhabitants of the Middle East, north Africa and parts of sub-Saharan Africa, water scarcity is a growing problem for many people elsewhere (Falkenmark and Lundqvist 1998).

The unevenness of the distribution of resources has been thought by some to have implications for global justice. After all, the processes by which national borders have come to be drawn on maps and subsequently defended by military force – and as a result of which rivers, coalfields or seams of gold end up in one nation's territory rather than another's – are hard to defend from a normative point of view. They have often involved military conquest, colonialism, violent dispossession and even genocide. Given this murky history, can nation states be thought to deserve, or have a just claim to, the resources that happen to be found within their borders? Or should resources be seen instead as some kind of collective asset? From the point of view of distributive justice should we try to correct or compensate for the current unevenness of resource distribution? If so, how would we go about doing that?

These and similar questions have been receiving more and more attention in recent years. This chapter examines some of the normative issues surrounding the distribution, ownership and sale of natural resources, to see whether we can make progress in answering some of the questions mentioned above. We begin with a case study which raises the issue of the ownership of natural resources, and how it comes to be achieved and recognised in practice (box 5.1). In section 5.1 we return briefly to Charles Beitz and his argument for a resource redistribution principle (which we originally discussed in chapter 2), a principle which tries to ensure that inhabitants of resource-poor countries do not suffer disadvantage. We also re-examine John Rawls's resistance to such a principle (Rawls believes that, since nations are able to prevent resource scarcity from translating into actual poverty, redistributing resources is unnecessary).

In section 5.2 we turn to two accounts which discuss the ways in which natural resources come to be 'owned' and then sold on global markets. Specifically, we address Thomas Pogge's and Leif Wenar's arguments about the 'resource privilege' and the distribution of 'resource rights'. Both of these focus, most importantly, on the fact that developed countries and their citizens are prepared to buy natural resources from illegitimate governments in the developing world. They argue that developed countries should not buy these resources, and that if they continue to do so then wealthy states, and their citizens, are partly responsible for trapping poorer states in a cycle of war, dictatorship and poverty.

Claiming that we should avoid buying natural resources unless 'the people' of a given nation state are able to give or refuse consent to that sale seems to assume that 'the people' or 'the nation' are the rightful owners of 'their' natural resources. Indeed for many people this will appear obvious; it seems to be a very common-sense fact about the way the world works. But is the idea of national ownership actually defensible? What is its normative basis? Section 5.3 addresses that question, and also discusses some alternative views on resource ownership. Rather than individual nations owning resources we might be said to own the natural resources of the world in common, or else we might each, individually, have an entitlement to an equal share of natural resources. We examine Hillel Steiner's advocacy of a global resources tax as an example of the latter kind of argument. Section 5.4, the further issues section, will focus on one specific, and very important, resource – water – and examine some suggestions for achieving a more just allocation of rights over it. By the end, the commonplace idea that nations own 'their' natural resources will have been subjected to real scrutiny, and we shall also have a much clearer picture of the way in which conventions on resource ownership and sale may actually sustain global injustice.

Box 5.1. **Case study: the struggle over natural resources**

The idea that natural resources are the property of the nation states in which they lie has been solidly enshrined in international law, at least since the years following the Second World Law (Schrijver 1997). The 1966 International Covenant on Civil and Political Rights, for example, asserts that 'All peoples may, for their own ends, freely dispose of their natural wealth and resources' (UN 1966).

But assigning ownership over resources can be a little more tricky in practice. For example, many resources span national borders. Examples would include rivers and oilfields. The recent history of conflict in the Middle East has as one of its recurring themes the struggle for control over key rivers and waterways such as the Jordan river, the Shatt al-Arab, or the Suez Canal. These conflicts in the Middle East are often intense, but they are not exceptional. Armed conflict is increasingly bound up in struggles to control natural resources (see e.g. Westing 1986). Moreover, the availability of valuable natural resources itself bankrolls many conflicts, allowing protagonists to buy more weapons and to recruit supporters – as illustrated by the civil wars in Rwanda and Sierra Leone during the 1990s.

A slightly more peaceful version of this struggle over resources is currently being waged over many resources which had not previously been claimed by anyone. Many countries are now asserting their right, under international law, to any resources contained under the seabed within 200 nautical miles of their coastlines. In some cases they appear to be emphasising claims over little-known island groups for just this reason, and even arguing for extensions of the zone of control beyond 200 nautical miles. In recent years Britain, for instance, has registered claims to the resources contained within 350 miles of Ascension Island, which is over 4,000 miles away from Britain in the South Atlantic (Philp 2008), and a similar claim with regard to the Chagos Archipelago in the Indian Ocean (Boycott 2010). It is said to be considering making a similar claim with regard to the Falkland Islands, although the history of dispute with Argentina over these islands (which Argentina calls the Malvinas) would make such a claim even more contentious.

The resources of the Arctic region have become another key arena for competing claims over natural resources. In recent years Russia, Norway, Canada, Denmark and the United States have each made claims to the UN over the Arctic region, keen to secure rights to the huge quantities of oil and gas which are believed to lie under the frozen surface. At present their control is limited to a zone within 200 nautical miles of each of their coastlines, but countries are able to make greater claims to land which occupies the same 'continental shelf' as their national territory. In 2007 a Russian explorer, Artur Chilingarov, used a submarine to plant a Russian flag on the Arctic seabed. Peter MacKay, the then Canadian Minister of Foreign Affairs, responded by declaring that 'these are Canadian waters and this is Canadian property. You can't go around the world these days dropping a flag somewhere' (Reynolds 2008). More recently the Russian Prime Minister Vladimir Putin has called for a more restrained approach, balancing national interests with the need for international co-operation (Harding 2010). But struggles for control over these and other key resources look likely to remain intense, especially given rising prices for fossil fuels. Such struggles throw into sharp relief the questions about the ownership of natural resources which we shall examine in the rest of this chapter.

5.1. A resource redistribution principle?

Does the uneven scattering of natural resources across the earth's surface raise issues of distributive justice? The global egalitarian Charles Beitz argued that the distribution of natural resources is morally 'arbitrary' (Beitz 1979). The dispersal of resources is a matter of mere luck – in the sense that no one is responsible for bringing it about – but unfortunately impacts hugely on individuals' life chances in different countries. In effect, the fact that some countries come to control disproportionate shares of natural resources leaves others seriously disadvantaged. In response, Beitz argued for a 'resource redistribution principle' according to which each nation state would be given the resources necessary to allow it to develop just institutions. Such a principle might require major transfers of resources between nation states, so that all states were able to meet their citizens' basic needs (Beitz 1979: 141). A similar argument was also suggested by Brian Barry, who likewise claimed that the distribution of resources improperly advantages some communities simply because of the good luck of where their national borders happened to lie (and national borders, as we noted in the introduction to this chapter, tend not to have been drawn in very just ways) (Barry 1982). As a result, a form of international taxation is necessary to transfer resources from rich countries to poorer ones. Specifically, a tax could be placed on the extraction of mineral resources, perhaps in addition to a tax on the value of land and other resources. If the proceeds were shared appropriately, Barry suggested, this would at least partly remedy the unjust disadvantage which currently arises from the uneven distribution of resources.

But not everyone is convinced that the distribution of natural resources should raise such concerns about justice and injustice. As we saw in chapter 3, John Rawls rejected any such principle in *The Law of Peoples* (Rawls 1999). If we looked around the world, he suggested, we should find that the relative wealth and poverty of peoples had little to do with resource distribution. Instead, it has a good deal to do with their propensity to work hard, their institutions and their different political cultures. Apart from a few exceptional cases, the lack of natural resources in abundance just does not stand in the way of economic advancement. As he put it,

> Historical examples seem to indicate that resource-poor countries may do very well (e.g. Japan), while resource-rich countries may have serious difficulties (e.g. Argentina). The crucial elements that make the difference are the political culture, the political virtues and civic society of the country, its members' probity and industriousness, their capacity for innovation, and much else. (Rawls 1999: 108)

Principles of resource redistribution like Beitz's are therefore designed to solve a problem that does not really exist. Rawls suggested that 'there is no society anywhere in the world – except for marginal cases – with resources so scarce it could not, were it reasonably and rationally organized and governed, become well-ordered' (Rawls 1999: 108). Since communities are able to prevent resource scarcity translating into poverty, redistributing resources is just not necessary.

Other minimalist theorists would tend to reach similar conclusions. Thomas Nagel has not directly addressed questions about natural resources. But we can easily imagine what his minimalist account would have to say about them. For Nagel, the distribution of natural resources can indeed be seen as a matter of chance, in the sense that no one has brought it about. But neither (or so we would expect Nagel to argue) is it established by coercive political institutions. On Nagel's account we need principles of distributive justice to correct inequalities to which institutions have given rise, and not those produced by 'nature' (Nagel 1997). As such, principles designed to correct for the distribution of natural resources are groundless. Their distribution just does not raise issues of distributive justice.

David Miller's position is slightly more complex. He once suggested himself that we might actually need a principle of resource redistribution to make sure that countries are not disadvantaged by a lack of resources. He suggested, apparently in contrast to Rawls, that 'nations cannot provide for the basic needs of their members ... unless they have a sufficient resource base to be economically viable' (Miller 1995: 105). The value of natural resources, he noted, is also affected by fluctuations on international commodity markets for which individual nations are not responsible, and for which they cannot claim credit. 'Since states are enriched and impoverished in seemingly arbitrary ways', he argued, 'this triggers an obligation on the part of resource-rich states to aid those who are resource-poor' (1995: 105). But this principle was not explored in any detail at the time, and does not appear to play any role in his more recent work – in fact it seems to run contrary to the general thrust of his subsequent arguments, which suggest that at the level of justice we owe other nations fair terms of co-operation, and *some* help in meeting basic human rights, but nothing more (Miller 2007). In his more recent work Miller tends, like Rawls, to emphasise the ways in which nations are responsible for their own fortunes. He has also suggested that nations have entitlements over their own resources because of the ways in which they have added value to them (see section 5.3).

So the dispute between global minimalists, including Rawls and Miller, on the one hand, and global egalitarians, such as Beitz and Barry, on the other, centrally involves disagreement over whether the distribution of resources raises issues of justice. For Rawls (and perhaps for Miller too, although his position may have shifted over time) societies are quite capable of succeeding economically regardless of how many resources they happen to possess, and so issues of justice do not arise. For Beitz and Barry the distribution of resources *does* disadvantage some societies through no fault of their own, and so issues of justice *do* arise. One key area of disagreement, here, is the empirical question whether the unequal distribution of resources really explains the differing fortunes of different societies. That is a difficult question to answer definitively, but the discussion in the next section allows us to advance the issue one stage further. Both Thomas Pogge and Leif Wenar, as we shall see, claim that the conventions or rules by which resources come to be bought and sold on global markets may themselves be the source of injustice. In that sense, although the *distribution* of natural resources may not necessarily cause poverty, the rules of resource *ownership* and *sale* may well unjustly contribute to its continuation. Regardless of whether injustice is involved in the initial distribution, there certainly is injustice in how resources subsequently come to be traded.

5.2. The ownership and sale of natural resources

John Rawls does appear to be right that there are some countries which have vast natural resources, but whose governments use them badly or corruptly and do not manage to convert their assets into healthy economic growth. Take a country like Equatorial Guinea, on the west coast of Africa. Equatorial Guinea has huge oil reserves which actually give it a national income which is higher, per capita, than that of the United Kingdom. But most of the inhabitants of the country remain impoverished, and excluded from any of the benefits which 'their' oil wealth might be expected to bring. Seventy per cent of the population live on less than $2 per day. A corrupt dictatorship led by President Obiang, on the other hand, enjoys a life of immense luxury (Wenar 2008a: 6–7).

Rawls might take this example as confirmation that we need not concern ourselves with the justice and injustice of natural resource distribution. Societies have the gifts that nature has given them, and it is up to them to make the best of them. Some do that well and some do it badly, but that does not raise issues of *global* justice. It looks, rather, like a matter of good or bad governance, or of wise or poor decision-making. In fact, puzzling though it may seem, it turns out that on average the greater a developing country's resource endowment, the *lower* its rate of economic growth (Pogge 2002: 163). So what Rawls would see as the failure to put resources to good use appears to be a widespread problem. However, both Thomas Pogge and Leif Wenar seek to convince us that there *is* an injustice at work here and it is not, or not wholly, down to the poor decision-making, brutality or the undemocratic nature of the dictatorships which exist in many resource-rich but underdeveloped countries. In stark contrast to Rawls, they emphasise the ways in which *global* factors are important in sustaining the injustice in question. In particular, they emphasise the crucial part which individuals, corporations and governments in developed countries play in sustaining unjust governments in the developing world, by continuing to buy natural resources from them.

5.2.1. Pogge on the 'resource privilege'

Thomas Pogge would reject Rawls's picture of the world, according to which poverty has essentially 'internal' or domestic causes, and focus instead on the many ways in which powerful external actors have *also* been complicit in the reproduction of poverty in developing countries. His position is not, as some critics have suggested, that poverty is simply caused by 'external' factors such as the global economic 'system'. Rather, the intention seems to be to paint a complex picture in which both internal and external factors are present, but in which we can legitimately focus on the role which external factors have played as *one* component in the reproduction of poverty. Pogge (2002) describes what he calls an 'international resource privilege', according to which global markets appear prepared to accept as legitimate owners of a nation state's resources just anyone able to command overwhelming military force within a given territory, and hence able physically to deliver up those resources. This privilege is not necessarily enshrined in any specific international law, but it is a fact of life within the global economy, since even an undemocratic regime, which has no regard for its people's human rights, will still be able to sell resources to the highest bidder. As Pogge puts it, the privilege

> allows any person or group holding effective power in a developing
> country to sell the resources of the country ... irrespective of whether
> that person or group has any kind of democratic legitimacy ... These
> privileges are very convenient for the rich countries ... However they are
> devastating for the populations of the developing countries because they
> make it possible for oppressive and unrepresentative rulers to entrench
> themselves with arms and soldiers they buy with money they borrow
> abroad or get from resource sales. (Pogge 2007b: 3)

This privilege has highly pernicious consequences, insofar as it actually *incentivises* the emergence of coups and dictatorships; for it becomes common knowledge that any armed group able to capture control within a territory will then be able to sell its resources and pocket the proceeds if it so wishes. As such the resource privilege 'is of great benefit to authoritarian rulers and a strong incentive to any predators aspiring to this role' (Pogge 2002: 165). But it is not *only*

the agents of such coups, or the dictators in question, who are eth-
ically responsible here. In fact both multinational corporations, and
indeed individual citizens or consumers in wealthy countries, can
be described as complicit in the impoverishment of people across the
world, for they regularly buy resources obtained from undemocratic
and tyrannical regimes – regimes which in many cases they otherwise criticise. The oil from Equatorial Guinea ends up on the fore-
courts of petrol stations across the world. And, according to Pogge,
when corporations, and ultimately consumers, buy that oil they are
responsible, in an important sense, for the ensuing poverty. While
they may not be the *only* agents responsible, they *are* nevertheless
responsible in the specific sense that they could, by refusing to buy
goods from such regimes, *dis*incentivise coups and the emergence
of dictatorial regimes. Thus while Pogge would not want to say that
developed countries are wholly responsible for global poverty, neither
would he want to say, with Rawls, that developing countries themselves are wholly responsible. The truth is more complex, and the
citizens of developed countries should confront their own role, and
recognise the negative impact that it has.

Citizens of countries like Equatorial Guinea obviously suffer if they
are subjected to brutal dictatorships, but it is also important to note,
for Pogge, that they are also excluded from their rightful share of
natural resources. We all have a moral right to a share in our country's resources, but authoritarian rulers exclude us from enjoying that
share, and also from being able to make decisions about what to do
with such natural resources. The developed world is also playing its
part in this exclusion. According to Pogge, citizens and governments
of developed countries are violating a negative duty of justice 'when
they, in collaboration with the ruling elites of the poor countries,
coercively exclude the poor' from enjoying the proceeds of their own
assets (Pogge 2002: 203).

What should we do about this state of affairs? Given that the nub
of the problem is that the citizens of some developing countries are
deprived of their fair share of resources, an obvious way to remedy
that deprivation, Pogge suggests, is to place a tax on natural resources,
and to use the money gained to try and improve the situation of the
world's poor. He therefore proposes what he calls a 'global resources
dividend' (GRD). Under this proposal a 1 per cent tax would be levied

on all natural resources at the point of their extraction. Although a 1 per cent tax is pretty modest, the proceeds would still be very considerable – raising several hundred billion dollars per year, according to Pogge's estimate. This money could then be spent, by an international panel of economists, lawyers and other experts, in such a way as to alleviate global poverty. The dividend would slow the depletion of resources and, just as importantly, it would help substantially in the drive to eradicate poverty, according to the World Bank's $2 per day standard. As Pogge puts it, 'Proceeds from the GRD are to be used toward ensuring that all human beings can meet their own basic needs with dignity' (2002: 197). Through such relatively straightforward mechanisms, Pogge tells us, we can make a significant dent in the apparently formidable problem of global poverty, and also mitigate the injustice whereby citizens of countries like Equatorial Guinea are prevented from benefiting from natural resources.

5.2.2. Wenar on the 'resource curse'

So it appears that one of the puzzles of economic development, which has been much discussed by economists, is that an abundance of natural resources does not reliably lead to economic and political development. This might be the case when a country has so much of one natural resource – such as oil – that it fails to develop other industries (indeed the very revenues gained from selling the oil might strengthen its currency, and thereby make its other exports more expensive and hence uncompetitive – this is the so-called 'Dutch disease'). But often, even where there is a reasonable spread of natural resources, these appear to lead merely to a vicious spiral of corruption, bad governance and underdevelopment. Economists have a name for this too. They call it the 'resource curse'. In fact it seems to be that in Africa, for example, the presence of reserves of oil, gas and minerals *increases* the risk of civil war, with all the resulting turmoil (Wenar 2008a: 3).

Why might this be? The broad reasons should already be familiar from Pogge's account: the presence of valuable resources, coupled with the fact that corporations or governments in developed countries ask few questions when they make their purchases, produces a powerful incentive for coups to happen. Anyone who succeeds in installing themselves as 'the government' in a developing country will be able to sell those resources and pocket the proceeds. Their legitimacy – or lack of it – does not appear to present much of an obstacle.

Like Pogge, Leif Wenar believes that our complicity in this trade is absolutely key in sustaining authoritarianism and injustice in the developing world. Wenar encourages us to concentrate, though, on a part of this picture which does not usually receive much attention. For Wenar, the willingness of citizens or corporations based in developed states to *buy* these resources is absolutely key. If they did *not* buy goods from dictatorships, the incentive towards coups and civil war would be much weaker. But, morally speaking, we ought *not* to buy these goods. After all, Wenar says, to buy goods obtained without the consent of the citizens of the nation states from which they come is rather like the knowing receipt of stolen goods – in fact, it *is* the receipt of stolen goods. Numerous instruments of international law – including the International Covenant on Civil and Political Rights and the UN Declaration on the Right to Development – stipulate that the resources to be found in a given nation state are the property of the national community as a whole, as we noted in the case study (box 5.1). This is not a particularly controversial idea – according to Wenar (2008a: 10) it is intuitively obvious to most people (although see section 5.3 for a critical discussion of the idea).

But this relatively uncontroversial principle of common national ownership is implemented very imperfectly. If resources belong to a country's citizens, what would count as a legitimate sale of a particular resource? According to Wenar, a legitimate sale would have to proceed with at least the general agreement of citizens. We would expect, for justice to be served, the owners (citizens) to be informed about the sale, to be able to safely express their dissent and to be able to stop the sale without fearing violence or intimidation. But in practice these basic standards are frequently not met. In countries like Equatorial Guinea resource sales proceed behind a veil of considerable secrecy, there is no strong and independent press capable of calling the government to account and citizens fear for their safety if they voice any dissent. As such, Wenar's standards would disqualify many sales of natural resources in the real world, which proceed in ways that (he claims) violate the principle of common national ownership recognised by the governments of wealthy states and by international law.

If a commonly recognised principle of international law is so clearly being violated, then it should be possible, Wenar suggests, for consumers and other interested parties to seek redress. In particular it should be possible for citizens to sue, in the domestic courts of wealthy countries, any corporations prepared to engage in this trade in stolen property. Litigants in countries such as the United States could launch lawsuits against corporations which bought 'stolen property' from illegitimate regimes. As Wenar puts it, 'Cases requiring the United States to follow its own principles in enforcing property rights are waiting to be made' (2008a: 26).

There is a challenge to be confronted here, however. What if US corporations stopped buying stolen goods, only to see corporations from other states filling the gap by continuing to trade with illegitimate regimes? If that were the case, the lawsuits would have achieved very little. Wenar does have a proposal to deal with this eventuality, however. If other states – such as China – continued to buy goods from African dictators, when this had already been ruled illegal in US courts, then it would be legal for the United States to raise tariffs against any imported Chinese goods. In effect, these tariffs would operate as fines, up to the value of goods which China had bought illicitly. Thus there would be no *incentive* for other countries to buy such goods from dictators. It would be economically self-defeating, because any benefits would be offset by fines on exports. The money gained from the tariffs in question, Wenar suggests, could be held in trust for the people of the resource-rich but illegitimate states in question, until such a time as a legitimate government came to power. That would in turn provide a powerful incentive for the emergence of a legitimate government, as considerable wealth would be available if an incoming government in a developing country met internationally agreed standards for legitimacy. It would also provide a strong incentive for wealthy countries and corporations to support political reform, because until it had been achieved they would be cut off from the supply of valuable resources. In this way Wenar argues that his proposals, taken as a whole, serve to reverse the incentive structure which currently feeds the resource curse. If his proposals were put into practice they would incentivise legitimate, as opposed to illegitimate, government:

If the only way for ExxonMobil or China legally to get oil out of Equatorial Guinea is for there to be minimally decent governance in Equatorial Guinea, then there will be. (Wenar 2008a: 31–2)

Although they both focus on the effective dispossession of citizens that occurs when ruling elites are able to sell resources without citizens' consent, the implications of Pogge's and Wenar's accounts are notably different. Pogge's goal is, in effect, to tax the dispossession in order to ameliorate poverty, which might strike us as a fairly normal and straightforward approach for a theorist of global justice to take to the problem of extreme poverty. Wenar's solution, on the other hand, is to outlaw the dispossession in the first instance – which represents a much less common strategy, focusing as it does on recourse to law courts, and to citizen action against an unjust trade in resources. In a sense Wenar's approach is the more direct one, though. If the sale of resources is illicit then we should not tax it, as Pogge suggests, but forbid it. After all, we do not tax people who sell stolen cars, but arrest them, and try to prevent thefts occurring in the first place. Wenar is not suggesting, as a result, the introduction of a tax on resources, with the revenues to be spent on a serious onslaught on global poverty, but simply a block on illegitimate resource sales. In fact it is open to question just what the impact of his strategy would be on global poverty. It might be that the *short-term* consequences for the excluded citizens of some developing countries would be very serious as their countries were immediately prevented from selling any resources. Even if ordinary citizens do not usually benefit *much* from the sale of those resources, the immediate outcome could be economic and political collapse. Sources of overseas revenue would be cut off and citizens would be obliged to sit tight until a legitimate government came to power and could resume selling resources, or else to take things into their own hands and try forcibly to install such a government. But nevertheless Wenar is clear that the consequences, over the *longer* term, would be the incentivisation of good governance – and in that sense the empirical outcome of serious attention to the just sale of natural resources might well be a reduction, over time, in grievous human rights violations.

5.3. Alternatives to national ownership of resources

The arguments discussed in the last section appear to take as their starting point the principle that 'the people' of a given nation state own the natural resources within their territory. But, actually, neither Pogge nor Wenar argues directly for that principle. Wenar is certainly prepared to cite the extensive backing for the principle which we can find in international law, and to describe it as a common-sense part of our understanding of the world – though he does not actually go so far as to provide a *justification* for national ownership himself. Pogge is still more ambiguous. He suggests that his argument for a global resources dividend depends on the relatively modest assumption that nations are not entitled to *all* the proceeds from their resource sales, but points out that in order to defend his position he does not need to suggest that they do not own them at all (Pogge 2002: 197). But that does not tell us quite what Pogge himself thinks about the rightful pattern of resource ownership. Similarly, when he tells us that the global resources dividend 'compensates' the poor for their exclusion from resource sales, he is unclear whether it is the poor of an individual country who are being compensated for the sale of *their* resources, or the poor of the world who are being compensated for the sale of the *world's* resources. If it was the former, it would make sense to ring fence the revenue from the dividend to make sure that each country's poor received the precise income gained from its *own* nation's resource extraction – but that does not seem to be what Pogge is suggesting (2002: 206–7).

This discussion might seem a little arcane to some readers. What does it matter whether Pogge and Wenar believe that nations really ought to own their natural resources? That's just how the world works, isn't it? It might well be how the world works, but political theorists will still – and ought to still – ask questions about the normative basis of that ownership. When we start to examine what the arguments for national ownership might be, however, we discover that it is a cornerstone of legal and political practice – and, perhaps, of common sense – that has not often been explicitly defended. In fact, even major theorists of global justice have only recently begun to turn their attention to laying out and assessing the arguments for national ownership of resources. While for some national ownership of resources is 'obvious' from a moral point of view, for others the opposite is true. On one strong view, 'national rights to wealth and resources, however commonly they are asserted, lack any coherent moral basis. What seems particularly evident is that the beneficiaries of national rights [over resources] are thoroughly undeserving of the special benefits they receive' (Jones 1999: 73). In the rest of this section, therefore, we shall briefly examine arguments in favour of national ownership before examining some alternatives, which defend either common or equal ownership of the earth's resources.

5.3.1. Defending national ownership of resources?

The arguments provided in favour of national ownership have so far tended to be brief, and not wholly conclusive. David Miller (2011) has suggested that since the citizens of a given nation labour over and improve the natural resources in their territory in various ways, and thereby increase their value, they are entitled to that increased value. And since the only way to ensure that they *receive* the value added is actually to grant them ownership of the resources themselves, then that is what we ought to do. If we started redistributing resources to achieve some kind of equality, we would actually be depriving some people of the fruits of their labour, and rewarding others who may *not* have conserved or improved the value of their resources. But although it has some initial plausibility, it is not clear that this is a strong enough argument to justify granting *exclusive* rights over *all* resources to individual nations. After all, some resources have lain untouched under the ground for centuries, and it is not clear what nations could have done to merit any claim to have improved them. Would it not be odd to grant nations ownership over such resources? Miller himself appears to concede that a nation could not be said to have created value in a resource simply by discovering it, for example (Miller 1995: 106). So more argument appears to be needed to strengthen an account based on the improvements that are sometimes made to resources, especially if it is going to be used to justify the very extensive control over 'their' resources which nation states currently enjoy under international law.

John Rawls, even more briefly, suggests that if resources are to be conserved and cared for, then someone needs to be given a stake in controlling them. If resources belong to a specific party, then that party will have an incentive to maintain them and improve their value. This party, he says, ought to be the governments of individual peoples (Rawls 1999: 8). But, again, it is not clear here that the initial assumption (that resources need to be cared for) justifies the conclusion (that individual states should be the agents which exclusively control resources). Presumably responsibility for – and rights over – resources could be spread over a variety of institutions. If what we care about is the conservation of resources, it is not obvious that giving total control over them to individual nation states is the best way to secure that conservation. Indeed, Rawls's work itself reminds us that many nations make very bad use of their resources, do not turn them to good use, and do not preserve them effectively. Of course, we do not have much information on what the best institutional spread of rights over resources would be, from the point of view of their conservation – political 'experiments' such as the European Union, which to some extent now governs the use of natural resources such as fish or forests, are still in their infancy. But it is interesting to observe that international law *seems* to be slowly developing in such a direction as to limit what nation states can do with their own resources, and to emphasise the common ownership of some key resources such as water (Armstrong 2011). At the same time, cross-border agreements to preserve some natural resources are already proliferating.

5.3.2. Common ownership of resources

Common ownership, broadly speaking, describes a situation where people are entitled to use resources non-exclusively – that is, where they are able to use them in such a way that using them does not deprive others of the ability to use them too. The inhabitants of a town might commonly own the water of a river that runs through it, and thereby be entitled to withdraw a certain amount of water per day, and also be forbidden to pollute or misuse that resource, or to exclude anyone else from using it. Although Rawls suggests that assigning ownership to specific users is necessary to their conservation, common or collect-ive ownership is, empirically speaking, a widespread and frequently successful response to situations where many people have interests in scarce natural resources and need to find ways of ensuring their sustainability (see e.g. Ostrom 1990). It is also notable that much his-torical political theory did assume something like common ownership of the earth. Rather than being seen as controversial, the idea that the earth was at least originally owned in common by everyone (or, perhaps, that it was given to everyone in common by God) provided a shared normative background for philosophers such as Immanuel Kant or John Locke. To be more precise, they tended to believe that the earth was *originally* commonly owned, but that individuals could secure private ownership of resources so long as certain conditions were observed. For instance, Locke believed that the requirement to leave ample resources for others to use placed limits on how much any one individual could remove from the common pool provided by nature (although philosophers have argued about the precise meaning of that limitation ever since).

Today the idea of common ownership continues to play a role in some accounts of global justice. Michael Blake and Matthias Risse, for example, argue that whereas natural resources are available for use by human beings, no one is actually responsible for creating them and no one, therefore, has any special claim to them. As they put it, 'Since the earth is simply *there*, with no one deserving credit for it, a plausible view on original ownership is that all humans have *some* sort of symmetrical claim to it' (Blake and Risse 2009: 134). Natural resources should be regarded as common or shared property, they argue, unless any less equal distribution could be said to be accept-able to everyone.

This idea has some resonance in contemporary global politics. Although international law, as Wenar tells us, does in general sug-gest that natural resources are the property of the countries in which they are to be found, it also establishes some resources as part of 'the commons' – parts of the common heritage of human-ity which cannot be owned by individuals or by nations. Examples have included the air, sunlight, the high seas and outer space. Likewise, whereas a contemporary struggle for the resources of the Arctic region is now being waged, the Antarctic region has long been recognised as *un*owned, or as part of the common heritage of humankind. Some have suggested that we expand the notion of 'the commons' to include other crucial resources such as the rainforests, which are presently poorly conserved. Such proposals are, however, controversial, since countries like Brazil are prone to viewing them as a major obstacle to their own economic development – an obstacle which would be placed by countries which had already developed themselves and squandered many of their own natural resources in the process (Conca 1995).

5.3.3. Equal ownership of resources

An alternative to common ownership – which essentially dictates that no one individually owns the resources of the world, but that everyone is entitled to make use of them – is the idea of equal ownership. The principle of equal ownership suggests that we all have an individual entitlement to an equal, but separate, share of resources. Common and equal ownership could be easily confused, not least since their respective supporters often wheel out quite similar justifications – such as the idea that, since no one has actually done anything to create natural resources – which are nevertheless key to everyone's existence – no one should be disadvantaged in their access to or enjoyment of those resources (see e.g. Blake and Risse 2009). Common and equal ownership are, though, distinguishable. A key element of common ownership is 'non-excludability' – that is, the idea that your enjoyment of a common resource should not deprive anyone else of the same enjoyment. That enjoyment should therefore be 'non-subtractive' – that is, it should leave just as much for all of your other co-owners to enjoy. It is easy to see how this could be applied to resources – like sunlight – which appear to be virtually boundless, although other resources – such as fresh water, or the rainforests – now look rather more limited than they once did. Equal ownership, though, does not assume non-excludability or non-subtractive use. If a group of individuals own a resource equally, they should each have a right precisely to remove their own portion and make use of it themselves, and to prevent others from using what is theirs. Although it is hard to see how that idea could be applied to resources like sunlight, it is much easier to see how it could be applied to land or mineral resources. Such resources could potentially be divided up equally between many people.

Hillel Steiner has argued for a version of equal ownership which emphasises equal claims not to natural resources themselves, but to their *value*. To be more specific, he argues for an equal claim to the *value* of unimproved natural resources – that is, the value which resources hold before such a time as they are improved, developed or managed by human beings (Steiner 2005: 35). Given that we do, in fact, use quite unequal portions of land, and in so doing deprive others of resources which they might otherwise use, we are obliged to compensate them. The privileged are, in a sense, unjustly squatting or occupying resources the value of which should be shared out equally with the less fortunate. In practice, Steiner argues, this means that nation states should pay a tax based on the value of the land that they occupy. Given that real estate is worth far more in Germany or Japan than it is in Chile, for instance, those countries would be taxed much more heavily. The revenues gained by levying the tax would then be paid into a Global Fund. Since everyone individually has an equal claim on the value of natural resources, the just way to disburse that money would be to pay it out equally to all humanity, either in the form of an equal individual lump sum, or an equal basic income for everyone. In that way individuals would enjoy the benefits of their equal right to the value of the world's resources. The impact of setting up such a Global Fund would, of course, be strongly redistributive (Steiner 2005: 36).

In some of its features, this suggestion resembles Thomas Pogge's argument for a global resource dividend. But it is more radical in character. Whereas Pogge's aims are more or less minimalist – they seek to protect basic human rights, and to help avoid serious poverty – the motivation behind Steiner's suggestion is clearly a global egalitarian one. Note that whereas Pogge envisages *partial* compensation for any dispossession that has occurred (and only at 1 per cent of the value of natural resources), Steiner's position calls for *full* compensation of the original value of land or resources.

One major objection to Steiner's proposal focuses on whether it is fair to tax the value of land or resources in the way he suggests. There has been an ongoing debate between Steiner and David Miller on this point, for instance (see Miller 2007, 2011; Steiner 2011). Steiner's proposal, recall, suggests that countries should be taxed according to the current

market value of their land. This appears, at least at first sight, to provide a clear, comprehensible and readily applicable way of measuring
the advantage which countries have derived from the resources within
their territories. But, from Miller's point of view, making Germans pay
more to the Global Fund because German land values are higher is
unfair, at least from one perspective. It is unfair because the fact that
land values are relatively high in Germany is not some simply arbitrary
fact. It represents, at least in part, the fact that countries have laboured
over their land, improved it, made wise (and sometimes unwise) decisions about how to use and preserve it, and so on. As such, it seems fair
to say that countries are *entitled* to at least some of the value they have
themselves created. To put it another way, although Steiner *could* be
right that nations are not entitled to the value of *unimproved* resources
within their territory, using actual real-estate values as a basis for calculating what each nation owes to the Global Fund is unfair, since
actual real-estate values are based on unimproved value plus any
improvements that have been made. And it is not right that nations
should pay more if they have made more improvements to their land
or resources. So Steiner's proposal itself seems 'arbitrary' (Miller 2007:
57–60). Given how formidably difficult it turns out to be to isolate the
'unimproved', 'natural' or 'latent' value of resources, 'we are left with
no way of determining when, in fact, a distribution of resources qualifies as an equal distribution – and therefore no way of implementing
egalitarian proposals such as Steiner's Global Fund' (2007: 62).

This reprises, of course, the argument advanced in section 5.3.1,
where it was claimed that nations are entitled to their resources – and
Miller would make the same claim about land – because they have
improved them and created additional value. So whereas a nation
may not have done anything to create the land or the resources in
its territory, it may be at least partly responsible for the *value* of that
land, or those resources. And this gives it some kind of claim to keep
those resources. This opens an interesting can of worms, however. On
the one hand Miller seems to be right that nations influence the value
of their land. On the other hand, it does not seem correct to say that
they solely create *all* of its value. International commodity markets,
for instance, have a major impact on the value of resources, as Miller
himself recognises (Miller 1995: 105). Is it possible to distinguish the
value which nations create in their resources from the value added

by other agents, or indeed any value they may have had before even being touched by anyone? Doing so would certainly be formidably difficult. Miller's response appears to be that since we *cannot* easily distinguish these different amounts of value, the only way to secure for nations the value that they have created is to give them exclusive rights over resources. But would this be any less arbitrary than saying (as Pogge does) that, however much value nations *are* responsible for creating, it cannot reasonably be more than 99 per cent of resources' market value, with the implication that a resources tax of at least 1 per cent would be justified? As I mentioned at the outset of this section, arguments for national ownership of natural resources are developing in depth and sophistication, but it is not likely that any justifications which might be produced for national ownership will be strong enough to entirely head off arguments such as Pogge's.

5.4. Further issues: water and global justice

Unlike some natural resources – such as gold or diamonds – water is an essential of life. We can safely say that each human being, just as they need air to breathe, needs water and some source of nutrition. Deprived of water, any human being will die in a matter of days. Human rights organisations estimate that the minimum water intake for the sustenance of human life is between two and a half and three litres per day (although much of this can be derived from foodstuffs). In addition, water is key to other human activities such as cleaning, growing plants, or providing food and drink for livestock. Indeed something in excess of 80 per cent of the world's total consumption of fresh water arises from agriculture (Hoekstra and Chapagain 2008). Taking into account these indirect water requirements, the UN estimates that, all in all, 20 litres of water per day are a minimum requirement for human existence (UN 2006).

Nevertheless, although it is an essential of life, access to and consumption of fresh water is radically unequal, globally speaking. The average North American uses almost 600 litres of water per day, compared with 6 litres for the average African (Barlow 2010: 19). Moreover, access to water proves to be time-consuming, dangerous and expensive for many people. It can be time-consuming insofar as reaching clean water can involve walking many miles. It can be dangerous in various ways: for one thing, available water is often not clean, but rather exposes the drinker to bacterial infection and disease; for another thing, the dependence of many families on their children to fetch water exposes them to risks to their safety. It is also, for many, very expensive. Inhabitants of slums in Latin America or the Philippines, for example, pay more – in absolute prices – per litre of water than do the inhabitants of New York and London (UN 2006). At the same time, water is consumed in vast quantities by the industries of many countries. Some sectors of the economy are highly water-intensive, and consumers in the developed world are usually able to treat the ready availability of cheap or even free water as a dependable fact of life.

What might we have to say about such facts from the point of view of justice? First and foremost, we might think that water is an obvious candidate for a human right, given its status as a clear essential of human existence. There is nothing culturally specific about saying that everyone needs access to water, for instance. If we are at all persuaded about the existence of the subsistence rights described in chapter 4 – and global justice theorists of both minimalist and egalitarian varieties suggest that they do exist – then we might think that water, alongside food and shelter, is one of the obvious things for which we have a basic need, and to which we might be entitled. Among scholars of global justice, water has received very little attention, but certainly does tend to be included in the list of basic human rights which should be protected (see e.g. Miller 2007: 184). Rather surprisingly, however, human rights law has not always recognised it as such. The 1948 UN Universal Declaration of Human Rights, and the 1966 International Convention on Economic and Social Rights did not include water as a human right – indeed neither of them even contains the word 'water' (UN 1948, 1966). Although the 1948 Declaration, for instance, includes references to what we might think of as less basic rights (such as the right to paid holidays, or the right to choose the form of one's children's education), nowhere in the document is water specified as a basic right. Food, shelter and medical care, by contrast, are singled out explicitly as key rights (UN 1948). Indeed, it was not until July 2010 that a resolution describing water as a human right was finally adopted by the UN General Assembly (UN 2010).

One reason for this appears to be disagreement about who, if anyone, has the responsibility to deliver water to meet this supposed human right. Although many countries supported the 2010 resolution, very few have actually enshrined a responsibility for the state to provide water to citizens within their own legal codes. And international organisations such as the World Bank and the UN have tended to encourage privatisation of water provision as a method (although often not a very effective one) of generating investment in infrastructure to provide water. As a result, the 2010 resolution does not specify that states have a responsibility to provide drinking water for their citizens directly. But, interestingly, the resolution *does* include an injunction on developed countries to 'provide financial resources, build capacity and transfer technology, particularly to developing countries, in scaling up efforts to provide safe, clean, accessible and affordable drinking water and sanitation for all' (UN 2010).

If we do believe in a human right to water, then what kinds of policy or institution might help to secure people's entitlements to water? How might we embrace and act on the 2010 resolution's apparent aim of securing the developed world's help in securing the basic water needs of people in developing countries? Although work on global justice and water is only just beginning, it might be worthwhile to investigate two possibilities: harnessing international trade to offset water insecurity, and a water levy to fund people's basic entitlements to clean water.

As we shall see in chapter 6, a standard justification for international trade consists in the idea that it allows countries to focus on producing the goods and services they are more efficient at producing and importing the goods which they cannot produce cheaply or easily. International trade is meant to make for a more efficient economy and to produce economic gains for all. Within this discourse of economic efficiency, very little if any attention is given to the efficient use of water. But there is good evidence that, empirically speaking, international trade does produce 'water savings', and that these savings might be increased still further if water conservation became one explicit goal of trade policy. Typically, water can be saved when an agricultural crop like wheat is grown in a country with plenty of rainfall and exported to a country with much lower rainfall, which would otherwise use more scarce river water to irrigate its own wheat fields. Studying the amount of water used to produce foodstuffs which are then traded internationally allows us to focus on cases where water is saved and cases where it is lost (as when a country uses a good deal of water to produce an import which could have been produced with less water in the importing country). Whereas wheat exports from the United States to Egypt, for example, produce a net water saving, rice exports from Thailand to Indonesia produce a net water loss (Chapagain, Hoekstra and Savenije 2006). The implication of all of this is that, whereas actually redistributing water between countries might seem an odd and expensive policy, international trade can itself help to alleviate water insecurity and spread the benefits of this increasingly scarce natural resource. Thus far, though, the fact that international trade leads to a large net water saving is more or less an accident: the efficient use of water has not been any kind of priority in evolving trade policy (Chapagain, Hoekstra and Savenije 2006). But there is surely potential for it to be more explicitly addressed as a possible goal of trade agreements.

The idea of a water levy has been floated in a number of countries but not yet adopted as a policy. For example, a proposal has been mooted by a number of non-governmental organisations (NGOs) in Italy to guarantee to all Italians a small quota of free water every day, but over and above that to place a 1 per cent per cubic metre tax on the use of excessive amounts of water. This would encourage more efficient water use, but, more significantly for our purposes, the proposal also suggests that the revenues from the water levy should be spent on assisting developing countries in improving their own water infrastructure and ameliorating water insecurity (Hachfeld, Terhorst and Hoedeman 2009). Rather like Pogge's Global Resources Dividend, the idea is that a tax which would hardly be felt by the richer citizens of the world could be used to guarantee (at least one of) the human rights of people in the developing world, and to protect the status of water as an essential and, hopefully, guaranteed element of any human life.

chapter 6

Global justice and international trade

When people protest or demonstrate in favour of global justice, a key element of their concerns, judging from the placards they hold, is often the justice (or injustice) of international trade. Each time the leaders of the most powerful countries meet to discuss trade issues – whether it be under the auspices of the G8 group of the largest economies, or the G20, or the World Trade Organization – the protestors give voice to profound concerns. International trade is held to be, in various ways, unjust – with the implication that we ought to redesign the rules, or allow developing countries a more equal chance to compete on global markets. Often the language used changes a little, so that instead of demanding distributive *justice*, activists and NGOs talk about *fairness*, perhaps alongside the need to avoid exploitation or a position where more powerful countries can abuse their superior bargaining power to set the terms of international trade to suit their own interests. This chapter examines just what international trade justice – or fairness in trade – might mean, and what the theories we examined in part I of this book can contribute to thinking about these issues.

Why, though, do we need a theory of justice in international trade? International trade is meant to be beneficial. The argument for 'free trade' suggests that some countries will enjoy a comparative advantage in the production of particular goods. One country may be able to produce computers cheaply and easily, but not dairy products; another might be better at producing dairy products, and less good at producing computers. Britons might have a great taste for bananas, but be unable to grow them without very expensive greenhouses. Caribbean countries might be happy to sell them to Britain, allowing them to buy the Japanese motorbikes their citizens crave. Japanese people in turn might buy Scottish whisky. If they traded with each other, each country could get what they needed more efficiently. They could enjoy the benefits of economic specialisation. International trade is also said to encourage the spread of technology, and allow countries to take advantage of economies of scale. Trade, in sum, is usually held to increase the total amount of goods that can be produced, and to avoid a situation where countries have to toil over producing goods which they are ill-suited to make. This argument has been widely accepted since the English political economist David Ricardo advanced it in the early nineteenth century. A world without any international trade, or so the theory goes, would have less specialisation, would be much less efficient and would see much slower economic growth.

But if international trade is meant to be beneficial, we can still ask questions (which economists have often failed to ask) about how those benefits are *spread*. For it might turn out that although Caribbean countries really are the best at producing bananas, there is simply not much profit to be gained from growing them. Really, most countries might prefer to be producing the motorbikes at which Japan excels, or even to be making a living from services such as oil refining, banking or tourism. But those markets can be very hard to break into. Sometimes producers of high-value goods in the developed world are protected by state subsidies – perhaps because they employ a great number of people and the politicians representing their constituencies have promised to protect their jobs. Even if there are no subsidised industries against which to compete, entering these markets can require a great deal of capital investment (buying expensive computers or machinery, paying for training and so on). And that capital investment would both be a big risk and take a long time to come good even if the gamble paid off, because in the foreseeable future established competitors in developed countries will continue to be able to sell their goods or services more cheaply than new entrants to the market. They might even decide to engage in 'dumping': they might decide, just as a developing country is in a position to start selling its new electronic goods or motorbikes, to sell their own rival goods at a loss, thus driving the infant industry into the ground.

As we shall see in this chapter, many of these fears are borne out in reality. Mainstream economic theory suggests that the liberalisation of international trade will be accompanied by 'convergence', or reductions in inequality between countries, as developing countries are able to take advantage of the opportunities which trade offers. However, although recent decades have witnessed extensive liberalisation of trade, they have not been accompanied by similarly substantial reductions in inequality. Although there has been a degree of 'convergence', this has overwhelmingly been the result of the economic growth of around ten Asian countries – particularly the large economies of China and India (Ghose 2004). Moreover, the precise relationship between the economic growth of those Asian countries and trade liberalisation is contested: some commentators believe that growth has been achieved to some extent *despite* liberalisation, and not merely because of it (Wade 2004).

A theory of trade justice, or of fairness in international trade, would try to respond to issues such as this: that the benefits of trade are spread very unevenly; that developing countries find it hard to break into the more lucrative industries, and hence may be condemned forever to supply the raw materials for other countries' lucrative industries; that some countries thwart the supposedly beneficial operation of the market by subsidising their industries or dumping goods on global markets. They will offer normative standards by which to judge whether trade is operating fairly, or whether more powerful countries are unfairly skewing the playing field in their own favour.

But trade also raises other normative issues. As well as a general concern for whether the playing field of the global economy is a level one, additional questions suggest themselves. Is it legitimate to buy goods from a country when we know that producers in that country employ children in their factories or that employees are forbidden to join trade unions? Do individual consumers have an ethical responsibility to buy so-called 'fair trade' goods, which are intended to protect suppliers, and guarantee them a fair and stable price for their goods? These questions suggest that the idea of 'fairness', as it relates to trade, is a complex and multifaceted idea (Miller 2010).

The chapter first considers a case study concerning the World Trade Organization and its latest, ongoing round of negotiations. Section 6.1 then moves on to examine how minimalist and egalitarian approaches to global justice might respond to the issues thrown up by international trade. The remaining sections address a series of specific, concrete issues. Section 6.2 examines arguments for changing the rules of international trade, particularly under the auspices of the World Trade Organization, in order to spread the benefits of trade more evenly. Section 6.3 examines the idea of 'fair trade' as a response to concerns about trade justice. Finally section 6.4, the 'Further issues' section, examines recent arguments for 'linking' trading rules with the protection of labour standards, so that trade rules would be used to encourage countries to avoid exploitative labour or the use of child labour, for example.

Box 6.1. **Case study: the World Trade Organization and the Doha Round**

The World Trade Organization (WTO) was established in 1995 as the successor to the General Agreement on Tariffs and Trade (GATT), and now comprises more than 150 member countries, which between them account for more than 97 per cent of international trade. It aims to supervise and liberalise international trade – to ensure the gradual reduction of barriers such as tariffs and subsidies to free trade, and to resolve the disputes which occur when countries accuse each other of breaking WTO agreements. WTO rules require countries to treat each other in a non-discriminatory way (that is, if they grant favourable access to their markets to one country, they ought to grant the same access to all). They also aim to reduce both tariffs (taxes which have to be paid on imported goods, making them less competitive on domestic markets) and non-tariff barriers (which discriminate against imported goods by, for example, requiring them to meet safety or environmental standards which domestically produced goods do not have to meet). The overall goal is a world of free trade in which the economic benefits of trade would be available to all countries.

Decision-making within the WTO officially takes a democratic form, with each country entitled to one vote in negotiations. But rather than voting, decision-making operates according to a kind of consensus-forming process, whereby countries debate possible rules in formal and informal settings. Any agreements must achieve the unanimous consent of the member states, and this consensus rule is held to secure procedural fairness.

Actual policymaking on international trade has proceeded in a series of 'rounds', and the current round is the so-called Doha Round (so-called because the first meeting of the round was in Doha, Qatar). The round began in 2001 with the explicit intention of enhancing the participation of developing countries, slashing subsidies and spreading the benefits of economic globalisation more widely. The WTO Ministerial Declaration of 14 November 2001 declared that

> International trade can play a major role in the promotion of economic
> development and the alleviation of poverty. We recognize the need
> for all our peoples to benefit from the increased opportunities and
> welfare gains that the multilateral trading system generates. The
> majority of WTO members are developing countries. We seek to place
> their needs and interests at the heart of the Work Programme adopted
> in this Declaration … We recognize the particular vulnerability of
> the least-developed countries and the special structural difficulties
> they face in the global economy. We are committed to addressing the
> marginalization of least-developed countries in international trade and
> to improving their effective participation in the multilateral trading
> system. (WTO 2001)

To date, however, the Doha Round has not concluded in agreement. The most significant stumbling block – although different parties predictably give different versions of events – appears to be the unwillingness of developed countries to cut back substantially on agricultural subsidies. In the absence of a new agreement, the goal of spreading the benefits of globalisation more widely remains an aspiration rather than a reality.

6.1. International trade and global justice

Trade justice is an 'applied' issue on which theory is developing rapidly, but where the judgements offered by the major theories of global justice often remain somewhat tentative. In part this may be because there are so many (contested) empirical questions involved, so that the potential impact of particular policies is not always clear. But we could still expect theories of global justice to offer general guidance on what normative standards, if any, we should apply to international trade. It is also worth noting that some of the arguments discussed in chapter 5 on resources – specifically those of Pogge and Wenar – bear directly on issues of trade (such as, for instance, whether it is legitimate to buy goods from oppressive regimes). Our focus here, though, will be directly on the issues mentioned in the introduction to this chapter – the WTO and trade rules, fair trade, and labour standards.

In this section we shall examine the broad contours of what global minimalists and global egalitarians have had to say about the issue of justice in international trade. Generally speaking, as we would expect, global minimalists have been concerned to set out minimal standards of fairness to which trade ought to conform. They have sometimes argued that it ought, for instance, to be broadly non-exploitative, and that the rules of trade should not be set by more powerful countries in their own interests. But minimalists are sometimes reluctant actually to apply standards of distributive justice to trade, or to argue that it is wrong, from the point of view of justice, if the benefits of international trade are spread unequally (indeed, some minimalists would wonder why there is a chapter on international trade in a book about global distributive justice at all; if there are normative standards to be applied here, they do not derive from concerns about distributive justice). So long as countries are able to participate in international trade on generally fair terms, and so long as the outcomes do not threaten their independence, we should not be concerned if the eventual outcomes are unequal.

Egalitarian accounts do often embrace a direct concern with the unequal outcomes which international trade produces. They do not necessarily argue for an equal distribution of the fruits of the global economy; but they may argue that the current rules of the game do not give developing countries an equal chance to access, and flourish within, global markets (they also tend to be much more comfortable with the idea that trade raises issues of distributive justice). As a result they often suggest reforms to organisations such as the WTO and policies intended to give developing countries a chance to 'catch up' economically. In this section we shall examine minimalist accounts first. We shall then move on to egalitarian accounts, and at the end of the section attempt to draw together some of the key points of contention between them.

6.1.1. Minimalist approaches

Although he did not want to embrace any substantial account of global distributive justice, John Rawls did address the issue of international trade justice in *The Law of Peoples* (Rawls 1999). His minimalist account suggested that imbalances in international trade might need to be corrected in practice. Specifically, the fairness of the 'Society of Peoples' might be threatened if more powerful actors were able to set the terms of economic co-operation to suit themselves. To avoid this possibility, peoples should set up 'cooperative organizations … and agree to standards of fairness for trade'. And 'Should these cooperative organizations have unjustified distributive effects, these would have to be corrected in the basic structure of the Society of Peoples' (1999: 115). Rawls also argued that well-ordered peoples should set up some form of world bank to assist development (see also Freeman 2006: 250).

   Rawls's comments, though, are very brief, and open to competing interpretations. He did not, for instance, tell us what 'unjustified distributive effects' would represent, or quite how we would distinguish justified from unjustified outcomes of trade. One supporter of Rawls's approach, David Reidy, argues that Rawls's brief comments nevertheless represent the beginnings of a substantial and satisfactory account of trade justice, which Rawls might have gone on to develop further had he lived longer. Since Rawls's primary concern is with the autonomy or independence of societies, the crux of this part of his argument is that 'No well-ordered people … is to use its economic power within trade relations or the international institutions governing them to undermine the well-orderedness or political autonomy of any other people' (Reidy 2007: 203). That much seems uncontroversial: any interference in the autonomy of well-ordered peoples is, for Rawls, illegitimate, and using trade policy to undermine the autonomy of other well-ordered societies would be wrong. We might still, however, have trade rules in place which did not jeopardise the actual autonomy of particular societies, but which nevertheless gave rise to highly unequal outcomes (Armstrong 2009a). Would there be a normative objection to trade relations which saw some societies remaining relatively poor – but independent – and offered much better opportunities to more fortunate societies?

Certainly Reidy himself wants to go further and argue that well-ordered societies are duty-bound to ensure that international trade is organised so as to help, and certainly not to hinder, the transition of burdened societies to well-ordered status. In that sense they should view trade relations as a part of their 'overall aid package' (Reidy 2007: 202). However, it is not clear that this is what Rawls wanted to argue. He does not explicitly say, in *The Law of Peoples*, that we should think about trade policy as some kind of extension of the duty of assistance. Whether we ought to extend it in that way is a moot point. But what is clear, as emphasised by Rawls's critics, is that on his account we ought not to be directly concerned about inequalities in international trade. One reason for this might be that Rawls saw participation in international trade as *voluntary*. Given that societies can become well ordered simply by wisely employing the natural resources at their disposal, participation in international trade is an option but not a necessity. The language of distributive justice is therefore out of place, given that abstention from international co-operation is a 'real possibility for each party to it' (Reidy 2004: 303). Principles of distributive justice, furthermore, apply to schemes of social co-operation, and as we saw in chapters 2 and 3 a number of minimalist theorists do not consider the global economy to represent genuine social co-operation.

David Miller's position on international trade is also not yet fully worked out. Recall from chapter 2 that, alongside his argument about basic rights as a global minimum standard, Miller also believes that we have 'a responsibility to offer [poor] societies fair terms of cooperation' (Miller 2007: 251). This means that the rules governing societies' interaction with each other – and Miller explicitly includes trade here – must be 'fair to both sides' (2007: 252). But he notes that it is very difficult to say what 'fair' terms of trade would be, especially since we lack a 'metric' by way of which to judge whether outcomes are equal (see also Miller 2010). Although some interactions are 'so one-sided in their impact as to be unfair by any reasonable standard', it is hard to say anything more definite than that. What he does say is that wealthy countries should not use tariff barriers to protect their own industries from competition from poorer states, and that we ought to take steps 'to stabilize the prices of commodities that are the staple exports of particular societies' (Miller 2007: 253). He also suggested in earlier work that nation states should refrain from exploiting each other (Miller 2000: 175), which can happen when more powerful states abuse their position to impose unfair terms of interaction on weaker states. This theme is unfortunately not explicitly developed in his more recent work, although it does raise some interesting questions. 'Exploitation' is a common term in political debate, but within political theory or philosophy its meaning is contested. What makes a transaction or relationship exploitative? Arguably, an account of exploitation demands an account of distributive justice itself – an account with which, at the global level, Rawls, at least, is reluctant to provide us. Like Rawls, in any case, Miller's concern seems to be largely with the minimal fairness of the international system, so that nations are able to interact on terms that are broadly fair, and which do not abuse their strength or jeopardise each other's independence. On the whole, then, minimalists show a basic concern with the fairness of international trade, but appear cautious about applying clear standards of distributive justice to its outcomes. The emphasis is on preventing more powerful countries abusing their power to create (or maintain) an uneven playing field within the global economy.

6.1.2. Egalitarian approaches

As we would expect, global egalitarians often present more demanding accounts of trade justice. Recall, for instance, that Charles Beitz argued that the rules of international trade could be redesigned so that they promoted redistribution towards developing countries (Beitz

1979: 174). He also wonders whether we might rearrange the tariff system so that developing countries could establish lucrative industries without competition from developed countries, but still gain access to the markets of the latter. In Beitz's case these proposals are represented as possible applications of a global difference principle: as a matter of distributive justice, we ought to pursue outcomes which advance the position of the poorest as far as we can.

Many broadly egalitarian approaches to trade justice are *relationist* in character – they suggest that trade embodies the right kind of relationship to trigger principles of distributive justice, and try to work out what the appropriate principles would be. A key question for relationists is, therefore, just what *kind* of practice international trade is. Two relationist theorists, Aaron James and Darrel Moellendorf, have suggested principles to govern international trade based on the specific kind of practice or relation that it represents.

Aaron James presents a broadly egalitarian approach to international trade which seeks to limit the inequalities that arise in the benefits from trade between particular *nation states*. In that sense it is an egalitarian account with global scope, but one which differs from most global egalitarian accounts in that it does not directly focus on the relative positions of *individuals* across the world. James (2009) suggests that international trade is 'an international social practice of market reliance'. It is a practice, that is, whereby countries rely on each other to produce and exchange goods and services, and make active political decisions to sustain that beneficial practice. As he puts it (2009: 6), 'the global economy is created and shaped by policies and rules adopted by different countries' which intend to benefit from free trade and the economic gains which specialisation brings. This mutual intention means that a concern with what James calls 'structural equity' is appropriate. He suggests, for example, that since the social practice of international trade is supposed to secure mutual benefit, then it ought to ensure that every participant is actually better off than they would have been if their country had not participated in international trade (2009: 14). As a normative standard, this will set the bar very high. For it is hard to imagine a country integrating itself within the global economy without making *someone* worse off, even if the gains for most people are considerable. James's argument is not that trade ought to benefit everyone *directly* and immediately, however. Rather, the argument seems to be that developing countries ought to be allowed to protect their members from the potentially damaging effects of free trade, if necessary by compensating them for their losses or erecting trade barriers to protect them from the effects of competition (see section 6.2). So developing countries should have the scope to ensure that participation in international trade benefits all their citizens, and should not be prevented – by WTO rules, for example – from doing this. A second implication is that the gains from trade are to be distributed equally between the countries party to it, unless unequal gains would be to the benefit of poorer countries. This suggests that James would apply something like the difference principle to the outcomes of international trade. That, again, sets a very demanding standard, and a much more challenging one than minimalists are prepared to embrace.

For Darrel Moellendorf, principles of justice apply to any association that meets four specific criteria. According to this relational account, the association must, first, be relatively strong; second, make up a significant part of the background conditions which influence people's lives; third, be largely non-voluntary in nature; and, fourth, be governed by norms which are under human control. Let's take these in turn, as they apply to the global economy. First, it is clear to Moellendorf that the global economy is 'not a fleeting phenomenon' (Moellendorf 2009a: 49). It is a long-lasting and far-reaching association. Second, it has 'profound effects' on people's interests. Countries' economies – especially in the case of small, developing countries – can be thrown into turmoil overnight by fluctuations in commodity prices. Trade itself is accompanied by a network of norms and institutions which sustain it, and which in many cases 'profoundly affect the domestic policies that countries may pursue'. States are forbidden to protect their own industries in certain ways, for instance, and are obliged to respect the intellectual property rights of people or corporations based in other countries (2009a: 50). On the third criterion, it is an issue of controversy whether participation in the global economy is voluntary or not. But Moellendorf believes that it is not, on the basis that there is 'no reasonable alternative development path' beyond participating in international trade (2009a: 50). Fourth, and finally, the global economy is under human control in the sense that the institutions, norms and rules governing it 'can be limited, directed or counterbalanced by deliberate public policy' (2009a: 51). The rules of the WTO, for example, can be, and regularly are, amended. It is therefore a valid normative question, for Moellendorf, in whose interests they *ought* to be amended.

Note that this is not necessarily an argument for an equal distribution of the proceeds of international trade. Moellendorf's argument is that the global economic association owes its members *equal respect*, which on his account generates a principle that any inequalities would have to be 'reasonably acceptable' to all its members (2009a: 59). This produces a *presumption* towards equality, but holds out the possibility that there might be good reasons for embracing some unequal outcomes – say, that needs are unequal, or that inequalities can produce incentives which benefit everyone including the worst off. But it is not clear whether any of these reasons apply to the inequalities which currently characterise international trade and, as such, Moellendorf's conclusion is that the global economy's huge gulfs in income and wealth represent serious injustices (2009a: 67).

6.1.3. Opposed approaches?

As we have seen in this section, there are several issues which divide theorists when they talk about trade. One is whether international trade is the right *kind* of practice or institution to which to apply principles of distributive justice in the first place. Most minimalist theorists are sceptical that it is, although they may set out conditions that we should, nevertheless, attach to international trade – that it should be non-exploitative, perhaps, or that it should not jeopardise the independence of societies, or that more powerful countries should not set the terms of international trade to suit themselves. For minimalist theorists these should really be sufficient to secure the requisite degree of fairness within international trade, insofar as we need to be concerned about fairness there at all. Many egalitarian theorists, though, want to apply full-blown principles of distributive justice to international trade, and to use them to argue for more substantial reform of the global economy.

That disagreement can also be witnessed with regard to a second, related issue, which is whether we should see participation in international trade as voluntary or not. For Rawls participation in trade *is* voluntary: since societies have, in all but exceptional cases, the natural resources that they need to develop, they also have the option of remaining self-sufficient if they prefer. While they might *choose* to trade globally, the fact that they can refrain from doing so seems partly to defuse any criticism that the actual outcomes of trade might be unequal. Thomas Nagel, whose minimalist account we discussed in chapter 3, also believes that participation in global economic institutions is voluntary in character. He concedes that the incentives to join such institutions are 'substantial', but nevertheless believes that since membership is not coercively imposed, their existence does not trigger concerns of distributive justice (Nagel 2005: 140). For global egalitarians like Beitz (1979) or Moellendorf (2009a), by contrast, participation in international trade is to all intents and purposes *non-voluntary*, in the sense that there are no reasonable alternatives to participating in the global economy. As such, the impetus towards using the language of distributive justice to evaluate the outcomes of that economy becomes stronger. On this point it is interesting to note that David Miller, a minimalist theorist, *does* believe that integration into the global economy is a 'precondition for economic growth' (Miller 2007: 253). But on his account that fact does not appear to lead to any direct concern, at the level of distributive justice, with the equality or inequality of the eventual outcomes.

All this suggests that egalitarians and minimalists diverge considerably on their approaches to trade justice. But it is important to note that theoretical disagreement does not always translate into practical disagreement. People with quite different theoretical positions can sometimes converge on roughly the same set of policy options, albeit they may do so for different reasons. Trade justice may be a good example of this – at least partial – practical convergence. For although minimalists often refuse to apply standards of global distributive justice to the outcomes of international trade, they might share with egalitarians an emphasis on reforming organisations such as the WTO, or the need to reduce tariffs to allow developing countries to advance economically. Minimalists may not make these arguments because they are concerned with the distributive injustice of the global economy – they might instead be concerned with the need to avoid some nations exercising undue influence over others, for example. But there is clearly some potential for common ground, and so the differences in theoretical perspective should not blind us to the possibility of practical agreement about pressing reforms to the trading system. When we examine the issues of WTO reform, fair trade and labour standards in the next three sections, it will often be the case that the differences between minimalists and egalitarians, on practical issues, will be differences of degree and emphasis.

6.2. Trade rules and the WTO

Theorists of global justice have often made the World Trade Organization the target of their arguments. Three reasons why this might be the case spring to mind. First, it is a ready target because it is one of the most powerful institutions governing the global economy. Second, its decisions have obvious distributional effects. Every time a WTO 'round' concludes, there will be countries who consider themselves winners, and those who consider themselves to have been hard done by. And third, WTO rules – and negotiations – explicitly invoke considerations of fairness. Although realists might claim that considerations of fairness are out of place in evaluating trade outcomes – perhaps because countries should be expected to ruthlessly pursue their own self-interest – negotiations are supposed to be (and are often publicly claimed to be) motivated by considerations such as reciprocity and non-discrimination, which are hard-wired into the rules of the WTO itself (Brown and Stern 2007). Rounds are themselves to be conducted by processes which aim at consensus, and which are formally democratic.

6.2.1. The WTO and fair decision-making

Critics of the WTO, however, suggest that decision-making is not a fair process in reality. Many of the packages of tariff reductions which are put up for discussion are worked up 'behind the scenes' by more powerful countries which discuss them in exclusive (although informal) 'clubs'. Developing countries often have little expertise on the (sometimes unnecessarily) complex issues which are discussed, and struggle to provide qualified representatives. It is also the case that whereas the requirement of reciprocity *seems* to guarantee procedural fairness, the unfortunate fact is that poorer African countries, for instance, have very little to bring to the negotiating table. If the United States can choose to sign a clothing-based tariff-reduction deal which will open up markets worth $10 billion with China, or a foodstuff-based deal which will open markets worth $0.5 billion with Eritrea, it should be of little surprise if it ends up reducing its tariffs on clothing but not on foodstuffs (Kapstein 2008).

We might think, of course, that the requirement of unanimity – the requirement that all members must agree to any new deal or else it will not proceed – would safeguard procedural fairness. But this may well not be the case, once we recognise the context of great inequalities in starting points. Given their precarious economic positions, very poor countries will be tempted to accept even minuscule advances rather than no advances at all. Furthermore, although poorer countries could reject the deal which emerges during any given round, in reality they would be confronting a choice between accepting that deal and, effectively, withdrawing from membership of (and protection from) the WTO altogether (Brown and Stern 2007: 294). It is understandable, then, that in the past poorer countries have – sometimes reluctantly – accepted deals which offered them very little in the way of progress in accessing global markets. Indeed, we might consider this a good example of the dictum that the degree of *voice* a party achieves in a negotiation will partly depend on how real and significant the threat is that they might *exit* if they do not like the eventual outcome (Hirschman 1970). In the case of individual developing countries, exit would damage their own interests substantially, but would hardly, in all likelihood, appreciably damage the interests of developed countries. And so it should not be surprising if their voice is often not heard when negotiations take place.

To address these concerns there have been many suggestions for organisational reform of the WTO. These suggestions aim to give developing countries a greater voice in negotiations. The Helsinki Process – a consultation on global governance jointly founded by the Finnish and Tanzanian foreign ministries – recommended in 2005 that 'The annual ministerial meetings of the WTO should be open to participation by non-state actors' such as NGOs or representatives of relevant UN agencies, which might possess the expertise to advance the interests of developing countries better. It also recommended that 'The negotiating capacity of developing countries should be strengthened … with sufficient technical assistance' (Helsinki Process 2005). The 2007 Warwick Commission on the international trading system also recommended that developing countries should receive more technical support in bringing complaints before the WTO to enable them to reap any benefits of membership more securely (Warwick Commission 2007).

6.3.2. The WTO and fairness of outcomes

If some criticisms of the WTO focus on the *process* – and whether decision-making is really as procedurally fair as it at first appears – others focus on the *outcomes*. Irrespective of the nature of the decision-making mechanisms, are the actual rules that arise from them, and the distributive outcomes those rules give rise to, fair or just? Here it is commonly argued that they are not. But there are at least two alternative positions on just why. One widespread view is that free trade, even if it is defensible in theory, has not been achieved in practice. A second view suggests that in the presence of deep structural inequalities the insistence on free trade can itself be unfair.

The first view, which suggests that what we need is more genuinely free trade, points out that the developing world is currently confronted with a world of 'rigged rules and double standards' (Oxfam 2002). Developed countries continue to place massive tariffs on agricultural products from the developing world, as well as other kinds of goods such as clothing and textiles. These make it very difficult indeed for developing countries to make money from those industries. Moreover, developed countries sometimes pay extraordinarily large subsidies to their own domestic industries, most especially in the agricultural sector, and these again thwart free competition. According to the UN's *Human Development Report* the average dairy cow within the European Union received a subsidy of the equivalent of US$913 per year – compared, for example, with the total income of $490 per year earned by the average inhabitant of sub-Saharan Africa, with $8 of it coming in aid from the EU. Japan's government spent $2,700 per cow per year (UN 2003). The United States, for its part, spent $10.7 million per day on subsidies to domestic cotton producers, and $3.1 million per day on aid to sub-Saharan Africa. Not only do these amounts dwarf the amounts paid in overseas aid; they may actually make it very much more difficult for developing countries to compete in the relevant markets.

The impact may be even more serious than that. Let's draw that out by focusing on the case of cotton. In 2005, the US government granted subsidies worth $4.2 billion to 25,000 domestic cotton farmers. Much of the cotton produced – for which there was insufficient demand within the US – was then sold on global markets with the aid of export subsidies, depressing the global market price and, according to many critics, damaging the chances of cotton producers in Africa turning a profit on their own crop (Oxfam 2006: 11). This so-called 'dumping' actually reduces the income that everyone outside the United States is able to gain from their own cotton products. Indeed, the harm which subsidies and the accompanying dumping creates might well outweigh any benefits arising from aid. In Thomas Pogge's language, while countries might be acting on a positive duty to aid poorer countries, they might at the same time be violating a more stringent negative duty not to harm them, or to prevent them from meeting the human rights of their members.

Our first view, then, suggests that the problem with free trade is that it has not been advanced consistently by developed countries, which demand access to overseas markets for their own goods but refuse to allow producers in the developing world to compete fairly in key markets. As Joseph Stiglitz – a former Chief Economist of the World Bank – puts it, 'In part, free trade has not worked because we have not tried it: trade agreements of the past have been neither free nor fair' (Stiglitz 2006: 62). This is not to say, though, that there is no argument in justice for protecting domestic producers, or subsidising the production of some crops. We could certainly try to construct such a justification. For instance, a country might want to subsidise the continued production of cotton, or grapes or cheese, for instance, not because it actually wants to depress global prices but because its people have a historical attachment to a landscape characterised by their production. It is not even clear that aiming to protect the jobs of domestic farmers is wholly objectionable. But at the very least critics would want to see those possibly legitimate goals weighed up against the costs to farmers in the developing world, who may have to operate without subsidies, who may have their access to markets restricted and whose livelihoods may be badly affected by dumping. The likely conclusion will be that the developed countries ought to reform their practices significantly.

It is open to question just how far we should take the argument for free trade, though, and this is where our second view comes in. For example, some theorists of global justice (including Beitz, James and Moellendorf) have argued that a degree of protectionism is acceptable on the part of developing countries which are attempting to nurture infant industries. These infant industries, if successful, would allow developing countries to break into more lucrative markets (recall the hypothetical example of bananas and motorbikes in the introduction to this chapter). They might enable developing countries to begin to narrow the gap between rich and poor countries – to making 'convergence' a reality.

But protecting infant industries – by subsidising them, or by placing tariff barriers on rival goods from overseas producers – obviously contravenes the idea of free trade. How might it be justified? One response has been to point out that historically, development on the part of countries such as Britain, the United States, Japan or South Korea has always been accompanied by protectionism – using tariffs and subsidies to protect infant industries in crucial periods of their development (see e.g. Stiglitz 2006: 71; Brock 2009: 223). Perhaps, rather than rushing to the liberalisation of trade, developing countries ought to be able to liberalise at their own pace, to minimise the damage to potentially lucrative industries. One global egalitarian therefore argues that 'there are good reasons to believe that a trade regime should sequence the requirement to eliminate protectionism so as to provide countries in the developing and underdeveloped world with more time to develop their infant industries' (Moellendorf 2009a: 96).

It might be that the answer, then, is in the timing. This is what the reference to 'sequencing' in the last quotation from Moellendorf implies. The idea behind sequencing is that poorer countries ought to be able to open up their markets in a gradual manner, liberalising different parts of their economies with care and forward planning rather than rushing, under pressure from international organisations, to open themselves up to the global market. But this does mean that, in the meantime, they should be allowed to maintain tariff barriers which developed countries should not for their own part be allowed to maintain. As such, it challenges the idea of strict reciprocity embedded in WTO rules (the idea that countries should match each other's tariff reductions). At best it replaces it with something looser, which we might have to call something like 'diffuse reciprocity' – and which would see wealthier countries making more substantial concessions than poorer ones (Kapstein 1999: 189–91). Alternatively we might point towards Rawls's view of reciprocity, which focused on the necessity for all, including the worst-off, to make gains from co-operation – but did not categorically require those to be equal gains (Rawls 1971). Either way, the WTO has gone some way towards allowing the 'special and differential treatment' of developing countries in practice – effectively allowing the poorest countries to maintain some tariffs which would otherwise contravene WTO rules, at least for a time – but, according to some critics, these moves have not gone far enough, or been pursued very coherently (Warwick Commission 2007). A somewhat more radical suggestion would be that the WTO's overarching goals should be revised, so that an emphasis on liberalising and regulating international trade was *supplemented* by a stronger focus on achieving development for the poorest countries and on safeguarding environmental sustainability. Although many of the WTO's pronouncements in recent years suggest an emphasis on such broader goals, they have not yet made much of an impact in reality (Deere-Birkbeck 2009: 10).

The disagreements between our first and second views revolves, in effect, around this question: will the supposed benefits of free trade always remain a mirage in the presence of very substantial differences in wealth and development between the various countries of the world? If we lived in a more or less economically equal world, then we might suppose that free trade could produce just outcomes. But since we do not, it may merely intensify existing inequalities. How to respond to that fact represents a serious challenge to theories of global justice, of both minimalist and egalitarian varieties.

6.3. Fair Trade

· ·

The idea of Fair Trade, as a consumer-oriented campaign, is distinct from the broader idea that international trade should be reformed to be more fair or equitable. We shall retain the capitals to make that distinction clear. Fair Trade goods are goods which are produced according to standards supervised by organisations such as the Fairtrade Labelling Organization. A distinctive Fair Trade logo on the outside of a packet of sugar, coffee or chocolate assures the consumer that the producer was paid a 'fair' price for producing the raw materials, and that certain labour and environmental standards were adhered to. It makes sense for the Fair Trade movement to be described as a consumer-oriented campaign because the emphasis is placed on individual consumers making choices with an explicitly ethical dimension: to buy a slightly more expensive variety of chocolate, for instance, and thereby to balance the supposedly 'normal' economic motivation (to buy the required goods as cheaply as possible) with an ethical one (to support sustainable industries, or the raising of labour standards).

As such Fair Trade – with capitals – is distinct from a general argument for fair international trade. It selects a set of producers, producing a specific set of goods, and attempts to raise standards within that sector of the global market. It does not aim to change the rules of the international trading system, or to reform the WTO – although people committed to buying Fair Trade goods might *also* be committed to that. It moves the pursuit of (an aspect of) trade justice into the home, or the supermarket.

The argument for Fair Trade does connect with concerns which are raised about trade generally, though. Take coffee as an example – one of the world's most traded commodities. Much of the world's supply of coffee beans is produced by peasant farmers operating small-scale businesses in the developing world. These farmers typically do not own the land they farm and are also obliged – through the lack of other options – to sell their produce to local intermediaries who will in turn sell it on at higher prices. It is estimated that farmers themselves receive between 1.6 and 5.7 per cent of the final price paid for a cup of coffee (Levi and Linton 2003: 410). The price of coffee is also subject to a good deal of volatility on global markets, and this risk is passed on to producers who do not know what price their product will eventually secure when they come to plant their crops. The ethical concern, then, is with the vulnerability of producers to fluctuations in market prices and their weak position at the bottom of a value chain which sees the vast bulk of proceeds going to wealthier intermediaries – traders and, often, retailers in the developed world. Fair Trade certification, by contrast, aims both to secure a predictable price for producers, and to grant them a higher portion of the proceeds by cutting out local intermediaries. Although he does not comment on it as a political strategy, Fair Trade might help meet Miller's goal of stabilising prices for 'commodities that are the staple exports of particular societies' (Miller 2007: 253). Moreover, small producers often form co-operatives to sell on to Fair Trade-certified importers, and those importers extend credit to farmers to enable them to purchase machinery, to improve production and to observe higher labour and environmental standards.

Fair Trade is a much-debated phenomenon, however. This is not to say that buying Fair Trade goods is held to be a bad thing. It is more the case that its critics see Fair Trade as strictly *limited* in its potential for securing the broader aims of a more just trading system. A first criticism of Fair Trade is that only a small part of international trade is touched, and that even here the influence is often rather slight. It helps a small number of producers by a certain amount (on one estimate, only 10 per cent of the 'premium' paid for a Fair Trade product goes to the producer; *Economist* 2006). But it certainly does not mean that trade as a whole is 'fair', or that we no longer need to address broader issues of trade fairness. Introducing Fair Trade as a 'niche' product at the higher end of a particular market 'is simply not enough if the ultimate aim is the transformation of the wages and working conditions of landless laborers as well as farmer-owners' (Levi and Linton 2003: 409). At their least forgiving, critics would argue that it makes very little real difference to international trade, but instead makes wealthy consumers feel better about their place within it: that it buys for them a sense of satisfaction in their status as 'ethical' consumers (Watson 2006).

A second criticism would be that Fair Trade actually distorts the market, encouraging people to produce goods when they cannot really compete on the global market and might be better off producing something else. It might be said that Fair Trade resembles government subsidies in that way, given that they also interfere with the 'normal' operation of the free market and allow producers to go on making products which are 'uneconomical' (Kurjanska and Risse 2007). In defence, it might be thought that there is an important normative difference between wealthy states acting to protect their own citizens *against* competition from citizens of poorer countries and individual consumers making decisions which actually aim (partly) to advance the interests of producers in poorer countries. But, either way, it could still be the case that the Fair Trade route is not the best development strategy. That is a largely empirical question, but we could still say, from the normative point of view, that buying Fair Trade goods certainly ought not to persuade citizens of wealthier countries that all their duties towards the world's poor had been discharged. Fair Trade might be a complement to the kind of reforms discussed in the last section, but it ought not to be a replacement for them.

6.4. Further issues: trade justice and labour standards

Although the argument in favour of free trade enjoys considerable support, and is in effect the official position of institutions such as the WTO and the International Monetary Fund, it is not, as we have seen, without its critics. One concern with which we have not yet dealt is that free international trade might drive down labour standards – or, to be more precise, that developing countries (or producers in developing countries) might only be able to compete with developed countries by offering very low pay and poor conditions to their own workers. We would then see a 'race to the bottom' as producers in developing countries competed to offer the lowest costs to multinational corporations seeking to base their manufacturing operations abroad. The 'anti-sweatshop' movement has, of course, made considerable progress in persuading consumers to boycott large corporations who use 'sweat-shop' labour, characterised by the prohibition of membership of trade unions, by rampant sexual harassment and sometimes by child labour or forced labour (Young 2007: 165). But it may be that individual consumers boycotting individual corporations is not enough. Perhaps very poor labour standards are an endemic feature of a global economy characterised by both free trade and substantial inequalities, with which consumer boycotts alone cannot be expected to deal. Perhaps multinational corporations can escape censure for employing sweat-shop labour by contracting out production in a supply chain sufficiently complex that blame cannot easily be attributed to them. Either way, it could be that we need a more concerted approach to the problem.

If so, what alternative approaches are available to us? One suggestion is that it is, normatively speaking, wrong to trade with countries which oppress or exploit their workers. Instead, there should be 'linkage' between rules on labour standards – monitored by organisations such as the International Labour Organization – and the trade rules monitored by the WTO. Countries which did not uphold minimal standards – which permitted child labour or the routine sexual harassment of workers, for example – could be expelled from the WTO. This would effectively cut them off from access to global markets, and that threat would act as a powerful incentive for them to improve their labour standards. This general idea has appealed to some global egalitarians. Moellendorf (2009a: 104), for instance, believes that participation in a trade regime should be conditional on conforming to a 'modest set of standards', including recognising the right to belong to a union, eliminating child labour and forced labour, and eliminating discrimination in employment. Mathias Risse also argues for at least a presumption against trading with countries which oppress sections of their own population (Risse 2007: 362).

This kind of linkage is, however, controversial. We might, for instance, suspect that it is counterproductive. Thus Martin Wolf has suggested that imposing such sanctions on countries with poorer labour standards effectively penalises them for their own poverty, 'while taking away the best ladder out of it' (Wolf 2004: 188). It is certainly widely suspected that developed countries use a focus on labour standards as a way of protecting their own markets from competition (Barry and Reddy 2008: 12). In effect, the insistence on labour standards then resembles a kind of non-tariff barrier to trade, which serves to keep competitors' goods out of domestic markets. Ensuring that good standards are upheld demands an apparatus for monitoring, which in turn demands effective governance – which is often lacking in developing countries. Even achieving basic health and safety standards for all workers could require the purchase of expensive equipment and protective gear. Although we might believe that such protection and monitoring is morally required, that demand is open to abuse if the intention is actually to exclude goods from developing countries.

On the other hand, we might say that the fact that standards can be abused is not a reason for abandoning them. Perhaps, instead, standards ought to be overseen by a global organisation such as the WTO, which could make impartial judgements about whether particular goods met agreed standards, and whether those standards were themselves necessary. But even if that were the case, we might worry that imposing labour standards on other countries, however impartially adjudicated, is still (unfairly) requiring *them* to pay for *our* preferences (Barry and Reddy 2008: 18). Moreover, the working conditions of sweatshop labourers are themselves a product, at least in part, of decisions made over the decades by wealthier countries and consumers (Young 2007: 170). Kapstein emphasises that developed countries' insistence that developing countries adhere to reasonable labour standards (or environmental standards, for that matter) can be 'well-meaning', but might still suffice to exclude the latter from world markets. If so, then refusing to trade with countries with poor labour standards might not achieve anything in reality: it might leave the same labour standards in place, but remove one pathway out of poverty for poorer countries. A more just solution, Kapstein suggests, would dictate that 'if the industrial countries take, say, the issue of child labor seriously, they should be willing to transfer funds to the South in order to build schools and enable these children to pursue their studies, as their talents permit' (Kapstein 1999: 204).

There are major disagreements about the merits of the proposal to link labour standards with trade, then. One general disagreement concerns whether this kind of linkage would be in the interests of developing countries or whether it would, on the contrary, make it still harder for them to achieve economic 'convergence' with developed countries. A number of critics are suspicious of such linkage, believing it to be an unwarranted interference in the market, or even a cynical ploy to exclude from developed-world markets goods from developed countries. Some supporters of labour standards, though, point out that it is not clear that ending child labour, for example, *would* be to the detriment of developing countries. It might well be to the detriment of the unscrupulous employers who wish to employ them. There is, however, evidence that removing children from the employment market frees up better-paid jobs for adults, and improves child health and education (Caney 2006: 129). We might also question whether we ought to consider the impact of labour standards in isolation. What Kapstein's argument, above, emphasises is that policies could be adopted alongside rules on labour standards which might mitigate or offset any negative impacts. If stricter labour rules were introduced at the same time as opening markets in developed countries to more goods from developing countries, for instance, then the overall effects could be beneficial. As such, these standards might be a valuable part of a general theory of global justice (Caney 2006: 129).

A further disagreement revolves around just *which* standards we ought to apply, if linkage is defensible in the first place. On Barry and Reddy's defence of linkage, the argument is not that developing countries should uphold exactly the same standards as developed countries; it is that the labour standards of developing countries should be *minimally adequate*, but also context-sensitive – that is, they could legitimately vary according to the economic situation of the country in question. This means that it might be appropriate to adopt lower standards in the least developed countries, standards which might then be ratcheted up over time as economic growth was achieved (Barry and Reddy 2008: 4). Although there are certain rules we should insist on for all – for instance, slave labour should obviously be prohibited (2008: 61) – other rules ought to be more flexible and take into account a country's level of 'development'. At this point, however, many an advocate of global justice might disagree – and some global egalitarians might be especially reluctant to embrace such context-sensitivity. For Barry and Reddy's proposal would effectively permit workers to suffer lower wages or inferior working conditions simply because of their nationality. Contrast this with Simon Caney's advocacy of equal pay for equal work, which suggests that workers in different countries should enjoy the same wages if the goods or services they produce are equally valuable (Caney 2005a: 122–3). That proposal would be extremely challenging – and Caney does not provide us with any indication of how it might be achieved – but it also forms a stark contrast with more incremental views such as those of Barry and Reddy.

chapter 7

Global justice and climate change

Our knowledge of human impact on the global environment has accelerated rapidly in the last few decades. In the 1970s, for instance, better understanding of the dangers of pesticide pollution or of 'acid rain' inspired governments to act in order to minimise risks to human health and natural ecosystems. While these represented something of a wake-up call to governments not used to taking environmental issues seriously, in recent years we have faced many further problems. One of the key features of many of these problems will be their *transnational* character: sulphur-bearing coal, for example, might be burned in one country but eventually lead to acidified rainfall in another country, damaging fish stocks and forests and causing illness in human beings. Another key feature of such problems is that their effects are often extended over *time*. A given generation might decide to burn fossil fuels or cut down its trees, but the environmental costs might be paid not by that generation itself but by generations to come. Both these features make thinking about environmental problems both important and challenging.

In this chapter we shall concentrate on the problem of climate change, which is both a politically salient issue and one where we can confidently say that the impacts will be felt across the world and also for many years to come. It is known that the concentration of carbon dioxide and other 'greenhouse gases' in the upper atmosphere is increasing (see the case study (box 7.1) for more details). It is also thought both that this is in large part the result of human action and that it will have – or may already be having – a serious impact on people across the globe. In some cases the people affected by climate change will have their very existences threatened, and be left unable to meet their basic needs. This is most obviously the case for inhabitants of some coastal areas or small island states which will be very vulnerable to the rising sea levels attendant on climate change. But other people may be affected in a whole variety of ways – by extreme weather conditions, by desertification or by the acidification of the oceans.

As is well known, the science of climate change is somewhat contested, and 'climate sceptics' question in particular whether humans are responsible for any climatic change which may be occurring. The scientific consensus behind climate change is actually very strong, but nevertheless we cannot be expected to settle that question here. Our interest is in the normative questions that arise *if* we accept that there will be serious impacts on people's life chances as a result (or substantially as a result) of carbon emissions which are in some sense under human control. If we accept that this is true, significant normative questions immediately arise. Is it *just* to damage others' basic interests in this way? Can we, instead, be required to make sacrifices to reduce the dangers associated with climate change? Assuming that meeting the challenge of climate change – which might mean either acting to reduce the impact of climate change, or adapting ourselves to its reality (and probably both) – will cost a great deal of money, how should we distribute those costs? Should we adopt a distributive principle for carbon emissions, so that everyone has a basic entitlement to emit, or even an *equal* one?

This chapter examines the contributions that the theories of global justice discussed in part I of this book can make to thinking about these and related questions. We begin with a case study which highlights the contribution of the Intergovernmental Panel on Climate Change to understanding the nature of that problem (box 7.1). We then shift our attention back to normative theory, and specifically contrast the contributions which minimalist and egalitarian positions can make to thinking about climate justice. In section 7.1 we examine the implications of minimalist accounts. Minimalists have not always had much to say about climate change, and in some cases – such as Rawls's – it is necessary to reconstruct what they *could* say, given the general features of their position. In David Miller's case, though, we do have a much more explicit response to the justice and injustice of climate change. In section 7.2 we shift our attention to egalitarian accounts. Here, an explicitly egalitarian principle, such as an equal 'right to emit' carbon dioxide, looks like a plausible response to the issue of climate change, and so we examine the arguments in favour of that principle. We shall, however, complicate matters by considering two difficult questions with which any account of climate justice will have to grapple. The first concerns just how we factor in *historical* considerations – that is, the fact that developed nations have *already* accounted for much of the increased carbon concentration in the atmosphere. Should they be held responsible for that? If so, how? The second question concerns how *broad* we want an account of climate justice to be. Is it appropriate to concentrate on the distribution of a single good – assuming that the right to emit carbon dioxide can be understood as a 'good'? Or should our position on climate justice be more wide-ranging in character, taking account, for example, of different nations' economic situations, their broader contribution to worsening or mitigating climate change and so on? Both challenges are difficult to meet, and in their own ways suggest that a simple egalitarian principle (such as an equal right to emit) may not actually be the most just response.

In section 7.3 we attempt to sum up our answer to the question, what guidance can theorists of global justice provide in thinking about how to spread the costs of climate change? Here we shall find that there is actually fairly broad agreement on the kinds of normative considerations that are relevant (with the contenders being equality, historical responsibility and ability to absorb costs), but nevertheless substantial disagreement on how to interpret each of those three ideas and on how to combine them to produce a compelling account of climate justice. Finally, in section 7.4, the 'Further issues' section, we discuss the plight of the populations of small island states whose very existence is threatened by climate change. We examine some recent arguments attempting to spell out the duties which people living in other, more secure countries might have in assisting, or even offering homes to, people displaced by climate change. This example brings the potential human consequences of climate change to the forefront, as well as the difficult issue of assigning responsibility for adapting to its consequences.

Box 7.1. **Case study: the Intergovernmental Panel on Climate Change**

One of the first things we need, if we are to make any progress in dealing with climate change, is a clear understanding of the nature of that problem. The Intergovernmental Panel on Climate Change (IPCC) was established in 1988 – by the UN Environmental Protection Program in co-operation with the World Meteorological Association – to help meet this need. Its remit is to provide UN members with a state-of-the-art understanding of 'the science, the impacts, and the economics of – and the options for mitigating and/or adapting to – climate change' (IPCC 2001: vii; see also Gardiner 2004: 559–63). Since 1988 it has issued four major 'Assessment Reports' doing just this (released in 1990, 1995, 2001 and 2007). The message of these reports has remained fairly consistent, and certainly has repeatedly emphasised the following major points:

- Annual emissions of carbon dioxide – the most important 'greenhouse gas' – increased by 80 per cent between 1970 and 2004.

- The average world temperature increased by 0.74°C between 1906 and 2005.

- By the end of the twenty-first century, global average temperatures are projected to rise by between 1.8° and 4°C.

- Sea levels are now rising at an average of 3.1 mm per year, compounded in part by the melting of glaciers and ice caps, and may rise by 59 cm by the end of the century.

- It is 'very likely' that the bulk of the observed increases in global temperature are a result of emissions of greenhouse gases for which humans are responsible. Emissions have also 'very likely' contributed to rising sea levels and to extreme weather conditions (including drought, heat waves and extreme levels of rainfall)

Source: IPCC 2007.

This last point is important. Although popular discussion was once preoccupied with 'global warming', in many ways this label is misleading. Human impact on the climate appears to be upsetting the balance of the earth's climate, but the effects are complex and hard to predict. In some areas the result may be a rise in average temperature, but in other areas (such as northern Europe) the reverse could be true. There is also likely to be a rise in extreme climatic patterns of all types.

The critical political (and economic) question is how to respond to these facts. The mission statement for the IPCC – cited above – refers to 'mitigating and/or adapting' to climate change. Here *mitigation* refers to concerted efforts actually to reduce the extent of climate change, for instance by cutting down on carbon dioxide emissions. Mitigation, therefore, seeks to *prevent* many of the worst effects of climate change. *Adaptation*, on the other hand, refers to the ways in which humans may have to learn to *live with* the consequences of climate change, and reduce their vulnerability to it.

It appears certain that both mitigation and adaptation will be necessary. Even if the world's leaders were to reach a secure agreement to reduce carbon emissions, it may already be the case that the earth's climate patterns have been upset in a way which will have consequences for many years. Human beings will therefore have to adapt to those consequences. Both mitigating and adapting to climate change will, in all likelihood, be extremely expensive (although not doing so may be even more expensive). Regrettably, a large part of the impact of climate change is likely to be felt in the tropical and sub-tropical zones of the world, where most of the world's poorest countries are clustered (Gardiner 2004: 569). In other words, the greatest impact is likely to be borne by those whose ability to adapt to it is weakest – unless some mechanism is put in place for helping them to adapt. Once we take into account the fact that the impact of climate change may be felt for many years to come, there is a very real danger that the costs of dealing with climate change will be felt by people who actually bear very little responsibility for bringing the problem into existence.

7.1. Minimalist responses to climate change

In this section we examine the responses which minimalist theorists of global justice could make to the issues raised by climate change. In many ways the issue of climate change seems to pose a serious challenge to minimalist accounts. Climate change appears to produce a clear issue of global distributive justice – after all, what we are talking about is how we ought to *distribute the burdens* of dealing with a hugely significant global problem. While some minimalist theorists have argued that for global justice to be at all relevant depends on the prior existence of social co-operation or the presence of coercive institutions, for instance, here we have a problem whereby people *are* having a pervasive impact on each others' life chances, and where this seems to call for a robust normative response. Institutions, in that sense, do not appear to be particularly important. Climate change is also an issue where a broadly egalitarian position – for instance, the principle that we all ought to have an *equal* right to emit carbon dioxide – has a good deal of initial plausibility.

We would not expect minimalist theorists to adopt such a position, not, in any case, if they are to hang on to the core of their position – which suggests that global inequalities are not inherently morally troubling. What, though, would a minimalist position on climate justice look like? To some extent, the process of answering this question has to be one of reconstruction. John Rawls, for instance, did not address issues of climate change, or environmental justice more broadly, in his work (and neither has Thomas Nagel). What Rawls did present was a brief account of intergenerational justice which others have suggested has implications for the issues thrown up by climate change. David Miller, by contrast, has recently addressed the question of how to distribute the costs of tackling climate change directly. In section 7.1.1 we shall examine the materials Rawls provides with which to construct a minimalist account of climate change. In section 7.1.2. we shall then examine David Miller's position, and pay close attention to his success in carving out a plausible position on climate justice without ceding too much ground to global egalitarianism.

7.1.1. Rawls and the just savings principle

John Rawls is one of the few major theorists of justice to have addressed the question of *intergenerational justice* explicitly. In a brief section of *A Theory of Justice*, he examined the attitude that present citizens should take towards the interests of citizens of the future (Rawls 1971: 284–93). It is important to be clear that Rawls therefore addresses intergenerational justice not as a *global* issue, but as one of how citizens should act towards future members of their *own* community. Rawls suggested that even this question 'subjects any ethical theory to severe if not impossible tests' (Rawls 1971: 284). From the outset it is not immediately clear how his general theory of distributive justice ought to apply to the issue of justice between generations. On the one hand, Rawls suggested that society could be seen as a system of co-operation over many generations (Rawls 1993: 274). On the other hand, there is no simple relationship of *reciprocity* between people currently alive and their future counterparts. To put it bluntly, while there is much we can do for future generations, there is nothing they can do for us (1971: 290). Indeed, Rawls appeared worried that current generations might in effect become morally enslaved to future generations, if they ended up being obliged to sacrifice their own interests in favour of vast numbers of future citizens. Instead of some very demanding principle of intergenerational equality, Rawls's view of our obligations appears to be very close in nature to the duty of assistance which we owe to non-nationals (see chapter 3). In essence, we have an obligation to allow future generations the opportunity to run decent social institutions of their own. We do this by creating stable institutions ourselves, and making sure that the material basis for maintaining them is in place for future generations (1971: 285).

Although Rawls's account here is brief, some theorists of the environment have tried to extend his ideas on intergenerational justice to the global environment, to produce a broadly 'Rawlsian' account of ecological justice (see e.g. Wissenburg 1999). The practical implication of Rawls's principle of intergenerational justice is that we ought to observe a 'just savings principle'. This suggests, as noted above, that we ought to leave enough capital or resources for future generations to have a chance of maintaining just institutions.

But, in the end, the ability of the just savings principle to provide guidance on how to distribute the costs of climate change is limited – which is not surprising, because this is not the job for which it was designed. For one thing, the exact implications of the principle are not very clear. Even if we restrict ourselves to intergenerational justice within a particular community, Rawls was reluctant to place a specific figure on how much of its capital a given generation is obliged to save. This is because saving a great deal would be inappropriate if a society were currently poor, but reasonably sure that future generations would be much more wealthy. If a society were already wealthy, on the other hand, it might be appropriate to save more (Rawls 1971: 287). But that in turn, of course, means that how much we ought to save *now* depends on estimating the likely wealth of generations far into the future (perhaps that problem, though, is unavoidable). A second limitation, for our purposes, is that the argument is not at all globally focused. Rawls's vision is obviously one of discrete communities extending indefinitely into the future, as if the world of more or less autonomous nation states is likely to be a permanent entity. It is certainly not a vision of ever-increasing global interdependence, or one which takes account of the impact we may have on future generations *across* the world – though this is, arguably, just what ought to be at the forefront of our minds when we discuss the justice of climate change. So at least as it stands, the guidance provided by Rawls's account is probably very limited.

7.1.2. Miller on climate change

Unlike Rawls, David Miller has directly addressed the question we are concerned with in this chapter: how, from the point of view of justice, should we distribute the burdens of mitigating and adapting to climate change? He has set out an answer to that question which is quite intriguing, because, at least at first sight, it appears to blend egalitarian commitments with more minimalist ones. In effect, Miller argues that richer countries should alone bear the costs of mitigating climate change, and that in so doing they should make *equal* sacrifices to their standards of living. But before examining whether Miller is thereby committing himself to what is actually a global egalitarian principle, we should sketch out the broad character of his proposal.

Miller accepts, with the mainstream of current scientific opinion, that current emissions of greenhouse gases are unsustainable. If we continue to emit as we are doing now, we shall be imposing serious harms, particularly on societies which are already poor. Indeed, were we to do so, we could even properly be charged with violating their human rights. So clearly emissions have to be reduced to some sustainable level. But this leaves the question of just *who* should do the reducing. As Miller asks, 'who exactly are the agents on whom the responsibility falls to act so as to prevent damaging climate change?' (Miller 2009: 120).

A first step, he suggests, is to absolve the poorest societies of *any* of the responsibility for mitigating climate change (2009: 145). Poverty is a serious enough issue that we ought to allow the poorest societies actually to *increase* their emissions somewhat if doing so is necessary to tackle their poverty (2009: 146). So societies in which poverty is *not* endemic should meet the costs of dealing with the problem. But how should *they* distribute the costs between themselves? This is our second step. Here Miller wants to reject a common proposal for reducing carbon emissions which suggests that we should all have an equal per capita right to emit (this principle is discussed further in section 7.2). He admits that it has an obvious intuitive appeal (2009: 139). But the problem with that principle is that it takes no account of societies' different capacities to reduce their emissions (2009: 148). If all societies were required to cut their emissions to the same level – equivalent, say, to one or two metric tonnes of carbon dioxide per person per year – this would be relatively easy for some of them (those which already emit less than or only somewhat more than that). It would impose very great costs, by contrast, on countries which were currently emitting at many times that level. This latter group of countries would in effect be required to absorb *all* the pain of dealing with climate change.

Instead, Miller wants to argue for a position whereby the costs of mitigating climate change are the same for each society; he calls this a 'principle of equal sacrifice' (2009: 146). The principle suggests, in essence, that given the seriousness of the problem we are facing, sacrifices will have to be made, 'and all those who can contribute without harm to their vital interests should do so on an equal basis' (2009: 150). So the proposal does not aim to come up with a figure of emissions per capita which we ought then to impose on all countries, regardless of the costs to each. Instead it starts from the total reduction in emissions which is necessary, and asks countries to make sacrifices to achieve that reduction which are equally *costly*. This means that some countries will make very large reductions in carbon emissions if they can do so without great cost to themselves, but also that some countries will make much smaller reductions if these prove to be very costly. The aim is to spread the costs of dealing with the problem and not to share the right to emit itself equally.

This is an intriguing principle, but two questions are worth asking about it. The first concerns whether it is just, and the second concerns just how much ground it concedes to the global egalitarians. On the first question, we have just seen that Miller's proposal does not actually set a figure specifying by how much a given society should reduce its emissions. Instead, it says that each society should make an equally painful sacrifice in relation to its current standard of living. But that means, almost certainly, that a country (like the United States) which is currently emitting far too much, proportionately, will continue to emit far too much once its own sacrifice has been made. A country which is emitting much less (such as Portugal) could even end up cutting its own emissions by more, if it could do so cheaply. Either way, the two nations would end up still emitting hugely unequal amounts of carbon dioxide. Not only would Miller's proposal not address that inequality, but in effect it would endorse it. Is this fair? Ought not the United States to be obliged to reduce its emissions further, given that it is making a disproportionately large contribution to the problem we are trying to deal with? Those who believe that it should might be attracted to the kind of egalitarian principle discussed in the next section.

The second question actually runs contrary to the first, since it tries to point out that while Miller's is not an egalitarian principle in one sense (it does not require equal emissions), in another sense it apparently is (because it argues for equal sacrifices to deal with the problem). Does this mean that Miller has actually embraced a global egalitarian solution to the problem of climate change? Miller seems to believe that he has not. At one point Miller points to a distinction between 'deep' and 'shallow' reasons for preferring an equal distribution of some good or other (here the costs of mitigation). A deep reason would suggest that equality is to be preferred because it expresses or reflects an idea of ourselves as equals – as equal citizens, say, or as people who deserve to have some kind of equal standing. Shallow reasons really only suggest that equality is to be preferred when there is no obvious reason to depart from it. This is a simple principle, which can command respect in the absence of an alternative which is clearly superior. And in the present context, where what we really want to do is reach a binding agreement, this ability to command respect is significant.

In any case, Miller claims that we only have shallow reasons for accepting his 'equal sacrifice' principle (2009: 140). We should accept it because it is capable of commanding support, and not because the equality which it achieves is intrinsically valuable (2009: 149). It is a simple idea which could command widespread endorsement, but it does *not* reflect some background idea that we might have of people across the globe enjoying equal standing. There is something to be said for Miller's distinction between deep and shallow reasons for preferring equality, but it still seems to mark at least a change of emphasis from his previous position, which held that egalitarian principles do not even enjoy any normative appeal at the global level. Instead he now seems to be saying – at least in this case – that we have *some* reasons to endorse what is basically a global egalitarian principle – but that these reasons are rather thinner than the reasons a global egalitarian would herself usually give for endorsing it. Still, it is hard not to suspect that Miller's outright opposition to global egalitarianism is a little weakened by this concession.

7.2. Egalitarian responses to climate change

A global egalitarian will likely be concerned not just about the impact of climate change on people's basic interests, but also about the glaring inequalities in how people in different countries are currently utilising the world's environmental resources. Simply put, if the atmosphere has a limited capacity to absorb carbon dioxide, it is clear that individuals in some countries are using far more than their fair share. Recall for instance the figures on global inequalities cited at the beginning of chapter 2. One of the key inequalities that we noted was in carbon dioxide emissions. The following are the figures, in metric tonnes of carbon emitted per person per year, for selected countries (World Bank 2009):

China 3.9

Denmark 9.8

India 1.2

Portugal 5.6

Sierra Leone 0.2

United States 20.6

These really are radical inequalities. The average American, as we noted in chapter 2, is responsible for more emissions than a hundred citizens of Sierra Leone. Moreover the fact that some are emitting so very much really does limit the ability of other people to emit their own carbon dioxide. To be precise, it is not so much that the scale of American emissions directly *prevents* citizens of Sierra Leone emitting more. But it certainly *is* the case that if everyone emitted in the same way as the average US citizen, we would be on a short cut to environmental catastrophe. So Americans are able to emit to this degree only because not everyone else does the same. Here, then, a global egalitarian will say, inequality really does seem to be the problem. The issue is not just that some countries do not have their basic needs met. It is that some countries are consuming *too much*. Moreover, many of the emissions of richer countries do not appear to serve basic needs. Rather they represent what Henry Shue (1993) calls 'luxury emissions', rather than 'subsistence emissions': they support consumption far beyond anything which could plausibly be called necessities. They support the consumption of food air-freighted from across the world, year-round air conditioning or frequent air travel, for instance.

These inequalities make it tempting to say that when it comes to responding to climate change, richer countries should bear the bulk of the costs. The point about 'luxury' emissions also suggests that significant changes could be made by the inhabitants of wealthier countries without their endangering their own basic interests. For instance, the World Bank's *World Development Report* for 2010 states that the emissions which would be necessary to provide electricity to meet the basic needs of 1.6 billion people in the developing world could be offset merely by converting the 40 million SUVs (and other large 'gas-guzzling' cars) currently driven in the United States to ones which met the average fuel economy standards of cars sold in the European Union (World Bank 2010).

So we can readily see that a global egalitarian is likely to be troubled by the current pattern of emissions. But what would they suggest by way of remedy? Just what would be the content of a global egalitarian position on climate justice? One principle which presents itself as an obvious contender is the idea that everyone should have an equal right to emit carbon dioxide. That principle is intuitively compelling, at least on first inspection, and has an appealing simplicity. In section 7.2.1 we shall examine the argument in favour of it. But, as we shall see, it is open to criticism on the grounds that it is a little *too* simple, and in fact many global egalitarians turn out to reject it. In section 7.2.2 we discuss some challenges to the principle of equal per capita emissions, which question whether we ought to adopt such a simple distributive solution to the issue of justice and climate change.

7.2.1. The principle of equal per capita emissions

The principle of an equal per capita right to emit carbon dioxide is to a large extent self-explanatory: it suggests that everyone, wherever they live, should be able to emit the same amount of carbon dioxide per person per year (or, to be more precise, that they should be responsible for the same emissions, wherever those emissions actually occur). It is not easy to specify exactly *what* that amount would be, of course. The answer to that question partly depends on what degree of climate change we think is acceptable; and even if we could agree on *that* it still might not be easy, scientifically speaking, to come up with a precise figure for sustainable carbon emissions. Whereas some sources suggest that one metric tonne per person per year would produce globally sustainable emissions, other sources suggest two tonnes.

But the principle itself is a very simple one, and it has proven attractive to a number of theorists (see e.g. Jamieson 2001; Baer 2002; Singer 2004). It also tends to be supported by developing countries such as China and India, which believe that their emissions should be permitted to *rise* to a sustainable level at the same time as those of developed countries ought to decrease. One justification for the principle, which would draw on an argument presented in chapter 5, would be that the atmosphere is a 'global commons' (see e.g. Baer 2002: 401; Vanderheiden 2008). As a 'commons', or part of humanity's common heritage, everyone should have the right to use it, but no one ought to deprive others of the same ability. Peter Singer's argument runs roughly along these lines. Essentially, he suggests, we should conceive of the atmosphere as a global 'sink', into which we can pour a fixed amount of carbon dioxide before there are serious and irreversible effects on the climate. The question then becomes one of how to distribute rights to pour carbon into this 'sink'. And, as Singer puts it, 'If we begin by asking "Why should anyone have a greater claim to part of the global atmospheric sink than any other?" then the first, and simplest response is: "No reason at all." In other words, everyone has the same claim to part of the atmospheric sink as everyone else' (Singer 2004: 35; see also Moellendorf 2009b: 257).

In practice, this principle would lead to what ecologists call 'contraction and convergence', whereby the emissions levels of different countries met or 'converged' at a fixed and equal level. The 'contraction' would apply to developed countries which would be obliged to cut their emissions very substantially. It is interesting to note that the implications of this principle run in a quite different direction from Miller's solution (discussed in section 7.1.2), even if Miller's solution is also egalitarian in its own way. For Miller, we should try and distribute the *costs* of dealing with climate change equally (Miller 2009). We need not, though, distribute the actual *right to emit* carbon dioxide equally. Singer's argument takes the reverse position. We certainly should distribute rights to emit equally. This will mean that the costs of responding to climate change are distributed very unequally, but so be it. There is no good reason why developed countries should be able to go on emitting far more than their fair share (Singer considers various arguments for continuing to allow them to emit disproportionately, but rejects each one. See Singer 2004: 36–43). Allowing developed nations to continue emitting a disproportionate share simply because they are already doing so, or because changing their ways would be expensive for them, would be morally unacceptable.

The impact of Singer's scheme on rich countries could be severe, then. Indeed, he concedes that the cuts could require fundamental changes to the economies of wealthier states (Singer 2004: 43). But still, it might be morally permissible for rich countries to try and avoid having to make such changes, so long as developing countries could be persuaded to agree. Specifically, Singer accepts the idea of *emissions trading* (see also Moellendorf 2009b; Caney 2010). Emissions trading works like this: if we managed to get agreement on an equal distribution of rights to emit carbon dioxide at some sustainable level – however many metric tonnes per year that turned out to be – then developed countries would end up having to cut back their own emissions substantially. Some populous developing countries, though – such as Bangladesh – will not actually use up their 'quota' of carbon emissions; this is because right now they emit much less than one or two tonnes per person per year. Emissions trading would allow Bangladesh to sell the unused part of its emissions quota to the highest bidder. In practice, this is likely to mean that it would sell part of its quota to countries like the United States, which would then use it to meet their own obligations.

In some ways we might think that the idea of emissions trading is morally suspect – because it allows the wealthy to continue polluting far too much, just because they can afford to buy rights from the poor – rights which *they* cannot use at present *because* they are poor or 'under-developed'. But according to Singer we could still accept a policy of emissions trading, for two reasons. First, and more pragmatically, we are not trying to punish anyone for emitting too much carbon. Our task – and a very urgent one it is too – is to reduce carbon dioxide emissions to sustainable levels. An equal distribution of emission rights coupled with an emissions trading scheme would still achieve that goal. In fact, allowing developing countries to trade their spare emissions quotas actually creates additional incentives for them to keep their emissions low. Second, Singer notes with approval that emissions trading would result in transfers of wealth from richer to poorer countries. Richer countries would spend large sums of money buying the spare emission rights of poorer countries, and if we think that greater global equality – or even the simple reduction of poverty – is desirable, then we should celebrate this side-effect of the scheme (Singer 2004: 46–7). An equal per capita emissions principle is potentially achievable, effective and just.

7.2.2. Challenges to the equal per capita principle

Singer is right that the equal per capita emissions principle has a great deal of normative plausibility. Indeed, it is not immediately obvious just how we could argue against it: after all, why should one person have a greater right to emit carbon than another? Why, to put it more pointedly, should richer countries have the ability to continue to emit substantially more carbon dioxide simply because they happened to industrialise first? But, as we shall see in the rest of this section, the principle is not without its problems, and these problems have been recognised both by global egalitarians themselves and by their critics. The major problems with the principle, it turns out, lie with what it ignores. It ignores, for one thing, what has been done *historically* to bring about the problem of climate change. It also ignores what nations might *currently* be doing to tackle the problem – or what their broader contribution to the problem of climate change is. We shall move on to discuss the first point – the neglect of history – in section 7.2.2.1 below. The second point – the neglect of the other impacts, both positive and negative, which countries have on the environment – is then addressed in section 7.2.2.2.

7.2.2.1. Historical emissions

The principle of equal per capita emissions is a *forward-looking* one. That is, it tells people how much they are allowed to emit from now onwards. Achieving agreement on that principle would be a terrific success, but it would leave one moral issue unaddressed – the issue of historical responsibility. Suppose we all agreed that each person should be able to emit the same amount – somewhere between one and two metric tonnes of carbon dioxide per year. Suppose we also thought that that level was sustainable. We would think so if we knew that, when added to the existing concentration of carbon dioxide in the atmosphere, it would not tip the balance towards some kind of climate catastrophe.

The equal per capita principle treats the current concentration of carbon in the atmosphere as some kind of baseline, asks how much more we can increase it by, and then divides the atmosphere's spare capacity between the earth's inhabitants. But treating current carbon concentrations as a baseline is morally misleading. There are important questions to be asked about *how* we got to that concentration and who was *responsible* for it – issues which the per capita principle, taken by itself, simply ignores.

Historical emissions have in fact been radically unequal. Some countries have made a far greater contribution to the current concentration of carbon dioxide than others. As such they are, we might think, substantially responsible for the situation in which we now find ourselves – a situation where carbon emissions must be strictly rationed. Peter Singer recognises this. He suggests that developed countries have already used up a very large part of the earth's ability to absorb carbon dioxide, so that developing countries simply cannot have – at the cost of planetary catastrophe – the advantages already made the most of by developed countries (Singer 2004: 31). Singer points towards theories of property such as John Locke's, which at least on one interpretation suggests that it is acceptable to appropriate resources from nature so long as enough is left over for others to do likewise (see chapter 5). But this is clearly not what developed countries have done. They *have* appropriated the atmosphere's capacity to absorb carbon; but they have *not* left enough of that capacity to ensure that others can do likewise.

If we take issues of historical responsibility seriously, we might be led to the conclusion that, since richer countries have absorbed more than their fair share of the atmosphere's absorptive capacity, then they ought to accept the bulk of the costs of dealing with climate change (see e.g. Shue 1999: 533). This suggests that the equal per capita principle is actually too favourable to developed countries. Its forward-looking nature offers them a clean slate, and does not require them to bear the costs of their past actions. If we wanted to combine a forward-looking emissions principle with attention to the *backward-looking* principle of historical responsibility, we might end up with a position which said that developed countries should now be allowed to emit *less*, per capita, than their relatively blameless developing counterparts. Although Singer recognises the moral significance of

these historical considerations, by accepting an equal right to emit we
might think that in practice he lets developed countries off the hook
for their historical emissions. This is both morally questionable and
also perhaps politically problematic, given that a demand of many
developing countries is that developed countries *should* in some way
make amends for their historical emissions.

Not everyone is convinced by this argument about historical
responsibility, however. For one thing, practically speaking the science of climate change makes it very hard to be sure just when and at
what level emissions actually started to become harmful (Miller 2009;
Caney 2010: 206–7). But an advocate of historical responsibility also
has to address some tough *moral* questions: is it acceptable to hold
developed countries responsible for historical emissions even though
they may not have known the impact those emissions might turn out
to have? Is it acceptable to hold current generations of Spanish or
Swiss people responsible for the actions of past generations within
their countries?

In response to the first question, the fact that we may in the past
have been ignorant about the impact of our emissions is undoubtedly
significant, and has inspired some commentators to suggest that we
should *not* hold developed countries at all responsible for their historical emissions (e.g. Jamieson 2001). But this is too quick a conclusion.
The carbon concentration of the earth's atmosphere has increased by
roughly a third in the last 250 years. But fully *half* of that increase
has occurred since the 1970s, during which time concern about climate change was certainly present, if anyone had seen it as in their
interests to listen to it (Byravan and Rajan 2010: 243). David Miller
has suggested that we ought not to apply principles of historical
responsibility to emissions which occurred before, roughly, 1985 –
that is, before it became reasonably clear that high carbon emissions
might have devastating consequences. 'But', he says, 'emissions after
that point have to be treated somewhat differently' (Miller 2009: 136).
In the case of emissions since 1985, it seems appropriate to conclude
that nations which have contributed disproportionately to the problem 'must pay a heavier share of the resulting costs' (2009: 137).

We might also want to say that even if richer countries were *not*
aware of the impact of their actions, this is not necessarily a knock-
down argument against making them bear the costs. If a wealthy

person accidentally and quite unknowingly harmed his poorer neighbour, and was easily able to rectify the harm at little cost to himself, we might still think that he ought to do so. When we discussed human rights in chapter 4, we took from David Miller (2007) the idea that when distributing responsibility to help, factors like our *capacity to help* might also matter. So we might want to say in the case of climate change, too, that while ignorance might be morally important, we should not assume that it is *all*-important.

The second question is obviously difficult to answer, too. Even if we can say that historical emissions were damaging, the fact remains that many of the people responsible for emissions in 1985, for instance, are likely to no longer be with us. And many of the people who would bear the costs of making amends for historical injustice may not even have been born in 1985. Is it right that they should bear the costs of choices made by their (recent) ancestors? This is also a formidable objection to applying the idea of historical responsibility to issues of climate change. But within his broader account of historical responsibility, Miller (2007) suggests that we ought to accord some weight to the fact that, whereas the people alive now did not necessarily make the crucial decisions, they may still be *benefiting* from them. In this case, inhabitants of countries such as Spain or Switzerland benefit from the infrastructure and institutions developed at a time when their forebears were busy emitting disproportionate levels of carbon dioxide. In the case of climate change, perhaps benefiting from an injustice committed by your forebears can produce obligations on you to set that injustice right (Miller 2009: 129; see also Shue 1999: 536).

7.2.2.2. Is focusing on emissions too narrow?

The principle of equal per capita emissions has some broad normative plausibility, as we have seen. Some theorists – such as Singer – have suggested that we need a good reason to depart from such an egalitarian principle. But perhaps we *can* think of good reasons to depart from equal per capita emissions. Here are three reasons which have at least some initial plausibility. First, to repeat the point we made in the last sub-section, it might be that developed countries deserve *less* than equal per capita emissions because of the sheer scale of their past emissions. Second, perhaps some countries have greater *needs*. Here we might say that countries in desperate poverty through no fault of their own ought to have greater than average entitlements to emit. Those countries which do not suffer from endemic poverty might then, as a result, appropriately bear a greater burden (see Miller 2009). Third, we might want to take greater account of the *other* things which countries do either to damage or actually to preserve the global environment. Perhaps some countries deserve greater than average rights to emit because in all other senses they behave impeccably, environmentally speaking. Perhaps some countries deserve less than equal rights to emit because they have a much worse ecological impact, overall, than most countries.

This third point is worth examining further. An egalitarian, by definition, will presumably care about how well or badly, when compared with one another, individuals' lives go. As a result, they will generally care about their access to all kinds of goods – income, education, health care, transport, political participation and so on. An egalitarian will *not* tend to say that 'Frank and Julie are equal when they have equal income' – because that would ignore all sorts of other inequalities that might afflict them (Julie might not be allowed to vote, for instance, or Frank might not have had any kind of education). Instead, egalitarians usually say something like 'Frank and Julie are equal when all of the goods that they enjoy, combined together, are roughly equal'. Focusing on one good alone is inappropriately 'atomist' – it makes a fetish out of equality in holdings of one good, at the expense of ignoring lots of other inequalities that should concern us. Many egalitarians will instead be 'holist' in their approach (Caney 2011). They will want to say that equality is about making sure that people's overall bundles of goods are roughly equal. Generally speaking, this will mean that we accept inequalities in the possession of some goods, so long as they are made up for by differences in the possession of *other* goods.

That may all sound very interesting, especially to political theorists and philosophers, but what has it got to do with climate change? Essentially, it allows us to introduce the charge that the principle of equal per capita emissions is *inappropriately atomist*. Perhaps, when it comes to considering the environmental impacts which different countries have, it is misleading to concentrate purely on the quantities of carbon dioxide they emit. David Miller has made just this point, arguing that 'even if you think that equal access to scarce resources is what global justice requires, it does not make sense to interpret this as requiring equality in access to any one particular resource, such as the opportunity to emit greenhouse gases' (Miller 2009: 142–3). Rather, equality in ecological terms would refer to something much broader. Equality might mean that countries placed equal demands on *all* the resources offered by the world, for example. That should also allow some inequalities to be *offset* by others. Perhaps country A emits much more carbon dioxide per capita than country B. But perhaps, unlike its neighbour, it maintains extensive carbon-absorbing woodlands. Perhaps it has spent billions on spreading green technologies throughout the developing world. Perhaps it has admitted thousands of 'climate exiles' displaced by rising sea levels (see section 7.4). A holist account of climate justice would suggest that all these contributions ought to be taken into consideration in assessing whether there is equality in the way we interact with the environment. (Indeed, it might well go still further than this, and suggest that our views on climate justice should themselves be integrated within a *broader account of global distributive justice*, rather than being considered in isolation from them. See Caney 2011).

All this has concrete implications, of course. If we were persuaded by a holist account of ecological justice, we might indeed allow a country engaging in 'technology transfer' to emit somewhat more than an equal share of carbon dioxide. Darrel Moellendorf, accordingly, has suggested that 'it could be permissible for states to earn credit against their target by investing abroad in a way that lowers emissions elsewhere' (2009b: 258). We might even want to say that states should be allowed not to lower their own emissions, just so long as they have the money to spend on encouraging other countries to lower *theirs*. We might also agree with Mathias Risse (2009) that a country admitting climate exiles could legitimately use that fact to offset reductions in carbon emissions that it would otherwise have to make. As we go further down this line, of course, we could potentially confront a situation whereby rich countries do not have to reduce their own emissions *at all*, just so long as they have the financial ability, and the willingness, to spend their money on green projects abroad. Would such a situation be morally acceptable? For an atomist – convinced as she is that everyone should be able to emit to the same degree – it will not be. But it does seem to follow from a holist account.

7.3. The complexity of climate change justice

Governments have spent considerable time and energy on trying to reach agreement on spreading the costs of dealing with climate change – or at least on giving the impression of trying. They have enjoyed only very limited success. The Kyoto Protocol – signed in 1998–9 by 191 countries and ratified by most of them, although not by the United States – set a number of emissions reductions targets for developed countries, and ensured some progress towards reducing their emissions. But it was frequently criticised as presenting an inadequate or incomplete response to the problem of climate change. First of all, it only placed firm duties to reduce emissions on developed countries. Developing countries did not have similar obligations. Although many developing countries had fairly low emissions in the late 1990s, some of them have been ratcheting up their emissions rapidly in the intervening years, and many believe that they should be set clear targets sooner rather than later. Second, the envisaged reductions in carbon emissions for developed countries were very modest – in the region of 5 per cent, compared with the reductions of 50–60 per cent (or even more) which many scientists believe are necessary to avoid serious climate change. Third, even though Kyoto did set apparently binding (although modest) emissions-reduction targets for developed countries, it provided only very weak mechanisms for monitoring those emissions and punishing any defaulters. Finally, it lacked a robust response to the problem of how developing countries would be able to develop economically without massively increasing aggregate global emissions. For that, it was said, some system of 'technology transfer' was necessary, by way of which developed countries would provide both funding and technological assistance to ensure that the development of poorer countries was less environmentally damaging than their own had been. On all of these issues Kyoto was weak on detail and on firm, enforceable commitments.

Progress towards establishing a 'post-Kyoto' framework which would include all countries, and include a satisfactory mechanism for funding 'green' technologies in developing countries, has been frustratingly slow. Intergovernmental meetings at which progress was hoped for tended to collapse in an atmosphere of mutual recrimination, as developing countries alleged that richer countries were not serious about making the required sacrifices to their own standards of living, and developed countries in turn accused some rapidly-developing countries (such as China) of deliberately scuppering deals so that their own rapid development could go on unimpeded by environmental considerations. There was therefore a sense of some relief when agreement was reached in Cancun, Mexico, in December 2010 to establish a system at least monitoring countries' carbon emissions. It also provided for a $100 billion per year fund to help poorer countries deal with the problem of climate change. Despite the sense of relief that some agreement had been arrived at, the Cancun system is still unsatisfactory in many ways. Although it proposes monitoring mechanisms to check that countries do not emit more than they have promised to, the *enforcement* mechanisms it describes are still very weak. Furthermore, there was no detail on how the $100 billion 'green climate fund' would actually be paid for.

We have a situation, then, in which the goal of restricting global temperature rises apparently has substantial international legitimacy. It has, after all, been accepted by institutions ranging from the UN Development Programme to the European Union (Moellendorf 2009b: 249). But progress towards acting on that goal has been frustratingly slow. Moreover, the efforts discussed above concentrate on mitigating climate change. They touch only very lightly, if at all, on the contentious issue of how to assist people who are *already* having to adapt to climate change.

For our purposes, the question is what theorists of global justice can contribute to thinking about our key normative question: how to spread the costs of dealing with climate change (whether that means the cost of mitigating or of adapting to it). On this point, we can detect a degree of convergence between global egalitarian accounts and the minimalist account of David Miller at least. The convergence suggests that *three* normative principles are relevant to this question. The first is some principle of *equality*, although there is disagreement about what shape that principle should take. Contenders include the principle that we should spread the costs of dealing with climate change equally – at least among countries not afflicted by serious poverty (see section 7.1.2); the principle that people should be able to emit an equal, sustainable quantity of carbon dioxide (see section 7.2.1); and finally a more wide-ranging principle which suggests that the degree to which people consume scarce resources – and make positive contributions to sustainability – should be equal in some overall sense (see section 7.2.2.2). Interestingly, this suggests that there is substantial agreement – although Miller, for instance, may be reluctant to say so directly – that egalitarian principles of some description ought to play a role in spreading the costs of the problem.

But egalitarian principles are not the only ones in play. A second principle holds that people ought to bear the consequences of their (damaging) actions – it applies, that is, some principle of *historical responsibility* to the issue of climate change. Once more we find disagreement about just how we should understand this principle, and just which emissions we should apply it to. But it is very commonly thought to be a relevant – indeed compelling – consideration in reaching a just response to climate change. Third, and finally, we often find recourse to a principle suggesting that *ability* or *capacity* to absorb the costs of dealing with climate change ought to influence the way we distribute those costs. There is, again, disagreement about precisely how to act on this principle. We can recall that in Miller's account countries are not required to bear any of the costs of dealing with climate change if they are afflicted by widespread and serious poverty (this, of course, is another way of saying that those who are able to pay more should do so). In Moellendorf's case, the principle is similarly embedded in his insistence that developing countries should not be required to forego their right to development (Moellendorf 2009b). If so, then those countries which are already developed will inevitably bear more costs than they otherwise would.

We have apparently quite substantial agreement, then, on which broad principles are relevant – equality, historical responsibility and capacity to bear the costs of change. This does not mean that we can detect some shortcut to theoretical consensus on this issue, however. One outstanding issue which we highlighted just now is that different theorists may well understand each of these three principles in quite different ways. A second issue is that there will be disagreement about how to *balance* or *weigh* these three principles against each other. Assuming that each of the three principles is relevant, how should we go about giving them all a role in some eventual agreement on climate change?

We saw in section 7.2.2.1 that the question of how to integrate considerations of historical responsibility is particularly difficult. Peter Singer effectively ducks the issue – he raises the argument, that is, that historical responsibility means that developed countries should deal with the problem of climate change more or less on their own. But he effectively drops that argument in favour of a principle of equal per capita emissions which forgives developed countries for their historical emissions. This might make reaching a deal on climate change more likely – which is undoubtedly part of Singer's motivation for arguing in this way – but it is not normatively very satisfying. Miller presents a way of connecting historical responsibility with the other two principles which is perhaps more satisfying. He suggests that when dealing with the costs of mitigating climate change, then an egalitarian principle (equal sacrifice) combined with a version of the capacity-to-help argument (which absolves very poor countries of any obligations) is appropriate. But when we shift our attention to the costs of adapting to such climate change as is already unavoidable, historical factors may then become relevant (Miller 2009: 151). There are two drawbacks to this solution, however. First, whereas at the level of principles of justice this looks like a neat solution, at the practical level it is not clear how we could implement it. For applying the principle in practice would require us to be able to point to, for example, the rising sea levels affecting the inhabitants of Kiribati (see section 7.4) and say whether their plight is the product of historical emissions, or of contemporary emissions. As Miller recognises, this is formidably difficult in practice. Second, past emissions actually have two sorts of impact, as Shue (2001) notes. On the one hand, past emissions may generate negative climate impacts in the here and now to which we need to adapt. On the other hand, past emissions have also used up common resources – perhaps unjustly – and left less of these resources for other people (Singer 2004; see also section 7.2.2.1 above). Miller provides a response to the first issue but neglects to address the second.

There is a more direct way of integrating the backward-looking issue of historical responsibility with forward-looking claims such as equality. It is said that, if we take the period 1750 to 2050 as a whole, then the atmosphere looks to be capable of absorbing roughly a trillion tonnes of carbon dioxide without dangerous temperature rises occurring (Allen et al. 2009). We could, in principle, apply the equal per capita principle to this trillion tonne capacity, and thereby generate a total emissions entitlement for each nation over this whole historical period. We could then say that some countries have *used up* virtually all their total quota over the period, whereas others have a good deal of spare capacity left. This kind of approach manages to combine the per capita principle with the view that nations should be held responsible for the historical contributions they have made to the problem of global warming.

While it looks neat, however, this proposal also displays several drawbacks. First, it faces the familiar problems in specifying historical responsibility which we addressed in section 7.2.2.1 (such as the question why should current generations be responsible for what their ancestors did in 1750). Second, insofar as it applies the equal per capita principle to emissions it is still atomist – it neglects, that is, the wider impacts which each community has had on the environment, both positive and negative. And third, although it integrates historical considerations into the issue of mitigation (because it reduces the emissions a nation can make now in direct proportion to the emissions it has been responsible for in the past), it actually gives us no guidance on the question of how to fund adaptation. So whereas Miller's solution addresses the issue of adaptation but lets countries off the 'historical' hook when it comes to mitigation, this proposal addresses mitigation only to ignore adaptation. (This problem could in principle be addressed, of course. We could bolt on to the proposal a separate scheme for funding adaptation, perhaps based on the principle of capacity to pay, which it otherwise neglects.)

Climate change continues, then, to pose a very difficult challenge for contemporary theories of global distributive justice. While such theories *can* provide useful guidance on the issue, the complexity of the problems makes it difficult to provide a simple solution. But perhaps we should not expect one. As we have seen, an adequate response to the justice of climate change must address (at least) three thorny issues. First, it must provide us with an account of just *how* to integrate the various normative principles that seem to be relevant (including equality, historical responsibility and capacity to help).

Second, it must provide us with an account of how to deal not only with the challenge of mitigation, but also with the problem of adaptation. Third, and finally, it must determine whether it is appropriate to consider emissions of greenhouse gases (carbon dioxide chief among them) in *isolation* or as part of a wider account of climate justice. And if it takes the latter route it must determine whether that account of climate justice itself ought to be nested within a still broader account of global distributive justice, or whether it can be free-standing.

7.4. Further issues: climate change and small island states

Climate change may cause sea levels to rise by the best part of one metre during this century, and perhaps more. This in turn may render many low-lying areas of land uninhabitable. Although climate change is likely to affect very many people, sea-level rises will have a particularly significant impact: they will force many people from their homes, in some cases permanently. The scale of this problem could be enormous: an estimated 600 million people live in coastal areas which could be at threat (McGranahan, Balk and Anderson 2007). Countries with large, low-lying river delta areas – such as Bangladesh, Egypt and Vietnam – could be very badly affected indeed. But the situation is especially pressing for many small-island states, which may either disappear entirely or become largely uninhabitable over the coming decades.

For some commentators this raises particularly clear issues of justice. For one thing, inhabitants of these countries will have their very basic interests affected. They will literally be exposed to threats to their existence, or else be forced to flee for their safety and in so doing lose much of the social, economic and cultural infrastructure of their lives. For another thing, the countries affected will for the most part be ones which are already poor and vulnerable. And finally, these countries will themselves have made, on average, very modest contributions to the problem of climate change in the first place. In sum, people who are already poor will have their very basic rights or interests seriously threatened as a result of processes for which they are scarcely responsible.

Many of the threatened countries formed, in 1990, the Association of Small Island States (AOSIS) in order to emphasise their vulnerability to environmental catastrophe and to demand action from other states both to reduce emissions and to provide resources for adaptation to such climate change as cannot be avoided. In their Declaration on Climate Change of 2009, AOSIS declared that its members were increasingly vulnerable to ecological processes which they were unable to control. They asked, as a result, for the provision of increased levels of technological help, and for 'an urgent and significant scaling up of the provision of financial resources' (AOSIS 2009: 2). Their call focuses on the provision of money to assist adaptation – assuming, not unreasonably, that adapting to rising sea levels will be expensive and technologically complex. Some theorists of global justice have explicitly supported such calls. Simon Caney (2010: 222), for instance, has advocated the establishment of a 'global adaptation fund', paid for by wealthy states which are responsible for most historical emissions, and charged with helping less fortunate communities adapt their way of life in the face of the various threats produced by climate change. But perhaps providing money to fund local adaptation will not be a fully adequate response. It may turn out that *migration* is actually the only 'adaptation' strategy available to many inhabitants of AOSIS states, albeit a drastic one. By way of example, the president of Kiribati – an AOSIS member – has proposed a radical plan to scatter the entire Kiribati population of 100,000 people throughout the world before Kiribati is submerged (Risse 2009: 281).

How might we respond to the plight of such people – people who have been, or are likely to be, displaced as a result of sea-level rises? Two recent arguments have emphasised that the only just and practicable solution is likely to be a *right to immigrate* into other countries. Matthias Risse, first, has suggested a human-rights-based response. The core of his position is that, since we all live in a world which we collectively own (see chapter 5), then a just global order ought to guarantee that we are able to meet our basic needs (Risse 2009: 293). For people displaced by rising sea levels, the only way of doing so is to join another political community which is not threatened by sea-level rises. Byravan and Rajan, second, have addressed the same question, and have similarly argued for 'special rights of free global movement and resettlement ... in advance of disaster' (Byravan and Rajan 2010: 241).

But if there is a right to migrate as a result of sea-level rises, this presumably must be matched by corresponding duties on the part of unaffected countries to actually offer citizenship or permanent residence to these migrants. Here, we shall want to ask two familiar questions. First, what *kind* of duty are we talking about? One response might be that other countries owe a duty of humanitarianism or charitable assistance (this, in effect, is the underlying principle of the international refugee system at present, which is founded on humanitarian principles). But Byravan and Rajan want to present a rather stronger argument, emphasising a clear negative duty not to harm the basic interests of people in other countries – in this case by contributing to climate change. Given that developed countries have failed to observe that duty, they have a duty to help repair the damage – in this case, to admit what they call 'climate exiles' (Byravan and Rajan 2010: 250). This suggests – although it is not quite explicit in their argument – that they conceive of this duty as one of justice. Risse for his part is certainly clear that respecting the right to immigrate 'is not a matter of charity, but of putting into practice what the inhabitants of Kiribati are owed' as a matter of justice (Risse 2009: 293–4).

Second, whatever kind of duty it turns out to be, how do we *distribute* it between different agents? Byravan and Rajan believe that only states can help, since it is precisely states which have jurisdiction over issues of immigration and membership. So they are the right kind of agent to which to distribute responsibilities, even if we think that the duties initially arise because of the harm done by individuals or by corporations. This still leaves an important distributive question unanswered, though: *which* states should admit climate exiles? As we saw in chapter 4, even if we think that we have duties to help outsiders meet their basic interests, this still leaves difficult questions about precisely how to divide up the costs of doing so. We might think that *capacity to help* should again be important, so that countries which were *capable* of absorbing more exiles would be obliged to do so. But Byravan and Rajan instead emphasise *historical responsibility*: they suggest that it makes sense to lay the greater part of the burden of admitting climate exiles on the shoulders of countries which have historically made the greatest contribution to climate change (Byravan and Rajan 2010: 253). Risse's answer is a little more complex, insofar as he believes that both *ability to help* (measured according to national income) and *historical contribution* to the problem (assessed by measuring past emissions) should be factored in when distributing the costs of admitting climate exiles (Risse 2009: 296; Risse also believes that cultural connections between sending and receiving countries might be significant in distributing migrants (2009: 297). In line with the kind of 'holist' account of climate justice that we examined in section 7.2.2.2., Risse then suggests that the contribution made to rehousing climate exiles should be factored in when calculating a nation's overall obligation to bear the costs of dealing with climate change (2009: 297).

We could ask several questions about these proposals, of course. Revisiting a theme from earlier in the chapter, we might ask whether a tight enough link can be made between the plight of climate exiles, on the one hand, and the historical emissions of developed countries, on the other. Can we robustly say in response to the plight of the people of Kiribati that their situation was caused by *this* community emitting *this* much carbon dioxide over *this* period? We could also interrogate the idea that countries should admit exiles at least partly on the basis of their capability, as Risse suggests. How should we understand capability here? Risse suggests that we should interpret it in terms of per capita income, so that wealthier countries should, other things being equal, admit more climate exiles than poorer ones. But perhaps we should pay heed to other elements of capability. Many developed countries are very densely populated (as are many developing countries themselves, of course). Should we therefore place more of the burden on very sparsely populated countries, such as Canada or Australia? Finally, we might reprise the difficult question from section 7.2.2.2 of how countries might offset (or perhaps offload) some ecological duties by taking on others. Risse suggests that if developed countries were to admit climate exiles this might partially absolve them from the duty to make large cuts in their carbon emissions. In that sense a moral 'credit' on one side (admitting exiles) partly excuses a moral 'deficit' on the other (not cutting emissions). That suggests that what is important is making progress towards climate justice overall, and that we should not be too concerned with the precise *ways* in which individual nations make a contribution. But could we extend that argument slightly further, so that developed countries could pay *other* developing countries to rehouse climate exiles? In fact, could we reach a situation whereby developed countries did not have to admit any exiles – or indeed make any emissions cuts – just so long as they had the money to pay less wealthy countries to do so? Would such a situation be morally acceptable, or is there a point where we believe that citizens of wealthier countries *ought* to bear some direct (and not purely financial) sacrifices?

These questions are interesting and important, but they should not obscure the fact that some version of a duty to rehome climate exiles could in principle be endorsed by both egalitarian and minimalist theorists of global justice. Egalitarians might well sympathise with climate exiles' plight – with the way in which they are the apparent victims of other peoples' excessive carbon emissions. They might also be persuaded by Risse's argument that countries agreeing to rehouse climate exiles should be able to count that towards their obligations under any climate change reduction treaty. But since what we are discussing is in effect the defence of very vital or basic interests, the proposals could also appeal to minimalists. Although – as we saw in section 7.2 – David Miller is reluctant to place too much weight on historical responsibility when we distribute responsibilities to *mitigate* climate change, he does suggest that there could be a role for such considerations when we come to distribute the costs of *adaptation* to such climate change as may already be unavoidable (Miller 2009: 151). This is not to say that he would accept Byravan and Rajan's argument in favour of a right to migrate to richer countries, however. For someone might accept a duty of global justice to help climate exiles while also believing that nation states have a robust right to determine exactly who is able to become a member of their community. As we shall see in the final chapter of this book, the connection between theories of global justice and issues of migration is a complex one.

chapter | **8**

Global justice and migration

Throughout this book we have examined various views on the rights and duties people ought to have as a matter of justice, wherever in the world they happen to live. We have also noted the emergence of various human rights which aspire to guarantee a minimum level of provision for everyone. But it remains the case that people enjoy the vast majority of their rights and duties as *members* of the specific political communities in which they live. The world of separate nation states has proven an enduring feature of political life, and one which substantially affects the opportunities available to people. In that sense membership is perhaps the most significant good which is distributed between individuals, since *where* we are a member is hugely important in determining the other goods to which we shall have access (Walzer 1983: 63). Given the facts of global inequality, membership of some communities is a much better 'deal' than others.

All of this might not matter, of course, if people could simply change their membership at will. But for the vast majority of people this is not easy. For one thing, entry to another country is by and large at the discretion of the 'receiving' state. The nation states of the world operate relatively 'hard' borders, which they use military force to maintain. For another thing, even if entry to another state *was* granted, it is no small endeavour to save the money to relocate oneself (and perhaps one's family) and start a new life in an unfamiliar place. Little wonder, then, that for the vast majority of us the community in which we live is also the community into which we were born. As such most of us enjoy the rights and duties we have largely as a matter of *birth*.

This prompts a series of normative questions. Why should the governments of rich countries be allowed to refuse entry to people seeking a better life? Can good reasons be given for maintaining relatively closed borders? Should countries actually have a duty to *admit* immigrants? If they did, what would be the implications for global poverty and inequality? Just what is the connection between global justice and migration in any case?

This chapter will examine arguments about the justice of restricting immigration and will also consider, once more, the contribution that theories of global justice can make to thinking through the normative issues raised by the migration of people across borders. The case study will begin by noting the distinction between refugees and migrants and then briefly discuss, by way of example, the immigration policy of Japan (box 8.1). Section 8.1 then considers the connection, if any, between global egalitarianism and minimalism, on the one hand, and arguments for open or closed borders on the other. Can we say, for example, that minimalists will tend to be advocates of closed borders, and egalitarians advocates of open ones? In section 8.2 we move on to examine the most prominent arguments in favour of (relatively) open borders. Then, in section 8.3, arguments in favour of restricting immigration – or in favour of (relatively) closed borders – will be considered. Section 8.4 discusses the relationship between migration and distributive justice. Are open-border policies a good response to problems of global injustice, or a poor one? If wealthy states acted on their duties of global justice, would this make it acceptable for them to maintain closed borders? Finally, section 8.5, the 'Further issues' section, discusses how we should respond to the fact that some states not merely allow, but also *encourage* immigration. The specific case which will occupy us is the active recruitment by wealthy countries of health-care professionals from poorer ones, which is often said to have a negative impact on the latter. What, if anything, ought to be done to minimise the impact on poorer countries?

Box 8.1. **Case study: refugees, migrants and state policy**

Refugees and migrants

International law on migration draws an important distinction between *migrants* and *refugees*. The latter are a sub-category of migrants who are afforded a special legal status. According to the 1951 UN Convention Relating to the Status of Refugees, refugees are individuals who have a 'well-founded fear of being persecuted for reasons of … membership of a particular social group', such as race, religion or culture (UN 1951). As a result of this persecution, they have particularly urgent claims to admission to the safe haven of another country (Wellman 2010:14). Migrants, on the other hand, are generally speaking people who want voluntarily to move to a different country, to find a better life or advance their own personal goals (and who are often therefore called 'voluntary' or 'economic migrants'). Here international law is much more permissive, leaving it largely up to potential 'receiving' states to decide whether to admit migrants.

This division is not perfect. For one thing, the set of social groups whose persecution qualifies them as refugees appears rather arbitrary. Most notably, the refugee system offers no (or very patchy) protection for people persecuted because of their sex or their sexuality. But we might also ask more fundamentally why people who experience persecution should be exclusively entitled to an urgent claim to admission (Shacknove 1985). Persecution is, to be sure, a terrible problem. But if what concerns us about persecution is that it prevents someone living a life of minimal decency, let's say, then why shouldn't we accord the same 'urgent' status to anyone affected by severe poverty? If the concern is that persecution presents what we called in chapter 4 a 'standard threat' to refugees' basic rights, then it is not that difficult to point towards *other* such threats. We noted at the end of chapter 7, for instance, that so-called 'climate exiles' also have their basic interests seriously affected by sea-level rises. Why not treat them in the same way as refugees? Nevertheless, although the boundary between refugees and economic migrants might be questionable from a moral point of view, states themselves have stood firmly behind it.

Immigration: the case of Japan

Even in a world of relatively closed borders, Japan has for decades operated an unusually restrictive immigration policy. Just 1.7 per cent of the population of Japan is foreign or foreign-born – the smallest proportion of any industrialized country (Fuess 2003: 243). Its refugee policy has certainly lagged behind other industrialized countries: Japan did not ratify the 1951 Convention Relating to the Status of Refugees until 1981, and not until the late 1970s, under international pressure, did it begin to admit refugees in any significant numbers (in this case from Indonesia). Although subsequent waves of refugees have arrived on the shores of Japan – from Vietnam in the late 1980s, for instance – its participation in the international refugee regime has remained rather lukewarm. To be more specific, while Japan has declared itself prepared to *fund* the relocation of refugees, it has proven reluctant to actually admit them to Japanese citizenship.

Japan's policy on economic migrants has been similarly restrictive. The curious point about Japanese immigration policy, according to many external observers, is that it often appears to be at odds with its own economic interests. Demographically Japan is a country with a rapidly declining birth rate. Its population is predicted to fall from 127 million to below 100 million by 2055 (Harlan 2010). At the same time it has a rapidly ageing population. Both facts work together to produce pressure on the shrinking native working population, both to support the growing population of retired people and to care for them. Many developed countries face similar problems, and as a result have begun to pursue policies of 'replacement migration' (UN 2001). They have also admitted significant numbers of young workers from overseas, often with fixed-term visas, to work in areas of high demand such as health care. But Japan has stubbornly resisted such strategies. The broad emphasis of immigration policy has been to exclude unskilled workers and to admit highly skilled professionals only when strictly necessary. Although relatively small numbers of low-skilled foreign workers are admitted, they must pass a test – in Japanese, with a pass-rate of less than 1 per cent – or else return to their own country (Harlan 2010). Those who are permitted to stay are frequently designated 'foreign trainees' and paid well below the minimum wage for native citizens (Yamanaka 1993).

Despite its demographic and economic challenges, this restrictive policy enjoys substantial popular support. Opinion polls regularly reaffirm Japanese citizens' commitment to maintaining the ethnic and cultural homogeneity of their country (Fuess 2003). In this sense the Japanese government – and to a large extent the Japanese citizenry – appears to prioritise the maintenance of national culture over and above both their apparent long-term economic needs and any obligations they might be thought to have to admit migrants.

8.1. Egalitarian and minimalist approaches to migration?

The debate about the ethics of migration is often said to be waged between advocates of 'open borders' and advocates of 'closed borders'. But we should be clear at the outset that this is potentially misleading, for two main reasons. First, there is broad support for the international refugee regime, despite its many faults. So advocates of closed borders are not necessarily arguing that we should close borders to *refugees*. Other migrants, often called 'voluntary' or 'economic' migrants, are the target of their arguments. Second, even here the debate is not really between those who would throw borders open entirely and those who would refuse entry to any migrants whatsoever. Advocates of 'open borders' tend not to argue for *completely* open borders, but for a duty to allow a *substantially higher* level of immigration. They may believe that some arguments for restricting immigration are good ones, but nevertheless assert that contemporary nation states have got the balance wrong. So in section 8.2 we shall consider arguments for relatively open borders, by which we shall mean arguments for substantially increasing the inflow of migrants. Likewise, when we discuss arguments for limiting immigration in section 8.3 we shall not be considering arguments for denying access to anyone *at all*. Rather, we shall generally be considering arguments why states should be able to restrict immigration to a certain level. So here we shall talk of relatively closed borders. Advocates of relatively closed borders will be advocating *something* like the status quo of contemporary political practice.

Given that word of caution, can we observe any simple relationship between global egalitarianism or minimalism, on the one hand, and arguments for (relatively) open or (relatively) closed borders, on the other? The answer is: not really. Someone could be a global egalitarian and yet believe that immigration can legitimately be substantially restricted by receiving states. Indeed, she might believe that if we managed to move to a world which was much more equal than ours, there would be much less *need* for migration. Even in the meantime she might think that allowing relatively unrestricted migration would be a very bad means of ensuring greater global equality (we shall return to that idea in section 8.4).

By the same token, if someone was a minimalist about global justice this need not mean that he would also, automatically, support relatively closed borders. As it happens both Rawls (1999) and Miller (2008) have defended restrictions on immigration. But we should be clear that a minimalist about global justice *could* coherently support relatively open borders, either for reasons which flow directly from his account of global justice (for example, he might believe that more open borders would allow more people to meet their basic needs), or for reasons which are basically unconnected (our minimalist might just believe, very strongly, in a right to free movement across borders, for example).

That said, we should be aware that there are *some* connections between support for egalitarianism or minimalism, on the one hand, and support for relatively open or closed borders, on the other. For one thing, although key global egalitarians such as Beitz, Caney or Moellendorf have not said a great deal about issues of migration, defenders of open borders – as we shall see in the next section – have often employed arguments with which global egalitarians might be expected to sympathise. It has been suggested, for example, that one problem with a world of fairly closed borders is that it produces global inequality of opportunity, so that our opportunities depend on the 'morally arbitrary' fact of where we happen to have been born. Global egalitarians need not agree that achieving more open borders would be the best means of serving the goal of global equality of opportunity. But the kinds of *reasons* given for supporting egalitarianism and for more open borders overlap at least partially. So we could expect many of them to sympathise with the equality-inspired criticism of closed borders which we shall discuss in the next section, even if they do not necessarily agree about the best response to the problem.

We can make a similar observation about global minimalism and arguments for more closed borders. To be specific, the *reasons* given for restricting immigration partially overlap with the reasons global minimalists give for rejecting egalitarian redistribution across borders. This is most obvious in the case of David Miller, whose arguments for relatively closed borders we shall address later on. As we know from chapter 3, in his defence of the normative importance of nationality Miller emphasises the significance of a *shared culture*, which provides people with a valuable and stable set of moral horizons. That specific shared culture makes egalitarianism appropriate domestically. But the fact that achieving equality demands both shared cultural understandings and the motivation to make sacrifices for one's fellows counts against global egalitarianism as an approach to global justice. As we shall see in section 8.3, the importance to people of a shared national culture is also held, by Miller, to support limits on immigration. Another common objection to global egalitarianism is that it is incompatible with national self-determination (Miller 2007; but see Armstrong 2010). For some authors, a concern for the self-determination of individual countries is held to also support restrictions on immigration. Thus while there is no simple connection between egalitarianism and minimalism and arguments for open or closed borders, there is a partial overlap in the justifications sometimes offered for those positions.

8.2. Arguments for (relatively) open borders

The arguments we are going to consider in this section, then, are arguments for increasing the flow of immigrants into receiving states. Defenders of relatively open borders can admit that there are some normative considerations that count in favour of restricting immigration to which we ought to give weight when thinking about migration. But they believe that many nation states have not given sufficient consideration to the arguments in favour of more open borders. If they had, they would likely have allowed substantially higher numbers of immigrants to settle in their communities. Some of these arguments (especially arguments based on freedom, section 8.2.1) apply to all countries and suggest that migration should be an easier option wherever people happen to live. Others (especially arguments based on equality, section 8.2.2) seem to apply most obviously to a world in which *wealthy* countries exclude migrants from poorer countries, at the cost of preserving the radically unequal opportunities between their inhabitants.

8.2.1. Freedom-based arguments

Liberals typically argue that there are certain key freedoms (including freedom of movement, association, and thought and expression) which are so very crucial to a good life that they ought not to be restricted by the state at all, unless restricting them is necessary to defend *other* people's freedoms. That is why Rawls, for example, gives general priority to freedom over other normative values in his account of justice (Rawls 1971). But if freedom is so very important to people, it is a valid question whether the defence of at least some of these freedoms ought to be extended globally. Joseph Carens has made just such an argument based on the idea of *freedom of movement* (Carens 1992, 1987). He suggests that there is a *basic human right* to free international movement. As citizens, he notes, we are standardly allowed freedom of movement within whatever community we belong to. If I want to move upstate to be nearer my parents, or relocate to the north of my country to seek a better-paid job, or go to live in a major city where there are more people who share my religion or culture, I am free to do so – at least in minimally liberal states. But, Carens suggests, all the reasons why we might value that freedom of movement also apply *across* borders, at least for some people (1992: 27–8). People also regularly want to relocate across borders for reasons of love, work or religion, for example. If the freedom to do so is important, it is not clear why we ought to have a right to freedom of movement *within* communities but not the same right to relocate *between* communities. Carens suggests, to the contrary, that we have a good case for a human right to freedom of movement – and this in turn would have major implications for an account of the ethics of migration.

This argument has been disputed. David Miller, as we shall recall from chapter 4, claims that genuine human rights have to be grounded in basic human interests or needs. Basic human needs are those we need to fulfil in order to live a decent life. They may also be crucial in allowing us to secure our *other* needs or interests. But it is not clear, Miller suggests, that we do have a basic interest in being able to move across national borders (Miller 2005b). If we live in a well-functioning liberal state, and have our basic needs securely met, why, then, say that we have a basic interest in being able to migrate across borders? Is being able to move across borders really necessary to the fulfilment of our other basic interests? Of course we might well have a basic interest in free movement if we were the victims of persecution or starvation in the country where we lived. But if we *were* able to meet our basic needs within the community in which we live, then although we might have an *interest* in moving across borders (because that might allow us to advance the various projects which are important to us), this is not the kind of *basic* interest that would necessarily trump the right of other communities to control their own borders (see section 8.3). Miller's objection concedes, in effect, that many people do have a basic interest in migrating across borders, but denies that this basic interest is general enough for us to call it a genuine human right.

8.2.2. Equality-based arguments

The equality-based argument has a similar structure, which should be familiar by now: we generally believe in equality of opportunity. This is often taken to mean that 'Access to social positions should be determined by an individual's actual talents and capacities, not limited on the basis of arbitrary native characteristics (such as class, race, or sex)' (Carens 1992: 26). The defender of open borders, like the global egalitarian, wants to add *nationality* to that list of arbitrary characteristics which should not determine our opportunities (although see Armstrong 2010). Arguing that individuals *should* enjoy better or worse opportunities just because of their nationality is not easy, just as it is not easy to make the same arguments in relation to race or sex. Nevertheless the world of nation states violates equality of opportunity at every turn. Our opportunities *are* strongly influenced by our country of birth – and the system of nation states coercively maintains that inequality, by preventing the free movement of people.

Carens draws a comparison between this situation and the medieval feudal system which assigned lots in life based on birth:

> Citizenship in the modern world is a lot like feudal status in the medieval world. It is assigned at birth; for the most part it is not subject to change

by the individual's will and efforts; and it has a major impact upon that person's life chances ... limiting entry to countries like Canada is a way of protecting a birthright privilege. (Carens 1992: 26)

Different countries actually allocate citizenship in two general ways. Some assign it on the basis of birthplace, whereas others assign it on the basis of parenthood or sometimes ethnic or linguistic identity. Most commonly there is some mixture of the two principles. But neither really appears any less arbitrary than the other, in the sense that neither birthplace nor blood are the result of individual choice.

The very same comparison – between the contemporary system of national citizenship and a feudal society where status is assigned by birth – has been made by Ayelet Shachar and Ran Hirschl (2007). They, too, suggest that citizenship is a form of inherited 'birthright'. Inheriting citizenship from one's parents is rather like inheriting money from them (something to which many liberal egalitarians take exception). But in fact the inheritance of citizenship is even more worrying, because 'the incredible gaps in life opportunities created and perpetuated by birthright citizenship regimes are far deeper and more multifaceted' than any inequalities produced by the inheritance of wealth (Shachar and Hirschl 2007: 259). When a person inherits citizenship of a wealthy, liberal state, she also inherits (whereas those less fortunate do not) a right to vote, to enjoy free education, health and welfare provision and so on.

There is some disagreement as to what the right remedy for this continuing injustice is, though. Carens's suggestion is that to hold firm to their apparently liberal egalitarian principles, wealthy states should admit far more economic migrants than they do now. But Shachar and Hirschl recommend instead a 'birthright privilege levy', according to which citizens of wealthy liberal states should pay into a global fund which would aim to tackle serious global poverty. Rather than preventing wealthy states from excluding migrants, this would leave that privilege intact but try to reduce its drastic consequences for the life chances of people throughout the world. Their proposal would 'address the global distributive consequences of birthright citizenship by "taxing" [its] intergenerational transmission' (Shachar and Hirschl 2007: 278).

If we agree that the transmission of citizenship – and the other privileges that come along with it – through birth or blood leads to injustice, which is the more appropriate solution? Admitting more immigrants, or taxing the citizens of wealthy states in order to pursue the goals of global justice? At first sight neither approach looks likely to be fully successful in dealing with the problem it diagnoses. The birthright privilege levy would address global poverty, but it would not do much to tackle the global inequality which is condemned both by Carens and by Shachar and Hirschl. It would partially redistribute some wealth away from developed countries, but still leave their advantages largely intact. Carens's solution – to admit more immigrants – would also fail to end the disadvantage he diagnoses. If wealthy states admitted substantially more immigrants, this would benefit those immigrants greatly. But there is no suggestion that they should admit *everyone* suffering from poverty in the developing world. The numbers involved are just too large. What would Carens's solution do for those who remained? As we shall see in section 8.4, the usefulness of immigration policy as a vehicle of global justice is much in dispute.

Those who believe that the state has a right to decide whether to admit immigrants might prefer Shachar and Hirschl's solution, since it leaves that right intact. Thus Christopher Heath Wellman conjures up the example of a rich (but single) man, to whose great wealth the egalitarian objects. We could target that wealth in two ways – he could be made to pay taxes, or he could be forced to marry someone who is poor. The first solution appears much more appropriate, especially if we think that people have a right to decide who they want to associate with, and therefore marry (Wellman 2010: 10). In just the same way, Wellman suggests, we should prefer redistributing resources to forcing states to absorb immigrants they would rather not associate with.

However, this analogy is not necessarily all that straightforward. For one thing, Wellman has produced an example where we have to choose between helping one person (by allowing her to marry our rich man), and helping many (by taxing his wealth or income). In this case helping many people appears much more appropriate from an egalitarian point of view. But we do not face quite the same situation in the migration case – the debate really is about how best to help *many* people, and this makes the moral mathematics slightly more difficult. For another thing, Wellman is deliberately drawing on the repulsion many of us might feel at the idea of being forced to marry someone against our will. But we do not necessarily feel quite as strongly about merely sharing our community with immigrants. Advocates of open borders are arguing that admitting more migrants is required by justice. They are not arguing that justice requires anyone to befriend or marry particular immigrants, which might plausibly be left to personal choice. Finally, although Wellman has us focus on the rich man's ability to pass on his wealth through marriage, many people – or many egalitarians, anyway – will be much more concerned with his ability to pass on his great advantages to his *descendants* (who have presumably done nothing to deserve them). Many egalitarians, at least, feel that this is intuitively wrong. And if we agree with that, then egalitarians can again try to persuade us that passing on the many advantages of citizenship through birth is also morally suspect.

8.3. Arguments for (relatively) closed borders

Strictly speaking, if we are looking for an argument why nation states should be allowed to exclude potential migrants from their territory, we shall also need an argument why they should be allowed to control that territory in the first place. We cannot very well say that the French people can exclude Chileans from French territory without first knowing why it is actually *their* territory. But political theorists have very often failed to address that question directly (Kymlicka 2001: 249–50), and the broader theory of states' territorial rights remains rather in its infancy. For our present purposes we shall take it for granted that there are separate nation states, and that they are in principle entitled to exercise dominion over their own territories. *Even if* we accept this we still need to ask why they are entitled to exclude potential immigrants from that territory. Defenders of relatively closed borders want to argue that there are weighty normative reasons why nation states should be entitled to restrict immigration. The argument is not necessarily going to be that nation states can legitimately decide not to admit any immigrants at all. To the contrary, many of the arguments considered below suggest that it is the *scale* of potential immigration which makes it problematic. As a result – although it might be thought that contemporary states have sometimes been mistaken about the appropriate criteria for admitting migrants, or that they have often made bad policy decisions – arguments for relatively closed borders are arguments for something like the status quo, in which many richer countries in particular strictly limit the numbers of migrants they choose to admit, or admit them only when they have clear economic interests in doing so.

8.3.1. Culture-based arguments

Many contemporary liberal thinkers believe that a stable cultural background is vitally important in allowing individuals to lead fulfilling lives. The goals and relationships which define a fulfilling life are themselves determined within individual cultures, which provide a moral 'horizon' or 'background' against which we can understand our lives and our place in the world (Margalit and Raz 1990; Kymlicka 1989: 162–78). In Miller's view this cultural background is provided first and foremost by *national* communities, which bring along with them 'a rich cultural inheritance' (Miller 1995: 184). Nations, we might say, are 'communities of character' in the sense that they display consistent characteristics over time. They are also ethical communities in the sense that co-nationals can have special duties towards each other that they do not have to outsiders and that, given the right conditions, we can plausibly hold them collectively responsible for their decisions, and even for decisions taken by their ancestors.

According to this view a stable national culture is hugely important to people. If that is right, then, as Miller puts it, 'the public culture of their country is something that people have an interest in controlling' (2005b: 200). If a national culture was eroded, or if it changed too quickly, it would cease to provide that vital shared background. This interest in controlling a shared public culture, Miller believes, has consequences for the issue of immigration. Unfortunately the sheer flow of immigrants into a country could potentially outstrip the receiving country's ability to incorporate them into the dominant public culture. That culture might then fracture or disintegrate. Although another key theorist of global justice, John Rawls, remains almost entirely silent on issues of migration, he does gesture towards a similar argument at one point in *The Law of Peoples*. In a footnote he briefly suggests that peoples have 'at least a qualified right to limit immigration'. Although he does not quite tell us why they might have that right, he suggests one reason is 'to protect a people's political culture' (Rawls 1999: 39). So what are the practical implications of such an argument? Rawls does not provide us with an answer to this question. Miller's own claim, though, is not that *any* immigration would have a detrimental effect on a shared public culture. Nations are actually resilient communities which are capable of change over time (Miller 1995). The point is rather that there is bound to be some level of immigration which places unbearable strain on the shared public culture. Miller's concrete conclusion, then, is that using quotas to limit the flow of immigration is legitimate, so that immigrants can become integrated into the public culture without threatening its integrity.

There is a second, related culture-based argument. As we saw in chapter 3, Miller believes a shared national culture is hugely useful in getting citizens to accept the kind of sacrifices – and the kind of orientation towards the common good – which are essential if we want to uphold both social justice and democracy. The general idea here is that 'The sort of solidarity required by a welfare state presupposes that citizens have a strong sense of common identity and common membership, so that they will make sacrifices for each other' (Kymlicka 2001: 265). For Miller this common identity is only reliably secured by a shared nationality. As a result, too much immigration may well erode support for the welfare state (and perhaps for democracy too): 'a culturally divided society without a source of unity to hold its constituent groups together would be unlikely to support a democratic welfare state' (Miller 2008: 9). Immigration is worrying, then, if it erodes the public culture, and the erosion of public culture is worrying in turn if it leads to diminishing support for democracy or the welfare state.

There are two challenges that this culture-based argument has to address. The first disputes the claim that immigration weakens support for domestic institutions, and that this provides a good reason for restricting it. The idea that immigration erodes support for domestic institutions has been widely contested (see e.g. Abizadeh 2002; Banting et al. 2006; Holtug 2010). But so has the suggestion that if immigration *did* erode support for domestic institutions, this might provide a good reason for restricting it. To see why, we need to investigate just what advocates of the culture-based argument for restricting immigration are actually claiming. They might be claiming that new *immigrants* will fail to show adequate support for the welfare state or democracy, and that this will weaken such institutions. Or they might be claiming that *current citizens* will become disaffected from such institutions if migrants of diverse backgrounds enter their country. If the argument is the latter – as it often seems to be – then the culture-based argument is really arguing that we should make potential immigrants pay the cost of domestic prejudices. This appears morally suspect to say the least (Pevnick 2009; see also Carens 1992: 32).

A second challenge suggests that the culture-based argument is really best directed at the *type* of immigrant who might be admitted, and not just the *number* of immigrants. After all, concerns about the erosion of national culture – or the resulting erosion of support for institutions such as the welfare state – only follow if we presume that potential immigrants have a culture that is substantially different from the domestic population. If our concern is to preserve a broadly shared culture, then surely there would be no problem with admitting people who already share much the same culture as the receiving country (Wellman 2010)? If so, we might think that the government of New Zealand ought to be ready to admit any number of migrants from Australia (or Canada from the United States). But we also might think that it *was* entitled to deny entry to people who did not share its culture (whether from Africa, Asia or elsewhere). The suspicion is that the culture-based argument is better designed to defend excluding certain *types* of immigrants than it does to restricting numbers per se – but this is not the position that defenders of closed borders tend to have defended. Miller, for instance, wants to say that it *is* legitimate to restrict entry to those prepared to accept liberal democratic values – and it might, in some cases, be legitimate to enforce language requirements too (Miller 2008:

19; see also Meilaender 1999). But it would be *illegitimate* to make cultural background or ethnicity a criterion in selecting would-be immigrants. On one view, that would potentially show disrespect to both potential migrants and the existing domestic population (Blake 2003). Advocates of the culture-based argument tend to have steered clear, then, of culture-based criteria for selecting one kind of immigrant over another.

8.3.2. Self-determination-based arguments

It has also been said that robbing a country of the right to decide how many immigrants to admit – and perhaps also *which* immigrants to admit – robs it in turn of its self-determination as a political community. For a relatively early statement of this view, we could turn to Michael Walzer. Walzer famously argued that 'Admission and exclusion are at the core of communal independence. They suggest the deepest meaning of self-determination' (Walzer 1983: 62). It is hard to see how a community could be self-determining, Walzer suggests, if it did not have this basic right to determine the rules of membership. He draws an analogy between a nation state and a club. Just like a club, a country cannot refuse exit to members who want to leave. But it can refuse entry to people who want to join. Broadly speaking, Walzer also believes that individual countries should be able to operate their own criteria for selecting potential immigrants – with some possible exceptions. He does appear to be disturbed by cases in which countries employ racist criteria to deny entry to people of the 'wrong' origins, as many countries have done in the past. But even here it is not clear that he would reject the option entirely (1983: 47).

A similar kind of argument has been put forward more recently by Andrew Altman and Christopher Heath Wellman. They present a very strong defence of the case for closed borders, which holds that states even have a claim to refuse entry to refugees if they so choose (Altman and Wellman 2009: 158). Their account suggests that the right to control borders is a core part of self-determination, but they also emphasise the importance of a related value: freedom of association. Like freedom of movement, freedom of association is usually held to be a core liberal value. But, crucially, whereas freedom of movement is sometimes taken to justify open borders, Altman and Wellman take freedom of association to justify *closed* borders. For if we ought to be free to associate with others, that must include the freedom to *refuse* to associate with others if we do not want to. Just as no one should be forced to marry someone they do not want to marry, no community should be forced to admit immigrants whom it does not want to admit (2009: 159). The authors concede, in fact, that marrying someone is a much more intimate decision than admitting someone you may never meet into your country, but they maintain that both fall within the proper sphere of freedom of association. Individuals rightly care about their countries, and who is admitted into that country is legitimately a matter of no small concern to them (2009: 162–3). So in that sense the parallel with marriage still holds: any (legitimate) state should be able to decide just who it associates with, and this justifies a strong right to deny entrance to any potential immigrants. That said, Altman and Wellman share Miller's conclusion that it would be illegitimate to employ just *any* criteria for deciding who to admit into a country. Specifically, they are much clearer than Walzer that a racist criterion would be unacceptable. But, crucially, it would not be inadmissible because it fails to treat the potential immigrant with sufficient respect. Rather, refusing to admit, say, Mexicans into your country would show insufficient respect to the Mexicans *already* living in your country, who would rightly feel themselves marked out as 'inferior' by such a policy (Altman and Wellman 2009: 187; see also Blake 2003).

What challenges are faced by the self-determination-based argument? First of all, what of Carens's charge that this right to exclude potential immigrants entrenches global distributive injustice? Even if Altman and Wellman are right that a claim to be able to reject potential immigrants is an important part of self-determination, is this claim important enough to offset the good which admitting poorer immigrants might do in reducing global poverty? Here their response is simply that there are different ways of addressing global injustice, and individual states should be free to choose between them. They agree that we do have substantial duties of global distributive justice. But they also suggest that admitting immigrants would be a rather ineffective way of discharging those duties. Admitting migrants only helps a relatively small number of people, and may in fact harm 'sending' countries who could be deprived of vital skills. As a result 'sending aid abroad is a better way to rescue those imperilled by poverty' (Altman and Wellman 2009: 1274; see also Miller 2005b). We shall return to this issue in the next section.

A second challenge concerns whether the appeal to the idea of freedom of association is really sufficient to justify the conclusion that states are entitled to prevent outsiders from obtaining citizenship. For instance, we can return again to the question whether admitting someone to a country in itself violates a citizen's right to freedom of association. David Miller, for one, is doubtful that the mere presence of an immigrant in my community damages my interest in freedom of association. I am not forced, after all, to associate with the new immigrant any more than I wish to (Miller 2007: 210–11). In that sense sharing citizenship with someone is quite unlike being married to them (see also Fine 2010: 349).

Alternatively, we might grant the argument arising from freedom of association – and admit that being forced to share citizenship with someone *does* harm me in some way – but claim that this harm has to be weighed against the harm which could be done to someone when we *refuse* to allow them to immigrate. Sarah Fine (2010) suggests that refugees in particular may have their interests seriously harmed if they are refused entry to another state. Although Altman and Wellman's acceptance of global distributive duties is welcome, sending resources to a poor country is little consolation to a citizen being persecuted *right now* by its undemocratic rulers. For such people migration does appear to be the only way to escape serious harm, and it is difficult to see why that harm might be outweighed by the damage done to native citizens' interest in freedom of association. Moreover, even if we restrict our attention to freedom of association, we can easily point to *tensions* between *different* actors' freedom to associate with whom they choose. Altman and Wellman focus on the state as a whole, and suggest that forcing a community to admit immigrants is akin to forcing marriage on people. But ironically, one of the major reasons for migration in the contemporary world is family reunification. In this instance, the decision of a community not to admit immigrants will mean that some citizens are *unable* to live in the same state as their spouses or other family members. Such a decision clearly harms their own freedom of association in a very fundamental way, and suggests that the value of freedom of association can be used to criticise closed borders as well as to defend them.

8.3.3. Economics-based arguments

Within political debates and in the media, some of the most prominent arguments for limiting immigration emphasise neither shared culture nor self-determination, but the practical consequences of admitting 'too many' immigrants for the purse strings of a country. There are two main varieties of argument. The first suggests that admitting migrants from poorer countries will drive down wages and as such leave the 'native' poor worse off. The second suggests that immigrants will place unbearable demands on public services, and perhaps make the existing level of provision of education, health and welfare services unaffordable. This is different, note, from the argument (examined in section 8.3.1) which suggests that immigration will undermine popular support for public services. The argument here is independent of that claim, and focuses specifically on the *financial* cost of admitting more immigrants. Perhaps liberal welfare states are only able to be as generous as they are *because* membership is strictly limited.

The first argument is interesting because it suggests something of an 'egalitarian dilemma'. The fear is that if substantial numbers of immigrants are admitted, the wages of poorer workers will be driven down, and that this will count against rather than for domestic equality (Macedo 2007). Perhaps this is a case, then, where we have to choose between national and global egalitarian goals. Those with broadly global egalitarian sympathies, of course, may believe that if this is right, our choice should be clear. Given that inhabitants of wealthy states are currently deriving a morally arbitrary advantage from their location – here, very high wages, globally speaking – we should not be too worried if a little redistribution of earning power takes place.

Why, after all, do workers in richer (and capitalist) countries have a right to be protected from competition from overseas (Moellendorf 2002: 63)? But the empirical facts about the likely impact of immigration on wages are in any case complex and contested. One thing that is clear is that developed countries themselves exhibit clearly opposed economic interests. Whereas representatives of workers do sometimes bemoan the driving down of wages through immigration, employers themselves often lobby their governments to allow it to continue, believing that they benefit from the influx of often highly skilled and motivated workers. Immigration is often held to produce benefits in growth and productivity, which *might* improve the position of the worst-off overall.

The second argument points towards the strain which could be placed on the welfare states of richer countries by large rises in immigration. These welfare states are already stretched, of course, by an ageing population, and by budget cuts following on from the financial crisis of 2008 – and even before that they had been scaled back by the broadly 'neoliberal' reforms of the 1980s. Once again the suggestion is that there is a kind of trade-off, whereby we are forced to choose between pursuing equality 'at home' or abroad. And once again, some theorists with global egalitarian sympathies will be rather unmoved: if countries do not in fact deserve the wealth or resources that they currently have, perhaps we should not spend too much time worrying about their inability to continue lavishing spending on their own citizens (see e.g. Carens 1988). But others will be more concerned that increased migration will lead to a further dismantling of the relatively few functioning welfare states in the world. Once again we are faced with a complex economic question which it is not within our power to answer definitively. One counter-argument to this general concern, though, is that given the shrinking birth rate and ageing population of many wealthy countries, the functioning of their welfare states and health-care systems will likely become more dependent on migrant labour in the future (with Japan providing an interesting example). If so, then we should be careful not to exaggerate or over-simplify the tension between immigration and the cost of maintaining the welfare state.

8.4. Migration and global justice

The last two sections have examined arguments for and against opening borders to larger numbers of migrants. The arguments on each side have proven to be complex and contested. But now I want to pick up an argument which has raised its head at a number of points, but which we have not managed to address properly yet. More than one defender of closed borders has suggested that it would be permissible to close borders if a country adhered to its broader duties of global distributive justice – and in particular, if it redistributed resources abroad. Indeed even some critics of closed borders have suggested that sending resources abroad might be a better response to global injustice than opening borders.

Thus Altman and Wellman, as we saw in section 8.3.2, have argued that sending aid abroad would do more to tackle global poverty than opening borders to fixed numbers of poor migrants. They are not alone in this view (see also Pogge 2006; Miller 2005b). Will Kymlicka similarly suggests that it would be permissible for liberal democracies to deny entry to migrants so long as they paid up to a 'global resource tax' requiring them to 'share their wealth with poorer countries' (Kymlicka 2001: 271). Broadly speaking, this is also John Rawls's position. Rawls suggested that if well-ordered societies made good on the duty of assistance and ensured that all societies were able to become well-ordered, there would be no reason for a large degree of migration across borders. Once that happens 'the problem of immigration ... is eliminated as a serious problem' (Rawls 1999: 9).

At the same time, some critics of closed borders are themselves sceptical that opening borders would be the best solution to global injustice. That is certainly the view of Shachar and Hirschl, who advocate a 'birthright levy' by way of which richer countries would in effect compensate poorer countries for maintaining their own restrictive citizenship regimes. Kok-Chor Tan, likewise, suggests that it is the fact of extensive global inequality which makes the current regime of 'hard' borders morally problematic. If we could secure a more egalitarian world, though, hard borders might not be objectionable (Tan 2004: 176).

So there is almost a consensus, it seems, that redistributing resources might be a better option than admitting more migrants, if reducing global injustice is our goal. But do we have sound reasons for believing this? There appear to be two main concerns about the potential of more open borders to seriously erode global poverty. The first concerns just who will be helped by an open-doors policy, and the second concerns the broader socio-economic effects of migration.

First, then, there are good questions to be asked about just *who* would be better off if we made the borders of rich countries substantially more open to immigrants. Even if we made borders substantially more open, we would likely only make a small dent in the 1.3 billion people in poverty worldwide (Pogge 2006). Furthermore, there are good reasons for believing that many inhabitants of poor countries would prefer *not* to migrate to other countries even if that was possible – perhaps because they have strong ties at home, or attachments to their own national culture. We should also recognise that those who *do* currently choose to migrate tend to be wealthier and more economically advantaged than their compatriots. As it stands, then, it seems fair to say that 'international migration provides extremely generous returns to a very limited group of recipients' (Shachar and Hirschl 2007: 277). More open borders would expand that group of recipients, but many more people would still fall through the net.

But perhaps greater migration might help even those who remained behind? Do sending countries benefit from many of their more talented and wealthy individuals leaving? This directs us to our second concern, which focuses on the broader socio-economic effects of migration. Here the picture is mixed at best. On the one hand, migrants working in developed countries often send back money to their families, and these remittances can be hugely important. They might be spent on setting up businesses in the sending country or paying for better educational opportunities, for instance. On the other hand, as we shall see in the next section, there can be hugely negative consequences for domestic institutions when a large portion of the highly skilled population of a given developing country decides to up and move abroad in search of higher wages. The empirical effects of migration are strongly contested, but it has recently been suggested that in many cases this 'brain drain' effect could easily outweigh any positive effect of remittances (Kapur and McHale 2009).

Is the (partial) consensus – that reducing poverty directly is a better option than admitting more migrants – therefore correct? Might rich countries therefore be entirely justified in maintaining relatively closed borders, so long as they adhere to their duties of global justice? There are good reasons for accepting the first claim – that redistributing resources is a better idea than moving people, if we want to tackle poverty. But the case for the second claim – that wealthy countries would therefore be justified in closing their borders, so long as they did redistribute resources – is weaker. I want to suggest three reasons for suspicion about that claim. Taken together, they suggest a variety of reasons for believing that greater migration ought still to be a part of the picture if we are interested in moving to a more just world.

First, recall the two major arguments in favour of relatively open borders. We have seen that if what we care about is global equality of opportunity, for instance, or the eradication of poverty, then there are good practical reasons for sending resources abroad rather than opening borders. We might want to quibble with that argument, and say that admitting more immigrants is actually an entirely 'practical' response to global poverty and even, possibly, an easier one to achieve than sending resources abroad. But, in principle, we can accept that there could be good reasons for favouring redistribution of resources over migration as a strategy for global justice, not least if we think that most people would prefer to stay where they are, provided they could enjoy decent opportunities at home. But what about the freedom-based argument? If we give any credit at all to the idea that a world of closed borders unjustifiably curtails individual freedom of movement (or perhaps other freedoms, such as freedom of association), then maintaining closed borders and sending resources abroad begin to look like a less ideal solution. So even if we reduced the impact of closed borders on equality of opportunity, say, they would still operate as a serious restriction on our freedom.

Second, we can question whether redistributing resources is likely to be a fully effective response to the problems which sometimes prompt migration in the first place. Whether this is so depends largely on our view of global justice. If everyone enjoyed equal opportunities the world over, migration probably would dwindle considerably. But it is not clear that minimalist accounts would produce the same result. Redistributing resources to tackle poverty might not prevent the leaders of some developing countries persecuting or oppressing portions of their population. In that sense, individuals might retain a strong interest in migrating, even if their country was the recipient of increased levels of aid. Aid will presumably take a long time to translate into decent and effective institutions, and in the meantime provide scant consolation to people whose human rights are abused or neglected. On Rawls's account this is not supposed to be a problem, of course. After all, the duty of assistance would produce a world of well-ordered societies in which the basic human rights of all members were met (Rawls 1999). But remember that some members of a decent hierarchical society might well be banned from political office because of their sex, ethnicity or religion, and might enjoy hugely inferior rights to education, health care or legal representation (Buchanan 2006: 151). In rejecting an egalitarian approach to global justice, Rawls also refuses to rule out such disadvantages. But are we really prepared to say that people confronted by such disadvantages lack a basic interest in being able to migrate? At the very least we might want to say that redistributing resources will not eliminate the need for an international refugee regime as a safeguard against the abuse of state sovereignty. And if the degree of redistribution we have in mind will still leave in place substantial international inequalities, the drive to migrate to improve one's opportunities would remain. Do we share Rawls's confidence that states have a strong enough interest in maintaining their own territorial integrity and resource base to justify excluding potential migrants, even in the face of highly unequal opportunities?

Third, while we might think that, at the level of justice, redistributing borders would be a better solution to problems of global injustice than opening borders, would something be lost in a world of completely closed borders? We might well suspect that *something* of value would be lost in a world in which different national communities no longer came into close contact with one another. Advocates of multiculturalism, for instance, often want to say that there is actually something valuable in mutual contact between people from different cultures. Such mutual contact makes it possible for people to learn from one another, and at its best provides an enhanced understanding of human diversity and human similarity. A world which achieved global justice but also maintained closed national borders would see us missing out on that possibility.

These three arguments are not intended to question whether redistributing resources is likely to be more effective in tackling injustice than redistributing people. But they are meant to suggest that even in a substantially more just world, there will be good moral reasons for endorsing some degree of migration. As such, the issue of migration promises to command our attention for the foreseeable future.

8.5. Further issues: the international recruitment of health-care workers

So far in this chapter we have been examining arguments about the state's right to exclude potential migrants. That is a hugely important issue in a world characterised by massive inequalities, and in which many poor people would wish to migrate to developed countries. But if our task is to think through the justice and injustice of migration, we ought also to consider another part of the picture. Despite a general tendency to maintain relatively closed borders, the fact is that the governments of developed countries often not only *allow* but also *encourage* some migration from the developing world. Indeed they spend – or allow employers or the managers of public services to spend – large amounts of time and money *recruiting* foreign workers to meet the needs of their economies. But when they do so, their goal is to recruit specific *types* of foreign worker. In the case study (box 8.1) we discussed the example of Japan, which has tended largely to exclude unskilled or low-skilled workers, but (perhaps somewhat grudgingly) admits some professional workers whose skills are in demand in key sectors of the modern economy. Doing so represents a good deal, economically speaking, for the receiving country. Professional workers from overseas provide a ready supply of valuable skills, crucially allowing the receiving state to avoid the cost of educating and training its own domestic workers. And while they may pay tax in the receiving country, these foreign professionals will tend not to claim welfare benefits or state education for their children, or grow old and place demands on its health-care system. Unsurprisingly, then, Japan is far from alone in actively recruiting key professionals from overseas.

The workers concerned are often people from the developing world attracted by the much higher wages on offer – and in that sense migration appears to offer a good deal for them, too. If we concentrate on the sphere of health care, the flow of workers from the developing world to developed countries is a significant one. An estimated 31 per cent of doctors working within the United Kingdom's National Health Service (NHS) are now born overseas, with the majority of them originating from the developing world (Martineau et al. 2004: 3). But the United Kingdom is far from being unique in relying heavily on foreign health-care workers. Looking at the issue from the other point of view, some areas of the developing world have seen a very large outflow of their own health-care workers. Strikingly, roughly 60 per cent of doctors trained in Ghana in the 1980s have now left the country (Eastwood et al. 2005: 1893). Other countries, such as South Africa, Zimbabwe and Nigeria, have also faced substantial losses to their 'human capital' within health care. In total, around 23,000 academically qualified health-care professionals emigrate from Africa each year (Brock 2009: 198).

Does this so-called 'brain drain' have a positive or negative impact on countries which 'export' health-care workers? Will the loss of trained employees be offset by remittances sent home to those employees' families? Here the picture is very mixed, but state responses can provide a general clue as to the overall impact. Some countries appear to have increasingly oriented their economies around training health-care workers who will one day work overseas. There are currently around 150,000 nurses from the Philippines, for example, working abroad (Brock 2009: 198). In such cases, state policy does seem to reflect a belief that remittances will make the migration of health-care workers beneficial, overall, to the domestic economy (Faini 2007). But there are many other cases where remittances do *not* appear to off-set fully the losses to sending countries (Kapur and McHale 2009; see also Clark, Stewart and Clark 2006). Once more, state policy may provide a clue to the perceived overall benefits. We could note, for example, the keenness of many African leaders to curb the flow of their health-care workers overseas. Nelson Mandela, most notably, made a public appeal to the United Kingdom in 1997 to stop 'poaching' South African nurses (Nelson 2004).

So in many cases developing countries are, in effect, investing large sums of money in the 'human capital' of health-care profes-sionals, from which developed countries then go on to benefit. The United Nations has estimated that each such migrant represents a cost to Africa of $184,000 (Eastwood et al. 2005: 1894). Developed coun-tries such as the United Kingdom or the United States, by contrast, have a vast and increasing demand for health-care professionals, and appear to be engaging in 'a deliberate form of free riding' (Martineau et al. 2004). It suits health-care providers, after all, to recruit the best candidates for the jobs they have available. And it also suits the gov-ernments of those countries to spend less, rather than more, on expen-sively educating new generations of doctors and nurses. As a result, as Brock puts it, 'what is effectively happening is that poor countries are subsidizing the health care of citizens of affluent countries, while losing significant resources in the process' (Brock 2009: 199). One result of this is that citizens of developing countries often have even poorer access to medical care – in a context of existing deprivation, and where HIV/AIDS is already placing ever-increasing demands on stretched health-care systems – whereas citizens of developed coun-tries are able to make ever greater demands on their already advanced health-care services.

If there is an issue of distributive justice here – as many have thought – it does not necessarily reside with the migrating workers themselves, who are moving to improve their own prospects. Theorists of global justice are likely to agree that simply forbidding health-care workers to leave their home countries would be impermissible; even those who do not believe that there is a human right to *enter* another country of your choice nevertheless tend to believe that people have a right to *exit* their country should they wish (see e.g. Walzer 1983;

Rawls 1999; Miller 2005b; note, though, that in some instances this right might be circumscribed – perhaps for reasons of national security, for instance). Rather, the major issue presumably relates to the fact that those who sink money into training workers are not those who benefit from it. Moreover, the issue is most pressing in the very poorest countries, which pay the lowest wages to their own doctors and nurses (Martineau et al. 2004). Such countries appear to be deprived, by the actions of developed countries, from the ability to run effective health-care institutions of their own.

What guidance, if any, can the theories discussed in this book offer us in thinking about this issue? Do theories of global justice possess the resources to condemn developed countries' role in recruiting health-care workers, and hence 'free riding' on the training offered by African countries? What we appear to need in this case is an account of exploitation – that is, a general account of just when it is permissible, or impermissible, to benefit from the structural inequalities of the world economy. But we do not have such an account readily to hand; although some theories of global justice have suggested that exploitation exists within the world economy, we lack a detailed account of just what qualifies as exploitation, and where in the economy we should be looking for it. David Miller, for instance, has suggested that nations ought not to exploit each other. He tells us that exploitation occurs, generally speaking, when a rich party (or country) abuses its power when interacting with a weaker party to dictate unfair terms (Miller 2000: 175). But his brief contribution does not quite make it clear whether this principle should, or could, apply to the case of health-care professionals. Other accounts appear to fare less well. In Rawls's case, the *Law of Peoples* (1999) suggests a duty on the part of developed states to assist the least developed in achieving their own independence, and thereafter presumably a duty not to jeopardise that independence. But there are many ways in which a country can take advantage of its own economic superiority short of actually threatening the independence of other societies. Rawls appears to leave 'considerable scope for some societies, even in a Society of Peoples, to take unfair advantage of their weaker consociates' (Tasioulas 2005: 11). The uncompensated dependence of wealthy countries on health-care workers trained in the developing world appears to provide a good example of this (Armstrong 2009a).

If we are convinced that the uncompensated 'poaching' of health-care workers from the developing world provides a form of free riding or exploitation, what would be a suitable response? Two general responses have been suggested – the first of which focuses on cutting off the 'drain' on health-care workers, and the second of which focuses on reducing the disadvantages which that drain can produce.

The first strategy suggests that governments ought to recruit from developing countries only where they have the *permission* of that developing country. Broadly, we would then expect permission to be granted in cases where recruitment is not significantly damaging, or where it is adequately compensated for (see below). We would not expect it to be granted where the developing country in question has serious objections. By way of example, the United Kingdom's NHS, as a result of some international pressure, now officially does not recruit health-care workers from many designated African countries (including South Africa, Zimbabwe and Nigeria). This approach seems to offer a degree of protection to developing countries concerned about the sustainability of their own domestic health-care systems. However, it does not offer a complete solution. Notably, the United Kingdom continues to offer work permits to thousands of health-care professionals from these designated countries every year (Eastwood et al. 2005). One explanation for this is that whereas the NHS is not directly recruiting workers, the UK government is still allowing private-sector employers to employ workers from these countries, especially if they have not been 'actively recruited' but have submitted their own unsolicited applications. In practice, then, the policy has had only a limited effect.

Moreover, even if we could close such loopholes so that workers were only *ever* recruited in circumstances where the developing country in question agrees, it is not clear that that would represent a perfect solution either. On the one hand, it potentially cuts off a valuable opportunity for the workers concerned and for their families. On the other hand, we cannot be sure in any case that granting developing countries a veto on the recruitment of their workers would give them enough bargaining power to guarantee that disadvantage did not result. We might hope, of course, that developing countries would use their veto to ensure that recruitment only occurred when it was genuinely in their interests. But wealthy countries recruit from many developing countries, and the loss of workers from any one of them would not be a great setback from their point of view. The loss of remittances could be a great setback to the developing countries in question, though. The very inequality of the contemporary world economy, and the very prevalence of poverty, may well drive down the 'price' developing countries could realistically extract from wealthy countries.

The second strategy suggests that when health-care workers from developing countries are employed, sending countries should be *directly compensated* for the cost of their training, for lost tax income and/or for the loss of their services (Brock 2009: 202). The compensation in question could be financial, or could take the form of technical or training assistance which developed countries might provide. Notably, whereas the first response to the 'drain' of workers restricts their freedom and opportunities by banning their employment overseas, the second option allows the 'drain' to continue and focuses instead on tackling the disadvantages it can produce. Once again there have been some moves in this direction – albeit on a broadly voluntary basis – with some developed countries providing targeted development assistance to countries from which they have recruited large numbers of workers. But we lack both a mechanism for determining what constitutes 'fair' compensation, and binding rules or institutions capable of ensuring that it is paid. Gillian Brock has suggested that for compensation genuinely to reflect the losses of human capital, tax revenue and so on, the creation of an impartial international agency is necessary, with the power to broker compensation and to levy fines on defaulters (Brock 2009: 202). Alternatively, rules (and penalties) relating to recruitment could be overseen by the International Labour Organization or the World Trade Organization, thus 'linking' issues of migration with issues of trade and labour policy more generally.

Until such an institutional mechanism is in place, the loss of health-care workers to the developed world will likely endure, with the inevitable damage to health-care systems in some of the poorest countries of the world. The massive inequalities which characterise the contemporary global economy provide a great part of the explanation for this, insofar as the voracious appetite of developed countries for expensive health care provides opportunities for people seeking to earn their way out of poverty. But in the absence of enforceable rules this inequality also makes a solution much less likely, given the respective bargaining power of the different parties involved. As such, global inequality both intensifies the problem and makes it more difficult to solve.

References

Abizadeh, A. (2002) 'Does liberal democracy presuppose a cultural nation?' *American Political Science Review* 96(3): 495–509.

——(2007) 'Cooperation, pervasive impact and coercion: on the scope (not site) of distributive justice', *Philosophy and Public Affairs* 35(4): 318–58.

Allen, M., D. Frame, C. Huntingford, C. Jones, J. Lowe, M. Meinshausen and N. Meinshausen (2009) 'Impact of cumulative emissions of carbon dioxide: the trillionth tonne', *Nature* 458: 1163–6.

Altman, A. and C. H. Wellman (2009) *A Liberal Theory of International Justice* (Oxford University Press).

Anderson, E. (1999) 'What is the point of equality?' *Ethics* 109(2): 287–337.

AOSIS (2009) Alliance of Small Island States Declaration on Climate Change, available at www.sidsnet.org/aosis/documents/AOSIS%20Summit%20Declaration%20 Sept%2021%20FINAL.pdf.

Armstrong, C. (2006) *Rethinking Equality* (Manchester University Press).

——(2009a) 'Defending the duty of assistance?' *Social Theory and Practice* 35(3): 461–82.

——(2009b) 'Coercion, reciprocity and equality beyond the state', *Journal of Social Philosophy* 40(3): 297–316.

——(2010) 'National self-determination, global equality and moral arbitrariness', *Journal of Political Philosophy* 18(3): 313–34.

——(2011) 'Beyond national control over natural resources', ms.

Baer, P. (2002) 'Equity, greenhouse gas emissions, and global common resources', in S. Schneider, A. Rosencranz and J. Niles (eds.), *Climate Change Policy: A Survey* (Washington, DC: Island Press), pp. 393–408.

Banting, K., R. Johnston, W. Kymlicka and S. Soroka (2006) 'Do multiculturalism policies erode the welfare state? An empirical analysis', in K. Banting and W. Kymlicka (eds.), *Multiculturalism and the Welfare State* (Oxford University Press), pp. 49–91.

Barlow, M. (2010) 'Our water commons: towards a new freshwater narrative', available at www.canadians.org/water/publications/water%20commons/water%20 commons%20-%20web.pdf.

Barry, B. (1982) 'Humanity and justice in global perspective', in J. Pennock and J. Chapman (eds.), *NOMOS XXIV: Ethics, Economics and the Law* (New York University Press), pp. 219–52.

Barry, C. and S. Reddy (2008) *International Trade and Labor Standards: A Proposal for Linkage* (New York: Columbia University Press).

Beitz, C. (1979) *Political Theory and International Relations* (Princeton University Press).

——(1999a) *Political Theory and International Relations*, 2nd edn with new Afterword (Princeton University Press).

——(1999b) 'International liberalism and distributive justice: a survey of recent thought', *World Politics* 51(2): 269–96.

——(2001) 'Does global inequality matter?' *Metaphilosophy* 32(1/2): 95–112.

——(2009) *The Idea of Human Rights* (Oxford University Press).

Blake, M. (2001) 'Distributive justice, state coercion and autonomy', *Philosophy and Public Affairs* 30(3): 257–96.

——(2003) 'Immigration', in R. G. Frey and C. H. Wellman (eds.), *A Companion to Applied Ethics* (Oxford: Blackwell), pp. 224–37.

Blake, M. and M. Risse (2009) 'Immigration and original ownership of the earth', *Notre Dame Journal of Law, Ethics and Public Policy* 23(1): 133–66.

Boxill, B. (1987) 'Global equality of opportunity and national integrity', *Social Philosophy and Policy* 5(1): 143–68.

Boycott, O. (2010) 'Chagos Islands exiles amazed by speed of Foreign Office's opposition to seabed claim by Maldives', *Guardian*, 27 September, available at ⟨www.guardian.co.uk/world/2010/sep/27/chagos-islands-maldives-seabed-claim⟩.

Brock, G. (2009) *Global Justice: A Cosmopolitan Account* (Oxford University Press).

Brown, A. and R. Stern (2007) 'Concepts of fairness in the global trading system', *Pacific Economic Review* 12(3): 293–318.

Buchanan, A. (2000) 'Rawls's law of peoples: rules for a vanished Westphalian world', *Ethics* 110(4): 697–721.

——(2006) 'Taking the human out of human rights', in R. Martin and D. Reidy (eds.), *Rawls's Law of Peoples: A Realistic Utopia?* (Oxford: Blackwell), pp. 150–68.

——(2010) *Human Rights, Legitimacy and the Use of Force* (Oxford University Press).

Byravan, S. and S. C. Rajan (2010) 'The ethical implications of sea-level rise due to climate change', *Ethics and International Affairs* 24(3): 239–60.

Caney, S. (2001) 'Cosmopolitan justice and equalizing opportunities', *Metaphilosophy* 32(1/2): 113–34.

——(2002) 'Debate: a reply to Miller', *Political Studies* 50(5): 978–83.

——(2005a) *Justice beyond Borders* (Oxford University Press).

——(2005b) 'Global interdependence and distributive justice', *Review of International Studies* 31(2): 389–99.

——(2006) 'Global justice: from theory to practice', *Globalizations* 3(2): 121–37.

—(2007) 'Justice, borders and the cosmopolitan ideal: a reply to two critics', *Journal of Global Ethics* 3(2): 269–76.

—(2008) 'Global distributive justice and the state', *Political Studies* 56(4): 487–518.

—(2009) 'Global poverty and human rights: the case for positive duties', in T. Pogge (ed.), *Freedom from Poverty as a Human Right* (Oxford University Press), pp. 275–302.

—(2010) 'Climate change and the duties of the advantaged', *Critical Review of International Social and Political Philosophy* 13(1): 203–28.

—(2011) 'Justice, equality and greenhouse gas emissions', ms.

Carens, J. (1987) 'Aliens and citizens: the case for open borders', *Review of Politics* 49(2): 251–73.

—(1988) 'Immigration and the welfare state', in A. Gutmann (ed.), *Democracy and the Welfare State* (Princeton University Press), pp. 207–30.

—(1992) 'Migration and morality: a liberal egalitarian perspective', in B. Barry and R. Goodin (eds.), *Free Movement* (New York: Harvester Wheatsheaf), pp. 25–47.

Chapagain, A., Hoekstra, A., and H. Savenije (2006) 'Water saving through international trade of agricultural products', *Hydrology and Earth System Sciences* 10(3): 455–468.

Clark, P., J. Stewart and D. Clark (2006) 'The globalization of the market for healthcare professionals', *International Labour Review* 145(1/2): 37–64.

Collier, P. (2007) *The Bottom Billion: Why the Poorest Communities are Failing and What Can Be Done About It* (Oxford University Press).

Conca, K. (1995) 'Environmental protection, international norms, and state sovereignty: the case of the Brazilian Amazon', in G. Lyons and M. Mastanduno (eds.), *Beyond Westphalia? State Sovereignty and International Intervention* (Baltimore: Johns Hopkins University Press), pp. 115–46.

Cranston, M. (1973) *What Are Human Rights?* (New York: Taplinger).

Cullet, P. (2003) 'Patents and medicines: the relationship between TRIPS and the human right to health', *International Affairs* 79(1): 139–60.

Deere-Birkbeck, C. (2009) *Reinvigorating Debate on WTO Reform*, Global Economic Governance Working Paper 2009/50, University of Oxford.

Donnelly, J. (1982) 'Human rights and human dignity: an analytic critique of non-Western human rights conceptions', *American Political Science Review* 76 (3): 303–16.

—(1999) 'The social construction of international human rights', in T. Dunne and N. Wheeler (eds.), *Human Rights in Global Politics* (Cambridge University Press), pp. 71–102.

Eastwood, J., R. Conroy, S. Naicker, R. Tutt and J. Plange-Rhule (2005) 'Loss of health professionals from sub-Saharan Africa: the pivotal role of the UK', *The Lancet* 365 (28 May): 1893–1900.

Economist (2006) 'Voting with your trolley: can you really change the world just by buying certain foods?', 7 December, available at www.economist.com/node/8380592.

Evans, T. (2002) 'A human right to health?' *Third World Quarterly* 23(2): 197–215.

Faini, R. (2007) 'Remittances and the brain drain: do more skilled migrants remit more?', *World Bank Economic Review* 21(2): 177–91.

Falkenmark, M., and L. Lundqvist (1998) 'Towards water security: political determination and human adaptation crucial', *Natural Resources Forum* 22(1): 37–51.

Fine, S. (2010) 'Freedom of association is not the answer', *Ethics* 120(2): 338–56.

Freeman, S. (2006) 'Distributive justice and the Law of Peoples', in R. Martin and D. Reidy (eds.), *Rawls's Law of Peoples: A Realistic Utopia?* (Oxford: Blackwell), pp. 243–260.

—(2007) *Rawls* (London: Routledge).

Fuess, S. (2003) 'Immigration policy and highly skilled workers: the case of Japan', *Contemporary Economic Policy* 21(2): 243–57.

Gardiner, S. (2004) 'Ethics and global climate change', *Ethics* 114(3): 555–600.

Ghose, A. (2004) 'Global inequality and international trade', *Cambridge Journal of Economics* 28(2): 229–52.

Gilabert, P. (2005) 'The duty to eradicate global poverty: positive or negative?' *Ethical Theory and Moral Practice* 7(4): 537–50.

Griffin, J. (1986) *Well-being: Its Meaning, Measurement, and Moral Importance* (Oxford: Clarendon Press).

—(2008) *On Human Rights* (Oxford University Press).

—(2010) 'Human rights', rev. edn, *Stanford Encyclopedia of Philosophy*, available at www.plato.stanford.edu/entries/rights-human/.

Hachfeld, D., P. Terhorst and O. Hoedeman (2009) *Progressive Public Water Management in Europe*, Reclaiming Public Water discussion paper, available at www.tni.org/sites/www.tni.org/files/download/progressivewaterineurope.pdf.

Harding, L. (2010) 'Vladimir Putin calls for Arctic claims to be resolved under UN law', *Guardian*, 23 September, available at www.guardian.co.uk/world/2010/sep/23/putin-arctic-claims-international-law?INTCMP=SRCH.

Harlan, C. (2010) 'Strict immigration rules may threaten Japan's future', *Washington Post*, 28 July.

Helsinki Process (2005) *The Helsinki Process on Globalisation and Democracy Report: Mobilizing Political Will*, available at www.helsinkiprocess.fi/netcomm/ImgLib/53/164/hp_report_2005_mobilising_political_will.pdf.

Hinsch, W. (2001) 'Global distributive justice', *Metaphilosophy* 32(1/2): 58–78.

Hirschman, A. (1970) *Exit, Voice and Loyalty* (Cambridge, MA: Harvard University Press).

Hoekstra, A. and A. Chapagain (2008) *Globalization of Water* (Oxford: Blackwell).

Hollis, A. and T. Pogge (2008) 'The health impact fund: making new medicines available to all', Incentives for Global Health, available at www.yale.edu/macmillan/igh/files/hif_book_0a_front_matter.pdf.

Holtug, N. (2010) 'Immigration and the politics of social cohesion', *Ethnicities* 10(4): 435–51.

IPCC (2001) *Intergovernmental Panel on Climate Change Third Assessment Report: Climate Change* (Cambridge University Press).

—(2007) *Intergovernmental Panel on Climate Change Fourth Assessment Report: Climate Change* (Cambridge University Press).

James, A. (2009) 'A theory of fairness in trade', ms.

Jamieson, D. (2001) 'Climate change and global environmental justice', in P. Edwards and C. Miller (eds.), *Changing the Atmosphere: Expert Knowledge and Global Environmental Governance* (Cambridge, MA: MIT Press), pp. 287–307.

Jones, C. (1999) *Global Justice: Defending Cosmopolitanism* (Oxford University Press).

Jones, P. (2000) 'Global distributive justice', in A. Valls (ed.), *Ethics and International Affairs* (Totowa: Rowman & Littlefield), pp. 169–84.

Kapstein, E. (1999) 'Distributive justice and international trade', *Ethics and International Affairs* 13(1): 175–204.

—(2008) 'Fairness considerations in world politics: lessons from international trade negotiations', *Political Science Quarterly* 123(2): 229–45.

Kapur, D. and J. McHale (2009) 'International migration and the world income distribution', *Journal of International Development* 21(8): 1102–10.

Kelly, E. and L. McPherson (2010) 'Non-egalitarian global fairness', in A. Jaggar (ed.), *Thomas Pogge and His Critics* (Cambridge: Polity), pp. 103–22.

Kurjanska, M. and M. Risse (2008) 'Fairness in trade II: export subsidies and the fair trade movement', *Politics, Philosophy and Economics* 7(1): 29–56.

Kymlicka, W. (1989) *Liberalism, Community and Culture* (Oxford University Press).

—(2001) 'Territorial boundaries: a liberal egalitarian perspective', in D. Miller and S. Hashmi (eds.), *Boundaries and Justice: Diverse Ethical Perspectives* (Princeton University Press), pp. 249–75.

Lamont, J. and C. Favor (1996) 'Distributive justice', *Stanford Encyclopedia of Philosophy*, available at www.plato.stanford.edu/entries/justice-distributive/.

Levi, M. and A. Linton (2003) 'Fair trade: a cup at a time?' *Politics and Society* 31(3): 407–32.

Macedo, S. (2007) 'The moral dilemma of US immigration policy: open borders vs. social justice?' in C. Swain (ed.), *Debating Immigration* (Cambridge University Press), pp. 63–81.

McGranahan, G., D. Balk and B. Anderson (2007) 'The rising tide: assessing the risks of climate change and human settlements in low elevation coastal zones', *Environment and Urbanization* 19(1): 19–37.

Margalit, A. and J. Raz (1990) 'National self-determination', *Journal of Philosophy* 87(9): 439–61.

Martineau, T., K. Decker and P. Bundred (2004) '"Brain drain" of health professionals: from rhetoric to responsible action', *Health Policy* 70(1): 1–10.

Meilaender, P. (1999) 'Liberalism and open borders: the argument of Joseph Carens', *International Migration Review* 33(4): 1062–81.

Milanovic, B. (2005) *Worlds Apart: Measuring International and Global Inequality* (Princeton University Press).

Miller, D. (1995) *On Nationality* (Oxford University Press).

—(2000) *Citizenship and National Identity* (Cambridge: Polity).

—(2002) 'Cosmopolitanism: a critique', *Critical Review of International Social and Political Philosophy* 5(3): 80–5.

—(2005a) 'Against global egalitarianism', *Journal of Ethics* 9(1): 55–79.

—(2005b) 'Immigration: the case for limits', in A. Cohen and C. H. Wellman (eds.), *Contemporary Debates in Applied Ethics* (Oxford: Blackwell), pp. 193–206.

—(2006) 'Collective responsibility and international inequality in *The Law of Peoples*', in R. Martin and D. Reidy (eds.), *Rawls's Law of Peoples: A Realistic Utopia?* (Oxford: Blackwell), pp. 191–205.

—(2007) *National Responsibility and Global Justice* (Oxford University Press).

—(2008) 'Immigrants, nations and citizenship', *Journal of Political Philosophy* 16(4): 371–90.

—(2009) 'Global justice and climate change: how should responsibilities be distributed? Parts I and II', *Tanner Lectures on Human Values* 28: 119–56.

—(2010) 'Fair trade: what does it mean and why does it matter?', Oxford University Centre for the Study of Social Justice Working Paper SJ013.

—(2011) 'Property and territory: Kant, Locke and Steiner', *Journal of Political Philosophy* 19(1): 90–109.

Miller, R. (1998) 'Cosmopolitan respect and patriotic concern', *Philosophy and Public Affairs* 27(3): 202–24.

Moellendorf, D. (2002) *Cosmopolitan Justice* (Boulder: Westview Press).

—(2009a) *Global Inequality Matters* (Basingstoke: Palgrave Macmillan).

—(2009b) 'Treaty norms and climate change mitigation', *Ethics and International Affairs* 23(3): 247–65.

Moore, M. (2007) 'Justice within different borders: a review of Caney's global political theory', *Journal of Global Ethics* 3(2): 255–68.

Muzaka, V. (2011) *The Politics of Intellectual Property Rights and Public Health: In Sickness and in Wealth* (Basingstoke: Palgrave Macmillan).

Nagel, T. (1997) 'Justice and nature', *Oxford Journal of Legal Studies* 17(2): 303–21.

—(2005) 'The problem of global justice', *Philosophy and Public Affairs* 33(2): 113–47.

Nelson, R. (2004) 'The nurse poachers', *The Lancet* 364(9447): 1743–4.

Nickel, J. (2005) 'Poverty and rights', *Philosophical Quarterly* 55(220): 385–402.

Nussbaum, M. (1992) 'Human functioning and social justice: in defense of Aristotelian essentialism', *Political Theory* 20(2): 202–46.

—(2002) 'Women and the Law of Peoples', *Politics, Philosophy and Economics* 1(3): 283–306.

O'Neill, O. (1986) *Faces of Hunger* (London: Allen & Unwin).

Ostrom, E. (1990) *Governing the Commons* (Cambridge University Press).

Oxfam (2002) *Trade Report: Rigged Rules and Double Standards* (Oxford: Oxfam), available at www.oxfam.org.uk/resources/policy/trade/downloads/trade_report.pdf.

—(2006) *Briefing Paper: A Recipe for Disaster – Will the Doha Round Fail to Deliver for Development?* (Oxford: Oxfam), available at www.oxfam.org.uk/resources/policy/trade/downloads/bp87_recipe.pdf?m=234&url=.

Pevnick, R. (2009) 'Social trust and the ethics of immigration policy', *Journal of Political Philosophy* 17(2): 146–67.

Philp, C. (2008) 'British claim to Ascension seabed raises the stakes over quest for Falklands oil', *The Times*, 28 August, available at www.timesonline.co.uk/tol/news/politics/article4622286.ece.

Pierik, R. (2008) 'Collective responsibility and national responsibility', *Critical Review of International Social and Political Philosophy* 11(4): 465–83.

Pogge, T. (1989) *Realizing Rawls* (Ithaca: Cornell University Press).

—(1994) 'An egalitarian Law of Peoples', *Philosophy and Public Affairs* 23(3): 195–224.

—(2002) *World Poverty and Human Rights* (Cambridge: Polity).

—(2004) '"Assisting" the global poor', in D. Chatterjee (ed.), *The Ethics of Assistance* (Cambridge University Press), pp. 260–88.

—(2005) 'Human rights and global health: a research program', *Metaphilosophy* 36(1/2): 182–209.

—(2006) 'Migration and poverty', in V. Bader (ed.), *Citizenship and Exclusion* (Basingstoke: Macmillan), pp. 12–27.

—(2007a) 'Why inequality matters', in D. Held and A. Kaya (eds.), *Global Inequality* (Cambridge: Polity), pp. 132–47.

—(2007b) 'Interview with Professor Thomas Pogge', *Ethics and Economics* 5(1): 1–7.

Pogge, T. and S. Reddy (2010) 'How not to count the poor', in S. Anand, P. Segal and J. Stiglitz (eds.), *Debates on the Measurement of Global Poverty* (Oxford University Press), pp. 42–85.

Rawls, J. (1971) *A Theory of Justice* (Cambridge, MA: Harvard University Press).

—(1993) *Political Liberalism* (New York: Columbia University Press).

—(1999) *The Law of Peoples: With 'The Idea of Public Reason Revisited'* (Cambridge, MA: Harvard University Press).

—(2001) *Justice as Fairness: A Restatement* (Cambridge, MA: Harvard University Press).

Raz, J. (1986) *The Morality of Freedom* (Oxford University Press).

Reidy, D. (2004) 'Rawls on international justice: a defense', *Political Theory* 32(3): 291–319.

—(2007) 'A just global economy: in defense of Rawls', *Journal of Ethics* 11(2): 193–236.

Reus-Smith, C. (2001) 'Human rights and the social construction of sovereignty', *Review of International Studies* 27(4): 519–38.

Reynolds, P. (2008) 'Trying to head off an Arctic "gold rush"', BBC Online, 29 May, available at http://news.bbc.co.uk/1/hi/in_depth/7423787.stm.

Risse, M. (2005) 'What we owe the global poor', *Journal of Ethics* 9(1): 81–117.

—(2006) 'What to say about the state', *Social Theory and Practice* 32(4): 671–98.

—(2007) 'Fairness in trade I: obligations from trading and the pauper-labor argument', *Politics, Philosophy and Economics* 6 (3): 355–77.

—(2009) 'The right to relocation: disappearing island nations and common ownership of the earth', *Ethics and International Affairs* 23(3): 281–300.

Sangiovanni, A. (2007) 'Global justice, reciprocity and the state', *Philosophy and Public Affairs* 35(1): 3–39.

Scheffler, S. (2001) *Boundaries and Allegiances* (Oxford University Press).

Schrijver, N. (1997) *Sovereignty over Natural Resources: Balancing Rights and Duties* (Cambridge University Press).

Sen, A. (1997) 'Human rights and Asian values', *New Republic* 14 July: 33–40.

Shachar, A. and R. Hirschl (2007) 'Citizenship as inherited property', *Political Theory* 35(3): 253–87.

Shacknove, A. (1985) 'Who is a refugee?' *Ethics* 95(2): 274–84.

Shue, H. (1980) *Basic Rights: Subsistence, Affluence and US Foreign Policy* (Princeton University Press).

—(1988) 'Mediating duties', *Ethics* 98(4): 687–704.

—(1993) 'Subsistence emissions and luxury emissions', *Law & Policy* 15(1): 39–60.

—(1999) 'Global environment and international inequality', *International Affairs* 75(3): 531–45.

—(2001) 'Climate', in D. Jamieson (ed.), *A Companion to Environmental Philosophy* (Oxford: Blackwell), pp. 449–59.

Singer, P. (2004) *One World: The Ethics of Globalization*, 2nd edn (Yale: Nota Bene Press).

Steiner, H. (2005) 'Territorial justice and global redistribution', in G. Brock and H. Brighouse (eds.), *The Political Philosophy of Cosmopolitanism* (Cambridge University Press), pp. 28–38.

—(2011) 'Sharing mother nature's gifts: a reply to Quong and Miller', *Journal of Political Philosophy* 19(1): 110–23.

Stiglitz, J. (2006) *Making Globalization Work* (London: Penguin).

Sutcliffe, B. (2007) 'The unequalled and unequal twentieth century', in D. Held and A. Kaya (eds.), *Global Inequality* (Cambridge: Polity), pp. 50–72.

Tan, K.-C. (2000) *Toleration, Diversity and Global Justice* (Pennsylvania: Penn State Press).

—(2004) *Justice Without Borders* (Cambridge University Press).

—(2006) 'The boundary of justice and the justice of boundaries: defending global egalitarianism', *Canadian Journal of Law and Jurisprudence* 19(2): 319–44.

Tasioulas, J. (2005) 'Global justice without end?' *Metaphilosophy* 36(1/2): 3–29.

Taylor, C. (1999) 'Conditions of an unforced consensus on human rights', in O. Bauer and D. Bell (eds.), *The East Asian Challenge for Human Rights* (Cambridge University Press), pp. 124–46.

UN (1948) United Nations Universal Declaration of Human Rights, available at www.un.org/Overview/rights.html.

—(1951) Convention Relating to the Status of Refugees, available at www.unhcr.org/protect/PROTECTION/3b66c2aa10.pdf.

—(1966) International Covenant on Economic, Social and Cultural Rights, available at www.un.org/millennium/law/iv-4.htm.

—(2000) United Nations Millennium Declaration, available at www.un.org/millennium/declaration/ares552e.htm.

—(2001) *Replacement Migration: Is It a Solution to Declining and Ageing Populations?* United Nations Population Division Report ST/ESA/SER.A/206.

—(2003) *Human Development Report 2003: Millennium Development Goals* (New York: United Nations Development Programme).

—(2006) *Human Development Report 2006: Beyond Scarcity* (New York: United Nations Development Programme).

—(2007a) *Human Development Report 2007: Fighting Climate Change* (New York: United Nations Development Programme).

—(2007b) *United Nations Millennium Development Goals Report 2007* (New York: United Nations).

—(2009) *United Nations Development Programme Report 2009* (New York: United Nations Development Programme).

—(2010) United Nations General Assembly Resolution GA/10967, available at www.un.org/News/Press/docs/2010/ga10967.doc.htm).

Vanderheiden, S. (2008) *Atmospheric Justice: A Political Theory of Climate Change* (Oxford University Press).

van der Veen, R. (2008) 'Reasonable partiality for compatriots and the global responsibility gap', *Critical Review of International Social and Political Philosophy* 11(4): 413–32.

van Heerde, J. and D. Hudson (2009) 'The righteous considereth the cause of the poor? Public attitudes towards poverty in developing countries', *Political Studies* 58(3): 389–409.

Wade, R. (2004) 'Is globalization reducing poverty and inequality?' *World Development* 32(4): 567–89.

Waldron, J. (1987) 'Nonsense upon stilts: a reply', in J. Waldron (ed.), *Nonsense upon Stilts: Bentham, Burke and Marx on the Rights of Man* (London: Methuen), pp. 151–209.

Walzer, M. (1983) *Spheres of Justice* (New York: Basic Books).

—(2007) *Thinking Politically: Essays in Political Theory* (New Haven: Yale University Press).

Warwick Commission (2007) *The Multilateral Trade Regime: Which Way Forward?* (Warwick: University of Warwick).

Watson, M. (2006) 'Towards a Polanyian perspective on free trade: market-based relationships and the act of ethical consumption', *Global Society* 20(4): 435–51.

Wellman, C. H. (2010) 'Immigration', *Stanford Encyclopedia of Philosophy*, available at www.plato.stanford.edu/entries/immigration/.

Wenar, L. (2006) 'Why Rawls is not a cosmopolitan egalitarian', in R. Martin and D. Reidy (eds.), *Rawls's Law of Peoples: A Realistic Utopia?* (Oxford: Blackwell), pp. 95–113.

—(2008a) 'Property rights and the resource curse', *Philosophy and Public Affairs* 36(1): 2–32.

—(2008b) 'Human rights and equality in the work of David Miller', *Critical Review of International Social and Political Philosophy* 11(4): 401–11.

Westing, A. (ed.) (1986) *Global Resources and International Conflict* (Oxford University Press).

Wissenburg, M. (1999) 'An extension of the Rawlsian Savings Principle to liberal theories of justice in general', in A. Dobson (ed.), *Fairness and Futurity* (Oxford University Press), pp. 173–98.

Wolf, M. (2004) *Why Globalization Works* (New Haven: Yale University Press).

Wolff, J. (2000) *World Health Organization: World Health Report* 2000 (Geneva: World Health Organization).

—(2007) 'Equality: the recent history of an idea', *Journal of Moral Philosophy* 4(1): 125–36.

—(2009) *World Development Report 2009: Reshaping Economic Geography* (Washington, DC: World Bank Publications).

—(2010) *World Development Report 2010: Development and Climate Change* (Washington, DC: World Bank Publications).

—(2011) 'The human right to health' in S. Benatar and G. Brock (eds.), *Global Health and Global Health Ethics* (Cambridge University Press), pp. 108–18.

World Bank (2001) *World Development Report 2000/01: Attacking Poverty* (Washington, DC: World Bank Publications).

World Health Organization (1946) Constitution of the World Health Organization, available at http://whqlibdoc.who.int/hist/official_records/constitution.pdf.

World Trade Organization (2001) World Trade Organization Ministerial Declaration, 20 November, available at www.wto.org/english/thewto_e/minist_e/min01_e/mindecl_e.htm.

Yamanaka, K. (1993) 'New immigration policy and unskilled foreign workers in Japan', *Pacific Affairs* 66(1): 72–90.

Young, I. M. (2007) *Global Challenges: War, Self-Determination and Responsibility for Justice* (Cambridge: Polity).

Index